Wellington's Army

Wellington's Army

Colonel HCB Rogers OBE

LONDON

IAN ALLAN LTD

First published 1979

ISBN 0 7110 0903 1

Published by Ian Allan Ltd, Shepperton, Surrey;
and printed in the United Kingdom by
Ian Allan Printing Ltd

Contents

To my wife
who joins in the Author's tribute
to the Memory of the officers and men
in the Light Division

Acknowledgements

I am indebted to several sources for the information needed in the writing of this book. The Journals of the Society for Army Historical Research (to which I am proud to belong) contain a mine of learning relative to my subject; my membership of the London Library gives me access to a vast store of knowledge into which I have never searched in vain; the National Army Museum has, from its wealth of military pictures, enabled me to illustrate all the principal incidents affecting the British Army during the long war with Revolutionary and Imperial France; and Messrs Francis Edwards (and particularly Mr A. S. Gilbert of that indispensable haunt of the military book addict) have been able to provide me with those books which I have needed permanently at my elbow.

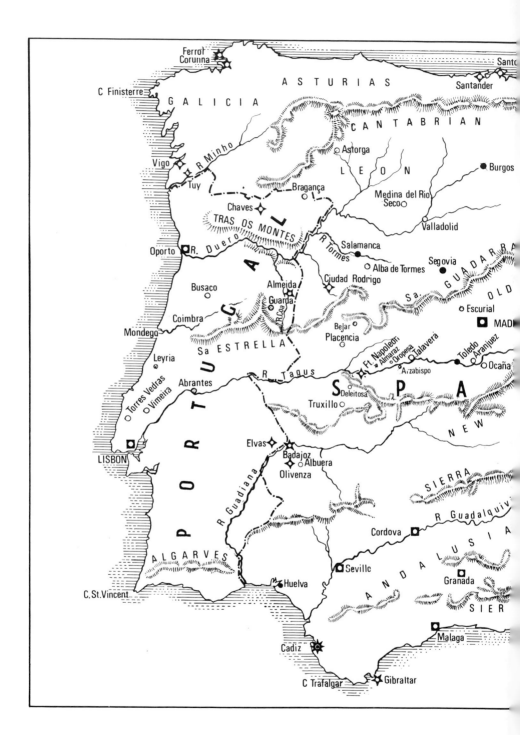

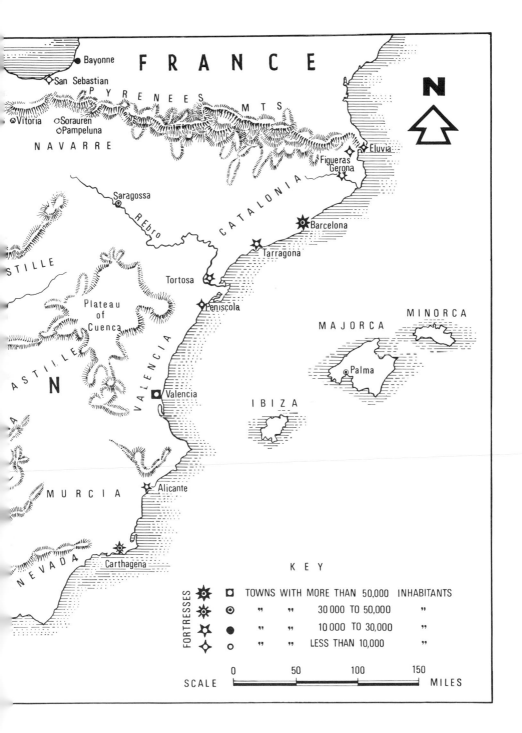

Bayonne
San Sebastian

F R A N C E

P Y R E N E E S   M T S

Vitoria   Sorauren
          Pampeluna

N A V A R R E

Eluvia
Figueras
Gerona

Saragossa

C A T A L O N I A

R. Ebro

Barcelona

Tarragona

STILLE

Tortosa

Plateau
of
Cuenca

Peniscola

M I N O R C A

M A J O R C A

ASTILLE

Palma

VALENCIA

Valencia

I B I Z A

N

MURCIA

Alicante

NEVADA

Carthagena

K E Y

FORTRESSES

⚝	◻	TOWNS WITH MORE THAN 50,000 INHABITANTS
⚝	◉	" " 30 000 TO 50,000 "
✦	●	" " 10 000 TO 30,000 "
✧	○	" " LESS THAN 10,000 "

SCALE   0   50   100   150   MILES

Introduction

It is perhaps an exaggeration to claim that Sir John Moore created the army with which the Duke of Wellington fought; but it is not, on the whole, very far removed from the truth. Moore's system of discipline and training gradually permeated the whole of the British Army, and it is noteworthy that amongst the few regiments that maintained their discipline and steadiness during the long retreat to Corunna were the 4th King's Own and the 52nd Light infantry, both of which had been under Moore's command at his famous Shorncliffe Camp. The Light Division, probably the finest fighting formation in Wellington's Peninsular Army, was Moore's military memorial.

Books dealing with the lives of Moore and Wellington still appear, and it is not the intention in this one to tramp again down these well-worn avenues, but rather to describe by arms, services, and staffs the army which drove Napoleon's legions out of the Peninsula and routed the Imperial Guard on the field of Waterloo. Military operations are only cited therefore to illustrate tactics, organisation, and the use of weapons. Nevertheless, in order to show how the various branches of the army functioned together in the field, the Coa River operations in the Peninsula of the famous Light Division have been chosen.

The army which entered France from Spain in 1813 was indeed a vastly different force from that which fought in Flanders 20 years before, and because this book is concerned to a certain extent with the whole of this lengthy period the first chapter is devoted to a brief narrative of the principal events in Europe and the Mediterranean in which the British Army was engaged.

At the close of the American War of Independence, 10 years before our period starts, the small British Army in the erstwhile Colonies was a very formidable fighting force. Its regiments had demonstrated their ability to dominate the battlefield, either in the close formation of conventional warfare, or in the loose order needed when fighting in forest or against guerilla opponents; they had been trained in the steady fire discipline of the one and in the individual fieldcraft of the other. It had, however, been very much an infantry war, primarily owing to the difficulty of transporting horses across the Atlantic or of procuring them in America. Of cavalry, only two regiments of light dragoons had been engaged in the war, and most cavalry regiments had seen little action since serving in the army of Prince Ferdinand of Brunswick in Germany during the Seven Years War, which effectively ended in 1762.

During the years immediately preceding the outbreak of war with Revolutionary France the readiness of the Army for active service had dropped to a low level, and the standards of discipline and training in many regiments had deteriorated badly. Major-General Sir Henry Bunbury, who was commissioned into the Army in 1795, writes, with probably some exaggeration:

'We have been so long accustomed to measure the efficiency and conduct of British troops by the standard of that noble army which fought and conquered in the Spanish Peninsula that men of the present generation can hardly form an idea of what the military forces of England really were when the great war broke out in 1793. Our army was lax in its discipline, entirely without system, and very weak in numbers. Each colonel of a regiment managed it according to his own notion, or neglected it altogether. There was no uniformity of drill or movement: professional pride was rare; professional knowledge still more so. Never was a kingdom less prepared for a stern and arduous conflict.'[1]

Apart from the readiness of the Army as a whole for war, the standards of individual regiments seemed to have varied considerably. According to Bunbury, at the opening of the campaign of 1793, 'Such was the condition of the British infantry at this time that two of Abercromby's regiments were left behind, as being unfit to appear in the presence of the enemy.'[2] Wellington, who commanded his own regiment, the 33rd, in Flanders in 1794, took a rather less pessimistic view than Bunbury. He wrote: 'There was a fellow called Hammerstein, who was considered the chief authority in the army for tactics, but was quite an imposter; in fact, no one knew anything of the management of an army, though many of the regiments were excellent: the 33rd was in as good order as possible.'[3] The Hon Edward Paget, commanding the 28th Regiment, also thought highly of his own regiment; for in a letter to his father, Lord Uxbridge, complaining of the transports provided to take the troops to the West Indies, he wrote: 'Can you form in your imagination anything more thoroughly disgusting than the transportation of the finest and best troops in England — I believe in the world — in ships . . . that nothing but the basest conception could ever have tempted men to have hired into our service. Oh, my poor dear 28th!'[4]

But Bunbury's overall assessment was undoubtedly right, and the reason for this lamentable state of affairs was largely political. Pitt, in his budget speech of 1792, said: 'Unquestionably there never was a time in the history of this country when, from the situation in Europe, we might more reasonably expect fifteen years of peace, than at the present time.'[5] In such a political climate a government is unlikely to spend much money on its fighting forces!

Whatever reservations Wellington may have had for the infantry of 1794, he had an unbounded amiration for them in 1815, for on 23 October he wrote from Paris to Earl Bathurst, Secretary of State for War: 'My opinion is, that the best troops we have, probably the best in the world, are the British infantry, particularly the old infantry that has served in Spain. This is what we ought to keep up; and what I wish above all others to retain.'[6]

Notes

1 Sir Henry Bunbury, *Narratives of Some Passages in the Great War with France* (London, Peter Davies, 1927 (Original edn 1854)), pxv

2 ibid, pxvii

3 Sir Herbert Maxwell, *The Life of Wellington*, (quoting De Ros MS) (London, Sampson Low, Marston & Co, 3rd edn, 1900), vol I, p13

4 ibid, (quoting *Letters and Memorials of General the Hon Sir Edward Paget* (privately printed, 1898)), p19

5 ibid, p9

6 *Selections from the Dispatches and General Orders of Field Marshal the Duke of Wellington*, ed Lt-Col Gurwood (London, John Murray, 1841), p901

Historical Outline

The Campaign in the Netherlands, 1793-1795

Hostilities with Revolutionary France had hardly started before the British Government decided to send military assistance to the Dutch, whose wealth had attracted a French invasion. The only force that could be sent immediately was a weak brigade of the Foot Guards of some 1,700 men together with a small element of artillery. These troops embarked on 25 February under the command of Major-General Gerard Lake, and were first used to reinforce the Dutch garrison of Dort. When the French retreated from Antwerp, Lake advanced to that important port, where he was joined by three weak battalions of the Line commanded by Major-General Ralph Abercromby. More troops from England, together with Hanoverians and Hessians from Germany, soon brought the strength up to about 17,000 all ranks, and the Duke of York was appointed to command them. The bulk of the force consisted of infantry, but in May 1793 some squadrons of light dragoons and a few companies of artillery arrived, and the Duke of York then marched to join an Austrian army on the French frontier.

The intention of the Allies was to capture the strong fortress of Valenciennes and thus open the way for an advance on Paris. Valenciennes was indeed captured, but then the British Government insisted that the Duke of York should besiege Dunkirk. Whilst on the march to undertake this operation, the Duke of York was asked by the Prince of Orange for assistance, as the French had driven his forces back from Linselles, about four miles south of Menin. The Duke of York sent Lake with the Guards Brigade; but, as the Dutch on the spot refused to co-operate, Lake attacked with his three battalions alone and retook Linselles.

The siege of Dunkirk was a failure, and after three weeks the Duke of York had to raise it and retreat in the face of heavy French pressure. At this time most of his army consisted of Hanoverians: at no time during 1793 did he have more than 3,000 British infantry and about 700 light dragoons.[1]

In the early part of 1794 there were three brilliant British cavalry actions. On 24 April the 15th Light Dragoons and the Austrian Leopold Hussars, together numbering only 300 sabres, attacked a French force at Villers-en-Cauchies, the British attacking in front, and the Austrians against the enemy's left flank. The 15th Light Dragoons, thought they were charging French cavalry in front of them only, but the latter wheeled outwards on either side to reveal a line of skirmishers and guns, with in rear of them two infantry squares, numbering altogether about 3,000 men. However, the 15th charged right through the guns and broke the squares, driving the enemy off in flight.

The second action occurred only two days later, when the Duke of York at Le Cateau was being threatened by two French columns from Cambrai. Making feigned attacks against the French right and front, he sent all his available cavalry against their left. This force consisted of the Blues, 1st, 3rd, and 5th Dragoon Guards, Royals, 16th Light

Dragoons and Austrian Cuirassiers. The regiments formed up unseen by the enemy in a hollow near Bethencourt and, making use of cover for their approach, broke suddenly on the flank of one of the enemy columns, some 20,000 strong. The mass of French infantry dissolved in flight, and the cavalry, pursuing them, came on the second enemy column on the march. Thrown into disorder by the fugitives, the men of this column also panicked and fled.

The third cavalry action took place on 10 May, and the regiments concerned were the Blues, the 2nd, 3rd, and 6th Dragoon Guards, the 1st, 2nd, and 6th Dragoons, and the 11th, 15th, and 16th Light Dragoons. The occasion was an attack by a French force 30,000 strong against the Duke of York's position at Tournai. The Duke ordered the cavalry to turn the enemy's right. As a result of a series of brilliant charges the French were driven back to the village of Willems and there their infantry squares were broken and their cavalry driven from the field.[2] Of these three charges, that of Bethencourt, or Beaumont as it is sometimes called, has been cited as the greatest day in the annals of British Cavalry and as a lesson in the correct use of ground.

But these cavalry exploits furnish some of the few bright reliefs in a dismal and depressing campaign. On 18 May 1794 the Allied forces were defeated at the battle of Tourcoing, owing to the failure of the inept Austrian command to co-operate, leaving the Duke of York to be crushed by vastly superior numbers. However, a very gallant action was fought by Major-General H. E. Fox's Brigade of the 14th, 37th, and 52nd Regiments at Pont-a-Chin, where, having been surrounded, the brigade fought its way out; though losing 580 men out of 1,120.

Shortly after this battle Lord Moira arrived at Ostend with another contingent of 7,000 British troops, including the 33rd Regiment commanded by Lieutenant-Colonel Wesley. By the time this contingent joined the Duke of York, the army under his command, abandoned by the Austrians, was making a rapid and difficult retreat. The retreat was to be continued, with stands of varying durations through Holland into Germany; the British troops ultimately embarking at Bremen for return to the United Kingdom. Wesley, it was noted, had handled his battalion extremely well in a counter-attack, and from October until January he had held with ability a covering position on the River Waal.

It was a ghastly retreat in one of the coldest winters on record, with all the canals and rivers frozen so hard that they offered little obstacle to the enemy advance. To make matters worse for the wretched troops, the commissariat and the medical services were grossly inadequate and inefficient due to the lack of preparation and provision during peacetime. However, there were lighter moments. Wesley, in a letter written on 20 December 1794 to Sir Chichester Fortescue, said: 'Although the French annoy us much by night, they are very entertaining during the daytime; they are perpetually chattering with our officers and soldiers, and dance the *carmagnol* upon the opposite bank whenever we desire them; but occasionally the spectators on our side are interrupted in the middle of a dance by a cannon ball from theirs.'[3]

The Expedition to North Holland, 1799

The next major British military intervention in Europe was an expedition to North Holland which, in conjunction with a Russian force, was intended to drive the French out of the area. During the five years that had elapsed since the Flanders campaign the Army had suffered grievously in the heavy losses, mostly from yellow fever, that had been incurred in the struggle for the West Indies sugar islands. It was however a better army: administration had been overhauled and improved and the soldiers' pay increased. In addition, a uniform system of drill and movement, worked out by General David Dundas and officially approved in 1792, had now been brought into universal use; and whatever the imperfections of the system, it was common to all regiments, in place of practices which varied according to the whims of their colonels.

The Duke of York was appointed to the command of the British and Russian expeditionary forces, and the first contingent of British troops under the command of Sir Ralph Abercrombie sailed from England on 13 August 1799. It consisted of 15 battalions organised in five brigades and numbering, with its accompanying artillery, some 10,000 good troops. Its initial objective was the Helder peninsula, with the aim of capturing the Dutch fleet in the Texel and destroying the naval magazines there.

Bad weather prevented a landing until 27 August. This delay gave the enemy time to prepare, and though they did not interfere with the slow and difficult manoeuvre of landing on the beach through a heavy surf, as soon as formed bodies of British troops began to move forward they encountered heavy opposition. However, the stout fighting British infantry, though no artillery had as yet been landed to support them, eventually drove back the 6,000 or so Dutch troops who were opposing them forcing them to retreat about six miles. The rest of the disembarkation went ahead without difficulty.

The Dutch squadron, which had been lying in the Texel channel, was uncovered by the withdrawal of the garrison of the protecting batteries and dropped inward as far as the draught of water would allow. On 30 September Vice-Admiral Sir Andrew Mitchell succeeded in leading his squadron through the shoals of the Texel channel to receive the surrender of the Dutch fleet. Major-General John Moore's Brigade had already taken possession of the Helder with the naval arsenal and storehouse, so the principal British objectives had been achieved. There remained the combined Anglo-Russian objective of driving the French out of Holland.

Sir Ralph Abercromby now moved forward and took up a strong covering position to await the arrival of the Duke of York with more British troops and the landing of the Russian force. The French General Brune with a large Franco-Dutch army attacked Abercromby's position on 10 September. After fierce fighting his troops were beaten off with heavy losses. An interesting aspect of the battle was the stubborn defence of the village of Krappendam by two battalions of the 20th Regiment, in which three-quarters of the men were volunteers recently received from the Militia.[4] An Act of Parliament had been passed in July 1799 to enable the ranks of regiments returning from the West Indies depleted by yellow fever to be filled by offering large bounties to militiamen to join the Regular Army. The men thus recruited were excellent material, but their standard of training varied considerably according to the Militia regiments from which they came, and their performance in action was consequently patchy. The 20th Foot were fortunate in the quality of their Militia recruits.

In mid-September the Duke of York arrived to take over command, bringing with him reinforcements that included a number of young regiments largely composed of militiamen. Two divisions of Russian troops had also disembarked. It was decided to mount an attack on the enemy's forces on 19 September, but this was a dismal failure owing to the incompetence and indiscipline of the right column of 12 Russian battalions, which were routed by Brune's troops. The other Allied columns had perforce to fall back to their starting lines. At the end of the day's fighting only three Russian battalions remained in a condition to fight and some of the newly formed Militia regiments were in great disorder. The majority of the British troops had fought extremely well and gained considerable success, before the failure on the right necessitated their retreat. As a result of this battle the Duke of York took a violent dislike to, and contempt for, the Russians, which he did not hesitate to voice.

On 2 October another general attack was made on the enemy. The French and Dutch were driven from their positions, but it was an inconclusive victory because of Russian inaction. On 6 October an unintended encounter battle started between the advanced posts on both sides resulting in heavy casualties and little else. By this time the Russians were completely unreliable, and the Duke of York decided to safeguard the British Army by retreating to the original defence positions. On 18 October he signed a convention with General Brune, undertaking to evacuate Holland by 30 November. However, Great Britain retained the prize of the Dutch fleet, which had been one of the original objectives.

The Campaign in Egypt, 1801

After various ineffectual attempts or projects to land in Italy, France, or Spain during 1800, the British Government finally decided to expel the French from Egypt, in conjunction with such help as the Turks might be persuaded to afford. Sir Ralph Abercromby was therefore despatched with 15,000 men to invade a country in which all the fortresses and harbours were in the possession of a French army of not less than 28,000 veteran soldiers.[5]

The British expedition sailed from Malta at the end of December 1800, with as a first objective the capture of Alexandria, the only suitable harbour on the Egyptian Mediterranean coast. On 2 January 1801 the force was concentrated in the Bay of Marmorica, on the southern face of Asia Minor, where Abercromby hoped to coordinate action with the Turkish command. He also wanted to procure horses for his artillery and dragoons, and hire suitable transport to carry them to Egypt. Major-General John Moore was sent to visit the Grand Vizier, commanding a Turkish army near Jaffa. He formed the opinion that as allies the Turks would be of little value, and in the light of Moore's report Abercromby decided to go ahead on his own in an attempt on Alexandria. A joint Army and Navy conference decided on Aboukir Bay as the landing point; detailed plans were drawn up; and practice assault landings were carried out at Marmorica.

On 22 February the fleet sailed and entered Aboukir Bay on 2 March. However, rough weather prevented a landing for some days, and as the ships were within sight of the French during this period all possibility of surprise was lost. The weather moderated on 7 March and Abercromby decided to land the following morning. The troops accordingly started to get into the boats at 2am, but this, and the marshalling of the boats into order, was a slow business and it was not till 8am that the long line of small craft started towards the shore. As they got within range the French opened a heavy fire, sinking some of the boats and causing many casualties. The landing, however, was a complete success, the soldiers leaping from the boats and driving the French defenders headlong from the beach. By the afternoon all the infantry and some of the artillery were ashore, and in the evening the army advanced inland for some two or three miles and established a strong defensive position.

The next few days were devoted to reconnaissance and the landing of ammunition and supplies. On 12 March the army moved forward and came into contact with the French cavalry screen. Abercromby deployed his troops into order of battle and the next day advanced to the attack. However, the enemy were doing the same thing, so that as the British columns approached an encounter battle developed. The French got the worst of this and withdrew to their main position. Reconnaissance showed this too strong for a frontal attack and Abercromby himself withdrew into a defensive position. He felt himself faced with an insoluble problem and was beginning to contemplate an assault on the enemy's position, followed, if it should fail, by embarkation, when the French themselves attacked. The French assault came before daybreak on 21 March. After a fierce struggle the enemy were driven off in defeat, but Sir Ralph Abercromby was mortally wounded. He was succeeded in command by Major-General Sir John Hutchinson.

Hutchinson isolated Alexandria by cutting an isthmus to let the sea into the dry bed of a former lake, and sent a force to capture Rosetta on the main western channel of the Nile. Next he left Major-General Eyre Coote to blockade Alexandria and moved his main body to El Hamed on the Nile south of Rosetta, in preparation for an advance on Cairo. The force available for this advance consisted of only 4,300 infantry, 300 dragoons, and 100 artillerymen — the last being short of horses to pull their field guns. Hutchinson began his advance on 5 May, marching along the left bank, but with a flank guard of one regiment and a small detachment of cavalry on the right bank, whilst a flotilla of gunboats moved up the river between the two bodies. Rahmanieh, the important junction of the roads from Rosetta and Alexandria to Cairo, was defended by the French in strength, but after some skirmishing on 9 May they withdrew.

In spite of strong opposition from his principal officers, Hutchinson decided to continue to Cairo with his small force. Away to the left of the British the Turkish army was now making its disorderly progress towards Cairo, preceded by a wild and unruly cavalry screen. The French commander in Cairo marched out to meet them, but, after checking their advance, became nervous of a rising in the city and fell back there. On 21 June Hutchinson's troops, with the Turks on their left, were at the city walls. The next day the French capitulated. Reinforcements now arrived from England, and Hutchinson was also joined by an expeditionary force from India commanded by Major General David Baird. On 26 August Alexandria surrendered, and this was the effective end of the campaign.

The Peace of Amiens and after

In March 1802 peace between Great Britain and France was arranged by the Treaty of Amiens. The immediate effect on the Army was that the Militia, which had been under arms for nine years, was stood down, and the Fencible (ie home service only) regiments of cavalry and infantry were disbanded. However, the peace was of very short duration for war broke out again exactly a year later. The Militia was accordingly re-embodied, an Act to levy an army of reserve was passed, and camps of instruction were established in Essex, Kent, and Sussex. The most important of these was at Shorncliffe, where Major-General John Moore introduced a new system of drill and movement. By 1804 the regiments of the Line were strong and fit for the field and the Militia was well disciplined.[6] It was none too soon for in 1803 Napoleon was marshalling his army for an invasion of England, and the threat lasted until autumn 1805.

In 1805 the Government decided to take steps to protect Sicily from invasion. Part of the Kingdom of Naples was occupied by French troops, and the seizure by the enemy of the Sicilian fortresses and harbours would have a dangerous effect on British power in the Mediterranean. A small force of about 4,000 men was therefore sent to the Mediterranean under the command of Lieutenant-General Sir James Craig, with Colonel Henry Bunbury as his Quartermaster-General. The force sailed on 19 April and, after sheltering from the French fleet in the Tagus and stopping at Gibraltar for a fortnight, it arrived at Malta on 18 July.

As part of an Anglo-Russian expedition under Russian command, Craig's force sailed from Malta on 3 November 1805. It then consisted of about 5,000 British infantry, 2,000 foreign infantry in British pay, 300 British light dragoons without horses, and 500 Royal Artillery. On 20 November the combined fleet anchored in the Bay of Naples. The French troops had been withdrawn to take part in the war against Austria. On landing the British troops set about procuring horses for the cavalry and artillery; and when this had been completed the allied armies moved forward to defend the northern frontier. This was plainly indefensible, and the return of French troops led to withdrawal and embarkation: the Russians sailing to Corfu and the British to Sicily. Craig's army arrived in Messina harbour on 22 January 1806, but it was not till 27 February that political objections to their landing were removed, and they took over the defence of the fortress of Messina. Shortly afterwards Sir James Craig had to return home due to his illness, and Major-General Sir John Stuart succeeded him in command.

The Battle of Maida, 1806

In June 1806 Sir John Stuart decided to cross to the mainland and attack the French forces there. The troops selected for this attempt were the light companies of nine regiments, formed into a light infantry brigade; 120 'flankers', or sharpshooters, taken from 'battalion' companies (ie those other than grenadier or light); seven infantry battalions; and an artillery detachment of six field pieces and ten mountain guns.

On 30 June the expedition sailed and anchored in the Bay of St Eufemia. The troops started landing at daylight on 1 July, and an enemy detachment that opposed the landing was routed. On 3 July information reached Stuart that General Reynier and the main French force were near the shallow Lamato River below San Pietro di Maida. Stuart, after a personal reconnaissance, ordered the troops to march at daylight on 4 July, leaving a detachment to hold the beach defences. As the British columns entered the lower part of the plain of Maida, the French army could be seen on the march, and Stuart promptly deployed his command in order of battle. Wheeling to face the French, the British force advanced in echelons of brigades; Kempt's light infantry on the right and in the lead, next to it Ackland's, then Cole's, and in rear of the centre and following in reserve Oswald's Swiss regiment De Watteville. The French cavalry manoeuvred across the front of their infantry, thus screening them from view. Suddenly, however, the cavalry moved off, and when the dust had settled the French infantry could be seen advancing, and in considerably greater strength than the British. The French 1st Light Regiment of three battalions struck Kempt's light infantry, but after a stern struggle they were routed. The British centre and left had a hard fight against the superior numbers of the French in this sector. Bunbury, anxiously watching French sharpshooters working their way round the British left, was informed that the 20th Regiment had landed and was coming up at the double. He immediately rode to meet them and explained the situation to their commanding officer, Colonel Robert Ross. The 20th promptly drove off the sharpshooters, scattered the French cavalry with a volley, and then, passing beyond the British left, wheeled right to open a shattering fire on the attacking French. This was decisive, and Reynier drew off his regiments in retreat, followed by the British.[7] As a result of this victory Lower Calabria was cleared of the enemy and communications with the insurgents in the upper provinces were assured.

The Second Expedition to Egypt, 1807

The British had evacuated Egypt in March 1803. Since their departure the country had been unsettled and the object of intrigue between various contending factions; though the Pasha, Mehemet Ali, was gradually gaining control. The British Government, however, were rash enough to take the advice of their incompetent Consul-General in Egypt that Alexandria was of importance to British interests and could easily be seized. Disaster was accordingly invited by the despatch of a small force of 5,000 men, of which 3,000 were British and 2,000 foreign troops. This detachment sailed from Messina under the command of Major-General M'Kenzie Fraser on 6 March 1807, and the first troops landed on 17 March. On 20 March the Turkish Governor of Alexandria surrendered, and the British Consul-General told Fraser that the town had been on the verge of famine. He recommended that Rosetta and Rahmanieh should be captured because they had the food on which Alexandria depended. Fraser had expected that Alexandria would have been able to provision his troops, and, reluctantly, he sent a small force to Rosetta. The troops entered the town without opposition, but walked into an ambush and had to withdraw after suffering heavy casualties. Fraser now sent a larger force under Brigadier-General W. Stewart to make another attempt. But after several days in front of Rosetta, faced now by a Turkish army in considerably greater strength, which was being constantly reinforced, Stewart decided to withdraw to Alexandria. Soon after his return it was discovered that there were, in fact, large stores of rice in Alexandria, and that the Arabs, if offered good prices, brought in ample provisions. The expedition to Rosetta, therefore, had been unnecessary. Fraser was reinforced by 2,000 troops from Messina; but a treaty was negotiated with the Turks in Constantinople and in accordance with this, the British force was withdrawn from Alexandria and Egypt.

The Expedition to Copenhagen, 1807

By the Treaty of Tilsit on 7 July 1807 the Tsar Alexander undertook not to interfere if Napoleon should seize the Danish fleet. This secret clause in the treaty came to the knowledge of the British Government. It was decided to anticipate Napoleon, and Lord Cathcart was placed in command of an expeditionary force of 27,000 men organised in two divisions, of which Sir Arthur Wellesley was given command of one and Sir David Baird the other. This force arrived off Copenhagen on 4 August and was there joined by the Pomeranian Legion under General Linsingen. The troops landed at Veldbeck and Cathcart decided on a regular siege of Copenhagen. He ordered Wellesley to operate with his division and Linsingen's against a Danish force of 14,000 men, mostly militia, at Roskilde. Linsingen was to turn the Danish left; but he was late, and Wellesley attacked frontally without waiting from him. The Danish militia were ill-trained and the result was an easy victory. On 5 September the Danes capitulated.

The First Peninsular Expedition, 1808

In November 1807 a French army under Junot marched through Spain into Portugal and occupied Lisbon; the Portuguese Regent fleeing before the invaders in a British warship to the Portuguese colony of Brazil. The excuse for this French aggression was that Portugal had refused to break off her relations with Great Britain.

In May 1808 Napoleon appointed his brother Joseph King of Spain, and, in consequence, revolts broke out all over the country. Various Spanish provincial governments were established and some of these appealed to Great Britain for help. The British Government supplied money and arms and decided to send an expeditionary force. As it happened, such a force had been prepared, but for action against Spain's colonies in the Americas; for up till this time Spain had been at war with Great Britain. Some 9,000 troops had been assembled at Cork for embarkation, and it was generally expected that Sir Arthur Wellesley would command them.

In June Wellesley, who had been promoted to Lieutenant-General on the previous 25 April, was appointed to the command and instructed to proceed to the Portuguese coast and cooperate with the Spanish and Portuguese commanders. The fleet sailed from Cork on 12 July. Wellesley boarded a fast frigate and went ahead to Corunna, arriving there on 20 July. However, the Spanish authorities there refused to accept British troops and suggested that Wellesley took them to north Portugal. On 24 July Wellesley arrived at Oporto. The situation there was no more satisfactory than at Corunna, and Wellesley departed the following day to confer with Sir Charles Cotton, commanding the British fleet off the Tagus, leaving orders for the expedition to remain at Mondego Bay. Cotton agreed that this was the best place to disembark, and General Spencer at Cadiz was ordered to go there by sea as soon as possible.

In the meantime, at home, the Cabinet had come to the conclusion that to land Wellesley's force of 9,000 men in the face of the very large French armies in the Peninsular might lead to disaster. Accordingly it was decided to increase the strength of the expeditionary force to 30,000 men. Lieutenant-General Sir John Moore, who had been sent on a fruitless venture to Sweden with 10,000 troops, was ordered to take this force to Portugal. Spencer's 5,000 from Cadiz, and another 5,000 to be sent from England would then bring the numbers up to the required 30,000. Moore was senior to Wellesley and should therefore have commanded the augmented expeditionary force; but he was not politically acceptable to the Government, who appointed instead Lieutenant-General Sir Hew Dalrymple, Governor of Gibraltar, with Lieutenant-General Sir Harry Burrard as his second-in-command. Both were senior to Moore. These alterations were notified to Wellesley, who received the dispatch on 30 July. At about the same date he learned of the surrender of a French corps to the Spaniards at Baylen on 18 July. This relieved Major-General Brent Spencer from his post of observation at Cadiz and he arrived at Mondego Bay on 5 August, by which time Wellesley's original force had just finished disembarking.

Wellesley now had under his command about 14,200 men. They were organised in six infantry brigades with supporting artillery; but there was only one cavalry regiment, and this lacked half its establishment of horses. Transport was lamentably deficient, and Portuguese cooperation was ineffective, and even replaced by obstruction.

On 10 August the British force began an advance towards Lisbon. Wellesley chose the coast road so that he could maintain close touch with the fleet. On 15 August French outposts were encountered at Rolica, and two days later the French advanced guard under General Delaborde was defeated. On 20 August the army reached Vimeiro, where it was reinforced by two brigades from England, commanded respectively by Brigadier-Generals Wroth Acland and Robert Anstruther. Wellesley intended to continue his advance the following morning, but Burrard had arrived and ordered him to await the arrival of Moore's force. Moore had started disembarking his troops at the Mondego estuary, but Burrard ordered him to re-embark and to land at the estuary of the Maceira River, near Vimeiro.

However, on the morning of 21 August General Junot, commanding the French troops in Portugal, attacked Wellesley's position with 13,000 men and was severely defeated. Burrard left Wellesley to fight the battle but refused his request to follow up the beaten enemy. Before nightfall Dalrymple arrived and assumed the command.

On 22 August an envoy arrived from Junot offering a convention under which the French should evacuate Portugal. This approach resulted in the Convention of Cintra of 30 August under which Junot and his army were to be conveyed to La Rochelle in British ships. The terms of the convention were ill received in Great Britain, and Dalrymple,

Burrard, and Wellesley, who had all signed it, were recalled home, leaving Moore in command.

The Government's plan for the further action of British forces in the Peninsula reached Moore at Lisbon on 6 October 1808. An army of 30,000 infantry and 5,000 cavalry was to be employed in northern Spain under Moore's command. Of these, 10,000 were to come from England and the remainder from the troops then in Portugal. It was left to Moore to decide whether these two components of his army were to be united in the course of a coastal voyage to the River Ebro, which was to be the area of operations, or whether junction should effected during a march into the interior. Moore chose the latter, and he was bidden to concert his plan of operations with the Spanish generals. However, no Spanish general was designated, so that Moore did not know with whom he should establish contact. Marches of 300 miles would be necessary before the two components of his army could unite, and there would then be another 300 miles to be covered to the Ebro. Moore was informed that the roads north of the Tagus along which he proposed to march were impracticable for artillery. But it was too late to change because the supplies were already moving towards Almeida, and most of the regiments were already on the move in the same direction. He had therefore to divide his army and send the artillery and its park, escorted by the cavalry and 3,000 infantry via Talavera. This column was commanded by Lieutenant-General Sir John Hope. Moore selected Salamanca as the concentration area for the whole army. According to Moore's information, the march and concentration would be covered by strong Spanish armies, so that there did not appear to be any risk to these widely separated columns.

Moore's headquarters left Lisbon on 26 October. In the meantime, the troops from England under the command of Lieutenant-General Sir David Baird had arrived at Corunna, but the local junta would not let them land, and kept Baird waiting for 15 days. On 8 November he was still at Corunna, whilst Moore had reached Almeida, and the artillery column was 120 miles south of him at Truxillo. By 23 November most of Moore's main body had arrived at Salamanca, but on this day Napoleon's troops had completed the rout of the Spanish armies and Moore had no cover in front of him at all. Three days later Baird's advanced troops were at Astorga, 80 miles away, and Hope's column was strung out between the Escurial and Talavera — a length of some 70 miles — with its head about 120 miles south-east of Salamanca and 24 miles north of Madrid. The situation was perilous, for Moore would need 20 days to concentrate his army. At first sight this appeared impracticable, and Moore's first decision was to retreat to Portugal; the main body direct by road and Baird's force by road to Corunna or Vigo and thence by sea to Lisbon. Hope, at this juncture, was conducting a rapid, able, and daring march across the heads of the French columns, and he eventually shepherded his charges safely into Salamanca.

At the beginning of December Moore was informed that the Spaniards were preparing for a desperate defence of Madrid. He changed his mind about retiring and determined to help them by advancing against the French communications in order to draw the whole weight of Napoleon's army against his own. On 11 December he started this movement, but preparations for a retreat still continued. The army reached and encamped at Sahagun, but here on 23 December a French despatch was intercepted, containing the news that Madrid had fallen but that Marshal Soult with a comparatively weak force was isolated in front of the British. Moore moved at once to attack him. However, the advance was almost immediately turned into a rapid retreat, for Moore had indeed brought the whole might of the French against him, and Napoleon in person was leading a thrust aimed at his flank and rear. Moore's army escaped, but a retreat under appalling conditions eventually ended at Corunna. Here, on 16 January 1809, Moore turned at bay to inflict a defeat on the pursuing Soult which enabled the Britsh Army to embark; but Moore was killed in the battle.

The Walcheren Expedition, 1809

In March 1809, according to information that had reached the British Government, a French squadron was in the port of Flushing and the French were building docks at Antwerp to provide a base for expeditions against the English coasts. At Admiralty instigation, a joint naval and military operation was planned to capture the island of Walcheren in the Scheldt estuary and demolish the new docks. The expedition sailed in July, the army element consisting of some 40,000 troops under the command of Lieutenant-General the Earl of Chatham. Flushing and the islands of Walcheren and South Beveland were captured by 15 August, the French retiring to the mainland. However, before an attack could be mounted against Antwerp, the troops were falling victims to the virulent Walcheren fever. On 20 August nearly 1,600 men were ill, and a week later the number of sick had risen to 4,000. On 28 August, with his own strength deteriorating so rapidly whilst that of the French was increasing, Chatham decided to abandon the expedition. After a further week, as evacuation was in progress, the sick list had doubled to 8,000. The effects of the Walcheren fever were long lasting, and four months later about a third of the troops who had taken part in this unfortunate operation were still unfit for active service.

The Douro and Talavera, 1809

After the battle of Corunna and the embarkation of Moore's army, the only British troops remaining in the Iberian Peninsula were some 10,000 left in Lisbon by Moore under the command of Lieutenant-General Sir John Cradock. Soult, who had been defeated at Corunna, seized Oporto on 29 March 1809, but he hesitated to advance on Lisbon in the face of Cradock's command. Early in the same month Major-General William Beresford was sent to Lisbon, with the local rank of Lieutenant-General, to reorganise the Portuguese Army, and was given the rank of Marshal in that army by the Portuguese Government.

On 2 April 1809 Sir Arthur Wellesley was appointed to command a fresh expedition to Portugal, and on 22 April he landed at Lisbon. A few days later he relieved Cradock, who was appointed Governor of Gibraltar.

The most immediate enemy threats came from Soult, who was at Oporto with 24,000 men, and Victor, who was at Merida east of Badajoz, with 30,000. Wellesley had about 22,000 British troops and was expecting to be reinforced by another 6,000. The force was organised in one cavalry brigade and nine infantry brigades, including the King's German Legion. He decided to attack Soult and recover the harbour of Oporto. Detaching a force to watch Victor, he concentrated the remainder of his army at Coimbra. Soult, aware of the weakness of his position, was already making preparations for a withdrawal and had ordered every boat to be brought to the north bank of the River Douro. On 6 May Wellesley detached Beresford with 9,000 Portuguese to secure the crossing over the upper Douro, about 40 miles above Oporto. On 9 May, by which time Beresford had had time to get into position, Major-General Rowland Hill's Brigade embarked in fishing boats on the Ovar Lake, an inlet from the sea that stretched 20 miles behind the French right which had been left unguarded, and landed at daybreak on 10 May on its northern shore, turning the French right. On the same day Beresford's crossing of the Douro turned the enemy's left. On 12 May Wellesley was surveying the French position from a height on the south bank of the Douro. With the help of local inhabitants, a staff officer secured barges from the north bank, and part of the 3rd Buffs were across the river before the alarm was sounded. Once a lodgement on the north bank had been made, more troops followed, and soon Wellesley had captured Oporto with less than 150 casualties and the French were in flight.

Wellesley pursued Soult 18 May; he then returned southward and was at Coimbra once more on 26 May. By the second week in June he was at Abrantes on the River Tagus, and towards the end of the month he left it, marching towards Spain. Wellesley had agreed a plan with the Spanish General Cuesta for an advance up the Tagus valley to Madrid.

On 18 June Wellesley had reorganised his army into one cavalry division and four infantry divisions, each of two brigades. He marched from Abrantes with 23,000 British troops, leaving Beresford with his Portuguese to watch the northern frontier of Portugal. Cuesta had about 30,000 men under his direct command, and another 25,000 under General Venegas. On 10 July the British Army was at Placencia, and Cuesta's force was at Almarez. Marshal Victor, with the immediately opposing French corps, about 23,000 strong, was at Talavera.

On 11 July Wellesley concerted a plan of operations with Cuesta, by which Venegas would move from the south by Ocana to Arganda, near Madrid, while Wellesley and Cuesta advanced to Talavera directly against Victor, and Beresford operated near Salamanca. The British troops, however, were already in dificulties owing to the Spanish failure to fulfil contracts for provisions and transport.

Contact with the French rearguard was gained on 22 July and Wellesley wished to attack the following morning; but Cuesta refused and a great opporuntity was lost. Meanwhile the Supreme Junta of Spain had countermanded Venegas's advance, and Soult, with the 2nd, 5th, and 6th Corps was marching from Salamanca to Plasencia in Wellesley's rear. On 27 July Victor attacked the Allied position at Talavera without success. The following day the French returnd to the attack, but after much bitter fighting they gave up the struggle and retreated from the battlefield. It had in fact been a very near thing, and Wellesley gave the credit for the victory to the 48th Regiment.

On 1 August information reached Wellesley that Soult had occupied Plasencia. He decided to give battle at Oropesa, 20 miles west of Talavera, leaving Cuesta to guard the military hospitals at the latter place. The British Army marched on 3 August, but to Wellesley's annoyance Cuesta joined him the following morning, having left the British wounded to fall into the hands of the French. Wellesley now learned that Soult was in far greater strength than he had thought. Seizing his only means of escape, he moved at dawn the next day, crossed the Tagus by the bridge at Arzobispo, and on 7 August was at Deleytosa. By this time his army was practically starving owing to the failure of the Spaniards to produce the promised provisions. The army finally went into cantonments in the frontier fortress of Badajoz.

In reward for his victories at Oporto and Talavera, Wellesley was created Baron Douro of Wellesley and Viscount Wellington of Talavera, whilst the Spanish Central Junta conferred on him the rank of Captain-General.

Marshal Masséna and the Lines of Torres Vedras, 1809-1810

By the end of 1809 the Spanish armies, as regular formations in the field, had almost ceased to exist. On 15 January 1810 Wellington, as part of his plan for the defence of

Portugal, left Hill's division at Abrantes and moved north across the Tagus with his main body, establishing his headquarters at Viseu, about 50 miles south-east of Oporto. Behind him he had arranged a formidable defensive position into which he could withdraw if necessary. Lisbon stands at the base of a tongue of land averaging some 25 miles in width, bounded on the east by the Tagus, and on the west by the Atlantic. It is crossed by two lines of mountains. In October 1809 Wellington had visited the area and had directed that these mountain chains should be fortified to provide two lines of defence. In almost the most northerly portion of the first line stood the little town of Torres Vedras.

Early in June 1810 Marshal Masséna began to besiege the Spanish frontier fortress of Ciudad Rodrigo, and this surrendered to him on 11 July. Masséna then advanced to attack Almeida, the corresponding Portuguese frontier fortress on the River Coa, in face of a rearguard action by Robert Craufurd's Light Division. Almeida capitulated on 27 August. On 16 September the French advanced into Portugal with 72,000 men in three corps columns, which formed a junction at Viseu. Wellington, his army now concentrated, had 25,000 British and 24,000 Portuguese troops.

Instead of retiring straightaway to his lines of Torres Vedras, Wellington decided to stand and check the French advance, both to stimulate the morale of his own troops and also that of the Portuguese Government and civil populace. He chose the ridge of Busaco, an immensely strong position which lay at right angles to Masséna's advance to Coimbra. Masséna attacked this position on 27 September with his 2nd, 6th, and 8th Corps; but after a fierce struggle the French were thrown back all along the line with heavy loss, whilst the British casualties were slight. In this battle the British-trained Portuguese troops behaved well.

Wellington fell back on Coimbra, and then, on 1 October, to Leira where he halted for three days. From there the British Army with its attached Portuguese troops moved into the Lines of Torres Vedras, in front of which a horrified Masséna arrived on 17 October. By the end of the month the lines were garrisoned by 29,000 British troops, 24,000 Portuguese, and 5,000 Spanish; whilst Masséna's army had been reduced by casualties and desertion to little more than 50,000. Sickness and lack of food made it impossible for the French to maintain their position, so on 14 November Masséna fell back to the more plentifully supplied region around Santarem and Thomar. There he remained until the end of the year.

The Campaign of 1811

At the end of 1810 Soult marched from Cadiz to open up communications with Masséna. On 27 January 1811 he invested Badajoz, and on 11 March the Spanish garrison capitulated. In the same month, however, Masséna retreated, covered by Ney's 6th Corps as rearguard. Wellington followed up strongly, but Ney handled his command with considerable skill, forcing the British advanced guard (generally the Light Division) to deploy, and retiring before a serious attack by the main body could be mounted.

After the fall of Badajoz Wellington had detached Beresford with a force to protect his right flank. However, the defeat of Marshal Victor by the British component of the Cadiz garrison under Major-General Thomas Graham at the battle of Barossa on 7 March directed Soult's attention to affairs in the south, and he returned with the bulk of his force to Seville.

On 21 March Masséna was back at Selorica and Guarda, almost on the Portuguese frontier. On 29 March Wellington attacked Masséna on the Heights of Guarda and the French fell back without attempting to hold the position; withdrawing across the River

Coa to reform on its right bank. There they were again attacked by the British forces on 3 April, and Masséna evacuated Portugal. Wellington now laid siege to the fortress of Almeida, and on 2 May Masséna, who had established his headquarters at Ciudad Rodrigo, advanced to try and relieve it. In the face of this fresh advance by the French, Wellington took up a position covering Almeida with his main strength about the village of Fuentes de Onoro. The first encounter took place on 3 May, when Fuentes de Onoro changed hands twice. On 5 May Masséna assailed the British position fiercely in superior strength and Wellington was only saved from defeat by the stout fighting of his troops. On the night of 7 May Masséna conceded the victory to Wellington and retired. A short time later Napoleon replaced Masséna by Marmont. Almeida fell to the British but the French garrison escaped.

In the south Beresford laid siege to Badajoz on 4 May, but the return of Soult forced him to raise the siege on 12 May, and he took up a position at Albuera in conjunction with a Spanish force. Soult attacked this position on 16 May, but after a bloody and indecisive battle he withdrew to Solano. Badajoz was invested again on 25 May, but the siege had to be raised once again because it was learned on 12 June that Marmont was marching to cooperate with Soult. Wellington followed suit and for nearly three weeks he faced Marmont with the bulk of his army, until the French Marshal gave it up and withdrew north of the Tagus. Wellington also moved northwards to blockade Ciudad Rodrigo.

On 21 September Marmont marched to the relief of Ciudad Rodrigo, and on 24 September he got a convoy of supplies into the fortress. The following day he deployed his troops against Wellington's and his cavalry, with artillery support, launched an unsuccessful attack against a British position on the height above the village of El Bodon. Having forced Marmont, with his considerably larger force, to show his strength, Wellington retired by stages to a strong position along the River Coa. Marmont, short of provisions, retreated, and Wellington resumed his blockade of Ciudad Rodrigo.

Sieges of Ciudad Rodrigo and Badajoz, 1812

On 1 January 1812 Wellington moved his troops forward for the complete investment of Ciudad Rodrigo. Eighteen days later the fortress was assaulted and captured. In recognition of this feat, Wellington was created an Earl in the British peerage, and the Spaniards made him Duke of Ciudad Rodrigo.

Preparations were now made for the siege of Badajoz, and as soon as the flooding of the rivers made it impossible for the French to invade northern Portugal, Wellington marched the greater part of his army southwards. The siege began on 16 March; on the night of 6 April the assault was launched; and at dawn on 7 April the French garrison surrendered. The capture of this strong fortress cost the attackers about 1,000 officers and men killed and some 4,000 wounded.

In Ciudad Rodrigo and Badajoz Wellington now held the northern and southern gateways from Portugal into Spain.

Salamanca and after, 1812-1813

During the siege of Badajoz Soult began to move forward from Seville and Marmont from Salamanca, but nothing came of these threats. After the fall of Badajoz, Soult returned to his blockade of Cadiz, whilst Marmont moved to Sabugal on the Coa River, some 40 miles south-west of Ciudad Rodrigo and south of Almeida. Wellington returned to the north to protect his frontier fortresses. Marmont having retired from his advanced position, Wellington prepared to advance into Spain. He now had an army larger than any he had yet commanded in the Peninsula. Under his immediate command were about 56,000 officers and men fit for duty (of whom some 18,000 were Portuguese and 3,500 Spanish), whilst Lieutenant-General Sir Rowland Hill's Corps in the neighbourhood of Badajoz numbered about 20,000 (including about 12,000 Portuguese).

Wellington began his advance on 13 June, Marmont falling back before him, and on 17 June British troops marched into Salamanca. Marmont had, however, left garrisons in the three forts that the French had built, and it was not till 27 June that these were taken.

Marmont, reinforced, returned to the offensive and tried to manoeuvre against Wellington's communications. However, on 22 July Marmont made a tactical error, and Wellington seized the opportunity presented to him to inflict a crushing defeat on him at the battle of Salamanca. In reward for this success Wellington was created a Marquess. Marmont was severely wounded in the battle and was replaced by General Clausel.

Following up the French retreat from the battlefield, the British Army marched into Valladolid on 30 July. Clausel continued his retreat to Burgos, but Wellington now turned south against the army under the direct command of King Joseph Bonaparte, which was retreating to Madrid. On 10 August Joseph evacuated Madrid and retreated towards Valencia, ordering Soult to leave Andalusia and to join him there. On 12 August Wellington's troops marched into Madrid. Meanwhile a force of 5,000 British troops from Sicily and 8,000 Spaniards from Majorca, all under Lieutenant-General Frederick Maitland, had landed at Alicante.

By the end of August Clausel had restored the efficiency of his army and was threatening Wellington's communications. Wellington sent Hill to Aranjuez on the Tagus to watch Soult and on 1 September marched north with four divisions, leaving two in Madrid. Clausel fell back before Wellington's advance, retreating through Burgos on 17 September. The French garrison of this strong fortress, however, remained as a formidable bastion, and Wellington, lacking adequate siege artillery, failed to reduce it in the time available to him.

In the meantime Masséna had been restored to favour, and Napoleon appointed him to command all the French forces in the northern provinces. Masséna promptly replaced Clausel by Souham and instructed the latter to relieve Burgos. Souham, reinforced by 12,000 fresh troops, advanced on 12 October, and three days later Wellington raised the siege of Burgos and retreated towards the Douro, ordering Hill to retire along the valley of the Tagus.

On 8 November Wellington, now rejoined by Hill, took up a position on the River Tormes. Two days later Souham arrived opposite him and was joined by Soult, who had been following Hill. Soult then crossed the upper reaches of the Tormes, threatening the British flank and rear. Wellington retreated again and by 17 December the British Army was back once more along the Portuguese frontier, and went into winter quarters.

The Campaign of Victoria, 1813

Wellington opened his 1813 campaign in the latter part of May. The army advanced in three columns: the left, and largest, under Lieutenant-General Sir Tomas Graham, consisted of six British divisions, two Portuguese brigades, and a large force of cavalry; the centre, under Wellington's direct command, comprised two British and one Spanish division, together with cavalry; and in the right column under Sir Rowland Hill were two British divisions. The left column advanced through the Tras-os-Montes and Zamora towards Valladolid; the centre via the road to Salamanca; and the right through Bejar towards Alba de Tormes. The left column turned the enemy right flank on the Douro and the French, under Joseph Bonaparte's supreme command, began a retreat which carried them right back to the line of the River Ebro, Burgos being evacuated without a struggle. This rapid advance was partly due to a swing in the relative strengths of the two sides. Whilst the French were still superior in the numbers of their regular forces, their quality had deteriorated because Napoleon had withdrawn some of the best troops, whilst Wellington had been reinforced and the Spanish forces had become more effective.

On 14 and 15 June Wellington crossed the head waters of the Ebro round the French right flank. On 20 June the British Army, with its Portuguese element and Spanish allies, encamped a few miles from the French concentration area in the neighbourhood of Vittoria. On 21 June Wellington attacked in three columns; the left under Graham, the right under Hill, and the centre under his immediate command. The result was an overwhelming victory, which included the capture of practically all the French artillery and the whole of their baggage. Wellington was promoted Field-Marshal for his victory and created Duke of Vittoria by the Spaniards.

By 8 July the Allied army had closed up to the French frontier. Of the French armies in Spain, only that commanded by General Suchet still remained there, and Wellesley expected Lieutenant-General Sir John Murray, then commanding the expedition in eastern Spain, to look after him. This expectation was not realised, for two days after the battle of Vittoria an ADC arrived from Murray with news that he had raised the siege of Taragona and embarked his army!

The Pyrenees, 1813

When Napoleon heard of the disaster that had be fallen his armies in Spain he despatched Soult to replace Joseph as commander-in-Chief and to protect France from invasion. Soult arrived in the Pyrenees on 13 July, and on 24 July he started an advance to relieve the fortresses of San Sebastian and Pamplona, which Wellington would have to capture before he could invade France. Soult attacked and seized the passes of Maya and Roncesvalles, taking the defending forces by surprise. Wellington, who was on a visit to the siege works at San Sebastian, heard of the heavy attacks against his right and rode off immediately to take command.

On 28 July Soult advanced in force from Sorauren, trying to turn the Allied left flank in this sector. This developed into the fiercely contested First Battle of Sorauren, and ended with the repulse of the French. On 30 July Soult, leaving Reille to face Wellington, switched his own attack against Hill on the Allied left, in an effort to relieve San Sebastian. Wellington foiled this move by attacking and defeating Reille in the Second Battle of Sorauren. He carried the French position and his pursuit brought him to the rear of the force attacking Hill. On the night of 30 July Soult retired, pursued by Hill, and leaving Wellington in possession of the passes.

In the meantime Lord William Bentinck had superseded the useless Murray, and he landed again on the east coast of Spain, forcing Suchet to withdraw north of the Ebro.

On 31 August San Sebastian was stormed, and on 8 September the castle, to which the garrison had retired, capitulated. Soult, on 31 August, made another attempt to relieve San Sebastian, but was stopped by the stout defence of a Spanish force under General Freyre.

The Advance into France, 1813-1814

The French had barred the way to Bayonne by two lines of strong defences. In the first was the precipitous mass of La Rhune, towering above the little town of Vera on the right bank of the River Bidassoa, which marked the frontier, and some seven miles from the sea. On 7 October, at low tide, the 5th Division waded across the mouth of the Bidassoa and stood on French soil. The following day the Vera pass was forced by the Light Division and the Spaniards captured La Rhune. Soult fell back on to his second line covering St Jean de Luz and on 31 October Pamplona surrendered.

On 10 November Wellington attacked Soult's new position, which was mostly south of the River Nivelle, and drove the French defenders from this line too. The Allies then went into cantonments and Soult entrenched a position to defend Bayonne. Wellington decided to clear the area between the River Adour and its tributary the Nive which, flowing from the south, joins the former at Bayonne. On 9 December British columns crossed the Nive. On 10 December Soult attacked the British position on the Nive while Wellington's forces were divided. Soult achieved surprise but was eventually checked, though he renewed his attacks unsuccessfully on 11 and 12 December. A further and heavier attack on 13 December was also defeated.

Operations were resumed on 14 February 1814, when Hill launched an attack against the French left. Then on 23 and 24 February Sir John Hope crossed the Adour between Bayonne and the sea. Soult fell back eastwards to place himself on Wellington's flank, but Wellington, leaving two divisions to besiege Bayonne, followed him up and at Orthez, in a stubbornly contested battle on 27 February, defeated Soult again.

Wellington now sent two divisions to occupy Bordeaux. Soult tried to take advantage of their absence by returning to the attack, but he was repulsed and on 18 March the British troops followed up the retreating French. On 24 March Soult entered Toulouse, a fortress with strong but rather antiquated defences. Mistrusting these, the French commander took up his main position on a range of heights to the east of the town. Wellington attacked on 10 April, driving the French back into the town and investing it. On the night of 12 April Soult slipped out of Toulouse, but Napoleon had abdicated on 30 March and hostilities were already officially at an end. On 11 May Wellington was created a Duke.

The Waterloo Campaign, 1815

On 20 March Napoleon, after his escape from Elba, entered Paris. On 5 April Wellington arrived at Brussels to take command of the British and Netherlands Army. On 14 June Wellington and Field-Marshal Prince Blücher, commanding the Prussian Army, learned that Napoleon's army was concentrating about Maubeuge.

The French offensive came two days later. On the afternoon of 16 June a wing of Napoleon's army under Ney attacked part of Wellington's troops in position at Quatre Bras, whilst Napoleon himself with the bulk of his troops attacked the Prussian position at Ligny. Ney was held at Quatre Bras, but the Prussians were beaten at Ligny and Blücher retired to Wavre. Napoleon sent Grouchy with the right wing of the army to follow Blücher and turned against Wellington with the remainder. Wellington, having withdrawn his troops from Quatre Bras, took up, on 17 June, a position on a low ridge across the Brussels road, just south of the village of Waterloo. Here, on 18 June, Napoleon attacked him all day without success, till, with the arrival of the Prussians on the French right flank, Wellington counter-attacked and Napoleon's army was routed.

Notes

1 Sir Henry Bunbury, *The Great War with France (1799-1810)* (London Peter Davies, 1927), pxviii

2 Captain Sir George Arthur, *The Story of the Household Cavalry*, vol II (London, Archibald Constable, 1909), pp519-25
3 Sir Herbert Maxwell, *The Life of Wellington*, vol I (London, Sampson Low, Marston, & Co, 1900), p14
4 Bunbury, op cit, p6
5 ibid, p53
6 ibid, p116
7 ibid, pp158-64

Infantry

General

After the end of the American War of Independence there were two conflicting schools of thought amongst those officers of infantry who studied their profession. Regiments which had fought in America had been trained in the loose order necessary in wood and forest against largely irregular foes, and had become convinced that the maximum volume of accurate fire was far more important than shock action with the bayonet. Many regiments, however, which had not served in America, remained wedded to the concept of the rigid lines which had served so well at Fontenoy and Minden. No common doctrine was at this time enforced in the British Army, so that colonels of regiments trained them in accordance with their own beliefs. The regiments from America believed in light infantry: most of the others did not.

In 1785 two officers witnessed the last Prussian Army manoeuvres to be carried out under the personal direction of Frederick the Great. One of them was Lord Cornwallis, who had commanded with distinction the British forces in the Carolinas; the other was Colonel (later General Sir) David Dundas, on the staff of the military headquarters in Dublin. Cornwallis, with the experiences of America fresh in his mind, was caustic about the Prussian exercise. He wrote, 'Their manoeuvres were such as the worst general in England would be hooted at for practising; two lines coming up within six yards of one another and firing until they had no ammunition left; nothing could be more ridiculous.'[1] Cornwallis was writing with the authority of his own brilliant victories at Camden and Guildford Courthouse. The other officer, however, received an entirely different impression. Dundas noted the measured movement of the infantry in their close-knit lines, three ranks deep, and the drill common to all battalions which enabled brigades to deploy and manoeuvre with exactness and precision. This, he felt, was the model upon which the British Army must be trained. Back in Dublin be began to put his ideas on to paper, and these were published three years later in a book entitled *The Principles of Military Movement*. In it Dundas commented as follows on the current over-emphasis on the importance of light infantry:

'During the late war, their service was conspicuous, and their gallantry and exertions have met with universal applause. But instead of being considered as an accessory to the battalion, they become the principal feature of our army, and have almost put grenadiers out of fashion. The showy exercise, the airy dress, the independent modes which they have adopted, have caught the minds of young officers, and made them imagine that these ought to be general and exclusive. The battalions, constantly drained of their best men, have been taught to undervalue themselves, and almost to forget that in their steadiness and efforts the decision of events depends, and that light infantry, Jägers, marksmen, riflemen, etc etc vanish before the solid movements of the line.'[2]

This book was expanded into *Rules and Regulations for the Formations, Field Exercise, and Movements of His Majesty's Forces*, and as such it received official approval and was issued under the authority of the Adjutant-General at the War Office on 1 June 1792, for adoption in all infantry regiments.

Although Dundas's drill was too rigid and formal, *Rules and Regulations* did provide a thoroughly sound system of training and it established tractical formations that could be modified as circumstances showed necessary. Furthermore, light infantry were included, though only nine of the book's 458 pages were devoted to them. The book was of great benefit to the Army, in spite of its shortcomings, for there was now a common doctrine to which all colonels of regiments had to conform.

Light infantry training was not, indeed, allowed to die, and in the Netherlands campaign of 1793-95 the activities of the French *tirailleurs*, or skirmishers, underlined its importance. In 1794, two years after the publication of *Rules and Regulations*, Lieutenant-General Charles (later General Earl) Grey formed a light infantry school in the West Indies, with the object of restoring 'the perfection of light infantry attained during the American War'. Captains Coote Manningham and the Hon William Stewart were two of Grey's officers at the school, and they were later to become Colonel and Lieutenant-Colonel respectively of the Experimental Rifle Corps. In 1796 Brigadier-General John Moore was posted to the West Indian island of St Lucia and doubtless became acquainted with Grey's school. Interest was now being awakened in England, largely in the light of Napoleon Bonaparte's remarkable Italian campaign of 1796-7, and in 1798 General Viscount Howe was directed to form a brigade on the coast of Essex for instruction in light infantry drill. Also in 1798 the 5th Battalion of the 60th Royal Americans was raised as a rifle unit from the remains of several corps of foreign light troops, mainly German, and Colonel Francis de Rottenberg was appointed to command it. This remarkable Austrian soldier had some years earlier written a book in German on light infantry drill and training, which, by order of the Duke of York, was translated into English and issued officially by the Adjutant-General's department on 1 August 1798 as *Regulations for the Exercise of Riflemen and Light Infantry and Instructions for their Conduct in the Field*. In April of that year de Rottenburg's battalion had been posted to Bandon, in Ireland, coming under John Moore, whose command already included 12 companies of Militia light infantry.[3] Moore's subsequent instructions for these Militia companies were mainly a mixture of de Rottenburg's and Dundas's 'Regulations'.

In January 1800 the Duke of York ordered the formation of an Experimental Corps of Riflemen. He gave the task to Moore, who had lately recovered from a wound received during the expedition to Holland the previous year. Moore sent a circular to the 13 regiments available in the United Kingdom, requesting each to send a detachment of three officers, a corporal, and 30 privates for instruction in light infantry work. These detachment were to be formed into a battalion under Colonel Coote Manningham. The response was not altogether satisfactory because six of the regiments seized the opportunity to get rid of their worst men. Moore, however, had now sailed for the Mediterranean and did not see the results of his circular, which was perhaps as well for the regiments concerned!

Lieutenant-Colonel the Hon William Stewart was soon posted to the Corps and placed by Manningham in charge of its training. At Stewart's request the Corps was sent to take part in the attack on Ferrol on 25 August 1800, and a few weeks later it was broken up at Malta. However, its nucleus remained in existence, and 33 Fencible regiments stationed in Ireland were each requested to supply 12 volunteers for the Rifle Corps. These volunteers were of a much better stamp than the men of the original detachments, and they were commanded by the officers originally selected for the Corps. *Regulations of the Rifle Corps* were drawn up, probably by Stewart. They were based on what he called the 'Company System', by which each comany formed a military family under its captain, bound by ties of honour, comradeship, and mutual confidence. This was something new in the British Army.[4]

Moore, after his arrival in the Mediterranean in 1800, went to Minorca, where he saw the 90th Regiment, which had been raised in 1794 as the Perthshire Volunteers and formed into light infantry. Its commanding officer was Lieutenant-Colonel Kenneth Mackenzie and the battalion had been trained in de Rottenberg's drill in Portugal under General Sir Charles Stuart. Moore, no stranger of course to the drill, thought the 90th's demonstration of it excellent.[5]

On 9 July 1803 Moore was appointed to command a brigade encamped in Shorncliffe, in Kent, consisting of the 4th, 52nd, 59th, 70th, and 95th Regiments He was already Colonel of the 52nd, which had been made Light Infantry in January 1803, and in response to his request Mackenzie, then in the 44th Regiment, was posted to command the 52nd.[6] The 95th was the number allotted to the Rifle Corps when it was brought into the Line in 1802.[7]

Sir John Moore has been associated particularly with the training of light troops, but in fact the most important part of his system was applicable to any type of infantry. Moore's Shorncliffe Brigade had not been formed for training, but for the defence of the coast from Deal to Dungeness against any attempted French invasion. An officer of the 4th (King's Own) Regiment, when it was under Moore's command, said that the soldiers 'acquired such discipline as to become an example to the army and proud of their profession.' He adds: 'It was the internal and moral system, the constant superintendence of the officers, the real government and responsibility of the captains, which carried the discipline to such perfection.' Moore insisted on the efficiency of the officers before that of the men, and newly joined officers had to learn their profession on the barrack square. He demanded of them knowledge of their duties, good temper, and kind treatment of their men. He ordered commanding officers of regiments to delegate power to their company commanders in regard to punishments, rewards, drill, food, and clothing. For punishments company commanders were to be assisted by courts martial with members drawn from the rank and file, presided over by a corporal, and with powers to award minor punishments, which could be inflicted, however, only in the presence of the company orderly officer. On 1 August 1803 the Duke of York inspected Moore's Brigade and was so impressed with it that he recommended to the King that the 4th and 52nd Regiments should be allowed a greater proportion of promotions than any other.[8]

Both the 4th King's Own and the 52nd Light Infantry were among the regiments chosen to form second battalions. The 1st Battalion of the 4th marched in due course to Horsham to join its 2nd Battalion, which had formed in that town, whilst the 2nd Battalion 52nd came to Shorncliffe. The 43rd Regiment had already arrived at Shorncliffe, so that, with the 95th, Moore now had under his command the three regiments which were to be permanently associated in Wellington's Light Division. However, whilst the 43rd and 52nd were Light Infantry regiments, armed with the smoothbore musket, the 95th was a Rifle regiment equipped with the muzzle-loading Baker rifle, and the specialist functions of the two were quite different. Light infantry were trained to act either as skirmishers in front of the main infantry body, or as close-ordered bodies in the normal infantry role. Riflemen, with their slow-loading but long-range and accurate rifles, were primarily employed in skirmishing, harassing, protection, and reconnaissance; though they too could operate in the same fashion as the heavy infantry in attack and defence.

Organisation

The organisation of the ordinary battalion of the Line is clearly stated in Dundas's *Rules and Regulations* to be as follows:

'The company is formed three deep . . . Each company is a platoon . . . Each company forms two subdivisions, and also four sections. But as sections should never be less than five files, it will happen when the companies are weak that they can only (for the purpose of march) form three sections.

'The battalion is in ten companies: 1 Grenadier, 8 Battalion, 1 Light. The eight battalion companies will comprise four grand divisions; eight companies or platoons: sixteen subdivisions; thirty-two sections, when sufficiently strong to be so subdivided, otherwise twenty-four for the purpose of march. The battalion is also divided into right and left wings. — When the battalion is at war establishment each company will be divided into two platoons. — When the ten companies are with the battalion, they may then, for the purpose of firing and deploying, be divided into five grand divisions.'

The last phrase was in reference to the prevalent custom, at the time that Dundas wrote his *Rules and Regulations*, of taking the flank companies (the light and grenadier companies) away from their regiments and forming them into light infantry and grenadier battalions respectively.

The company had originally been a purely administrative sub-unit, whereas the platoon was the tactical sub-unit in a battalion. On its peace establishment a company could produce only one platoon, or fire unit, but on the higher war establishment it could provide two. The organisation in grand divisions took place when a battalion formed in column of double companies (ie four lines, each of two companies, one behind the other).

An infantry battalion was normally commanded by a lieutenant-colonel. The other officers on the establishment were two majors, ten captains (one to each company) and twenty subalterns (two to each company). Of the subalterns, some were lieutenants and the others ensigns (or second-lieutenants in rifle regiments). A light infantry battalion had two lieutenant-colonels and an extra subaltern in each company.[9] Each step in rank had to be purchased, but if a vacancy occurred through death in action the next senior officer in a battalion was promoted into it without purchase. In 1797 a sergeant-major was first officially incorporated in the battalion establishment.

The normal marching rate laid down in *Rules and Regulations* was 75 paces of 30-inch length. This was known as the 'ordinary step' and applied to all movements on parade. It is the slow-march of the present time. In the 'quick step' there were 108 paces of the same length in the minute. This was used when moving from column into line and vice-versa, and in other parade ground changes of position. It was also approved for small bodies in column of march, and in practice it was probably used for all ordinary movements on active service. The 'quickest step' was 120 paces to the minute, and was intended for wheeling or when distances had to be made up.

The 10-company establishment was used throughout the Peninsular War, though in light infantry and rifle regiments the companies were all of the same type. The three-rank formation in line did not last. It was unpopular with many officers, particularly those who had served in America. The fire in the third rank could not be brought to bear, so that troops in three ranks only developed two-thirds of their fire power. In his camp at Shorncliffe, Moore abandoned three ranks as far as he could, but inspecting officers did not always share his views and often insisted on a third rank, at any rate in the battalion companies. When this happened Moore's instructions were that the fire of the third rank was to be held in reserve and the men were to remain with their muskets shouldered.[10]

In July 1809 there were 103 infantry regiments of the Line (ie excluding the Foot Guards) in the British Army. Of these all but 29 had two or more battalions, for by this time the expansion of the Army had resulted in a general formation of second battalions. The regiments were, of course, scattered all over the world: at home, in the Peninsula, Sicily, Malta, India, the West Indies, the Cape of Good Hope, Canada, Australia, Gibraltar, and Madeira. Second battalions at home supplied reinforcements to their first battalions serving overseas; so that when and if they themselves were posted overseas they generally embarked considerably under strength. In the field, if two battalions of a regiment were in the same theatre, the first battalion got preference and, as strength dropped, the rank and file of the second battalion would normally be transferred to the first battalion, and the officers and sergeants of the second battalion sent home as a cadre to recruit. Wellington, however, preferred to keep low strength second battalions under his command, and group them into 'provisional' battalions. He explained his reasons in a letter to Earl Bathurst, Secretary of State for War, on 9 March 1813, as follows.

'In answer to your letter of the 3rd February, in regard to the detention in this country of the second battalions, and their formation into provisional battalions . . . Every day's experience has proved to me that one soldier, who has served one or two campaigns in this country, is worth 2, if not 3, newly sent out; and it further appears, that it signifies but little from what part of the world regiments come, as those from Gibraltar, Ceuta, Cadiz and the Mediterranean, are equally inefficient with those from England and Ireland. The second battalions, some of which have been now been 4 years in this army, are the best troops we have, and will render good service in the next campaign in the way in which I have organised them.'[11]

At the start of the war with Revolutionary France, the infantry in the field was organised in brigades of from two to four battalions. In the light of experience in the war this simple organisation was gradually modified, primarily because of the introduction of light troops, first in the French Army and then in our own, and brigades were grouped in divisions.

Divisions were first adopted in the 1807 expedition to Copenhagen, and Moore organised his army in divisions on 1 December 1808. Wellington fought his Oporto campaign with no higher formation in his army than a brigade, but in June 1809 the divisional organisation was finally adopted. A few months before this, Wellington had begun to include a strong element of light troops in each infantry brigade to provide a screen against the harassing tactics of the French *tirailleurs*, operating in advance of the main enemy infantry columns. Each battalion of heavy infantry had one company of light infantry, and to these were added in each brigade a company of the 5th Battalion 60th Regiment, a rifle unit. Wellington further increased his proportion of light troops when in March 1810 he created the Light Division of two brigades, each having a nucleus of light infantry with smoothbore muskets for rapid close-range fire and a lighter element of riflemen with slow-loading rifles for long-range accurate fire. A few months later he posted to each brigade of the Light Division a Portuguese rifle battalion.

Weapons

The British infantry entered the wars with Revolutionary France armed with the old Brown Bess flintlock musket, of which the earliest example seen by the author is in the Tower of London and bears the date 1717 on the lock plate. In 1793 the barrel length was 42 inches and its bore was 11 or a shade over .75 calibre. The bullets were from 13½ to 14 to the pound, which would slip easily down a barrel of this diameter. The cartridge consisted of a tube of stout cartridge paper, sealed at both ends with pack thread. It contained six to eight drams of powder and a lead bullet. The soldier bit off the rear end of the cartridge, squeezed a small amount of the powder into the flash-pan, and emptied the remainder down the barrel. He then inserted the bullet and rammed it down the barrel, with the empty paper cartridge on top as wadding. Using this method of loading a trained soldier could fire about three rounds a minute; but with the loose-fitting bullet the weapon had a range of reasonably accurate fire of only about 50 yards. The private soldier had discovered a method of increasing his rate of fire to some five round of minute, though at the cost of still greater inaccuracy. He poured all the powder down the barrel and, leaving the pan shut, banged the butt on the ground, which both consolidated the charge and sent sufficient powder into the pan for priming. The bullet was then rolled down on top of the powder without using wadding and ramrod. (Of course if the musket was then presented in a less than horizontal aim, the bullet could roll out again.) The bayonet used with the Brown Bess musket had a triangular blade 17 inches long, and a four-inch long socket to fit over the barrel.[12]

The Brown Bess musket was used exclusively till 1794, and a large proportion of the infantry was probably armed with it until the reduction of the Army after the battle of Waterloo. In 1794, however, an increasing number of muskets of the so-called India Pattern were issued. This was not a new weapon, but the standard firearm of the East India Company's European and Native infantry. If differed little from Brown Bess, except in its shorter barrel of 39 inches. It was probably issued to British troops because there were large stocks available, whilst supplies of Brown Bess were running short.

In 1802 an improved pattern of Brown Bess musket had been devised, and this was first issued to the 43rd and 52nd Light Infantry in 1806. It became the standard army weapon and had three barrel lengths: 42 inches for heavy infantry, 39 inches for light infantry, and 33 inches for artillery. The bayonet was unaltered.[13] (The 52nd Light Infantry, when they became such, were first issued with muskets 'constructed on a peculiar plan; but experience proved them to be defective', and in consequence they were replaced by the new muskets in February 1806.[14])

Rifle regiments were armed with a muzzle-loading rifled musket designed by Ezekiel Baker, a gunsmith of Whitechapel, which had been chosen from a number of models submitted for a competition held on 4 February 1800 at Woolwich Arsenal. A 30-inch barrel and a bore of 20 (.615 calibre) were selected. The bullet was loose-fitting, but it was used in conjunction with a greased patch to give the necessary grip on the rifling. This made the fit very tight, and ramming bullet and patch down the barrel was consequently a slow process, with the result that two rounds a minute was the maximum rate of fire. A powder horn was issued with the Baker rifle, and this had a cut-off in the nozzle to measure the correct charge of powder to be poured into the barrel. Later this horn was replaced by the usual pattern of made-up cartridges, filled with the correct rifle charge. A special fine-grain powder was used for priming, however, and this was carried in a very small horn slung from a cord. For rapid fire, in an emergency, the weapon could be treated as a smooth-bore musket, and for this purpose a pouch filled with the appropriate cartridges was carried in the soldier's equipment. They were never used if it could be avoided because the grooves of the rifling got clogged up and had to be cleaned out before the weapon could be fired as a rifle again. The bayonet had a flat single-edged sword blade, 24 inches long, and was fixed to the rifle by a grip, slotted to fit over a lug at the side of the barrel and secured by a spring in the slot.[15]

In the heavy infantry the barrels of the smooth-bore muskets were burnished bright. Ensign George Bell of the 34th Foot writes: 'We marched away by moonlight; the men slung their arms to prevent the enemy seeing our line of march and calculating our numbers, for the barrels were bright in those days and might be seen glistening a long way off by moonlight. The daily polishing of the old flintlock gave the men an infinity of bother and trouble. Rainy days and night dews gave them a rust which was never permitted on parade.'[16] Light infantry in the Peninsular campaign, however, browned their muskets, and this practice seems to have been copied by some other regiments. Baker rifles were browned from the start.[17]

On flintlocks generally, Bell remarks that, 'Our wretched old flint firelocks would not burn powder at times until the solider took from the pocket in his pouch a trianglular screw, to knock life into his old flint, and then clear the touch-hole with a long brass picker that hung from his belt.[18] After the battle of Vittoria he noticed solders, 'their muzzles black with powder from biting their cartridges'.[19]

Trouble could also be experienced with flintlocks in heavy rain. In the action at Sabugal in 1811 there was 'A heavy fall of rain in the middle of the fight, and for a short time not a musket would go off.'[20] Bad flints were another cause of failure to fire. 'Sometimes after a volley nearly a fourth of the muskets were still loaded, owing to the inferiority of the flints then supplied.'[21]

Uniform and Equipment

The first break with the traditional dress of the eighteenth century came with the abolition of hair powder in July 1795. The following year the old tricorne hat, cocked in various fashions, was replaced by a very large bicorne cocked hat, worn cross-wise. It was ornamented with feathers of distinctive colours; red and green for battalion companies, white for the grenadier company, and green for the light company. It was worn by both officers and other ranks, except that the latter in the grenadier company wore bearskin caps (later discontinued on active service) and in the light company black leather helmet-caps. Officers of battalion and grenadier companies wore a long red coatee, but officers of the light company and all other ranks in the battalion had jackets with short skirts. All ranks wore white breeches with black cloth gaiters extending to the knee, except that in the light company the gaiters were only ankle height. In 1797 a service dress coat, short and without lapels, was introduced for all officers. In 1798 overcoats were provided for all other ranks; they replaced the blue so-called watch coats which had been held only in small numbers and issued to sentries as required. In 1800 there was a revision of the head-dress. The bicorne hat was now restricted to officers of the battalion and grenadier companies and worn fore-and-aft. Officers of the light company and all other ranks wore a stovepipe felt shako. In some regiments the hat was restricted to officers of field rank.[22]

The equipment worn by the soldier in the Egyptian campaign of 1801 is well described by Joseph Coats, one-time Sergeant-Major of the 28th Regiment, as follows:

'The first thing after dressing he puts on his side belt, then his pouch, containing sixty rounds of ball cartridges, then his haversack with four days provisions, then his canteen with water, if he chooses to fill it, but in a short time it gets too warm to drink with pleasure or to quench the thirst; then his knapsack, containing two shirts, two pairs of stockings, one pair of shoes, jacket and trowsers for fatigue dress, three brushes, black-ball, razors and shaving box, and a blanket or great coat buckled on the top; then his firelock with bayonet.'[23]

In 1802 chevron badges of rank were adopted for NCOs and were worn on the right arm half-way between elbow and shoulder. A sergeant-major and a quartermaster-sergeant wore four chevrons of silver lace with an edging of blue cloth, a sergeant wore three chevrons of white lace, and a corporal had two chevrons of the regimental pattern of lace.[24]

Although hair powder had been abolished, pigtails had been retained. They had been shortened to seven inches in 1804, but it was not till 1808 that they were abolished altogether. On the return of Moore's force from Sweden in that year, the transports anchored off Spithead. Adjutants and barbers were ordered to report to the headquarters ship, and on their return they announced that queues were to be cut off. This news was greeted with enthusiasm, and in the 28th Regiment each man kept his severed pigtail until the last man had been shorn, when they were all thrown overboard with three cheers.[25] The relief at the abolition of the queue is expressed in the following account of the landing of Moore's troops at Vimiero by Captain John Dobbs of the 52nd Light Infantry: 'We landed near Vimiero in a heavy surf, with only the clothes we wore, a blanket, and a few days' provisions in our haversacks; we had no change of clothes till we arrived in Lisbon, for our baggage had gone on thither by sea; we used to wash our shirts in the nearest stream and sit by watching till they were dry; but our men had great joy for they were *relieved from their hair tying*, which was an operation grievous to be borne.'[26] In 1808, also, blue-grey trousers were authorised in replacement of the unsuitable white breeches. Three friends, Lieutenant-Colonel Wynch commanding the 4th King's Own, Lieutenant-Colonel Ross commanding the 20th, and Lieutenant-Colonel Belson commanding the 28th, agreed to try different ways of wearing them during the operations in Walcheren. Wynch had them made tight and worn with the old black gaiters, Ross had them made into overalls, strapped under the insteps with buttons down the side, and Belson had them worn loose with half boots. When the King's Own returned to England their new trousers were in rags, as were also those of the 20th; but the trousers of the 28th were nearly as good as when they were issued. The result of this competition was that the method adopted in the 28th was copied by nearly every other regiment, though it was not till 1823 that it was officially ordered. With the trousers were worn either shoes or ankle boots and leather or grey cloth gaiters.[27]

The other major change in uniform was the adoption of the so-called Wellington shako, with a plume at the side — red and white for a battalion company, white for a grenadier company, and green for a light company. It was one of the most attractive headdresses ever worn by the British Army. In light infantry regiments a green plume was worn in front of the shako instead of at the side.[28]

Rifle regiments were always clad in dark green, instead of red. They originally wore the old light dragoon helmet, but this was changed to a tapered shako, also with a green plume in front. Highland regiments wore the same red jacket as the remainder of the infantry, but with feathered bonnet, kilt, red and white diced hose, and calf-length gaiters.

On service the baggage of a junior regimental officer was limited. In his haversack were clasp knife, fork, spoon, tin mug, and any provisions he might be carrying. The rest of his belongings were carried in two small portmanteaux, slung on each side of a mule. In one of these was a uniform jacket, two pairs of trousers, waistcoats (white, coloured, and flannel) a few pairs of flannel drawers, and a dozen pairs of stockings, of which half were worsted and half cotton. In the other were shirts, cravats, a fitted dressing case, three pairs of boots, two pairs of shoes, and a number of handkerchiefs.[29]

Officers' dress regulations of 1811 directed them to wear 'a cap of a pattern similar to that established for the line'. Their regimental coat was to be 'similar to the private men's; but with lapels to button over the breast and body'. The great coat was to be of grey cloth 'corresponding in colour to that established for the Line, with a stand-up collar and cape to protect the shoulders'. On foreign service officers were to wear 'grey pantaloons or overalls with short boots, or with shoes and gaiters, such as the private men's'.

Transfers between companies and regiments could entail considerable expense for officers on account of differences in uniform. In a letter of 10 June 1812, Lieutenant Robert Garrett of the 2nd Queen's said that he had been put into the light company, 'so have put aside my cocked hat and taken to myself a cap and a light company jacket, with a pair of trimming large bullion epaulettes'. The following year he was transferred to the Royal Fusiliers and on 17 March 1813 wrote: ' . . . I got a pleasant bill the other day from my tailor; he sent me two uniform jackets on my being appointed to the Fusiliers, for which he charges me 20 guineas each.'[30]

The load of equipment that the private soldier had to carry during the retreat from Madrid in 1812 is well described by Ensign George Bell as follows:[31] 'This was a hard day upon the men from the heavy rains. Many fell out, some sick, others disabled and footsore. Hundreds broke down overcome by the great weight they had to carry, in addition to the wet clothes on their backs — viz a knapsack, heavy old flint firelock, sixty rounds of ball cartridge, haversack with sometimes three days' rations, wooden canteen, bayonet, great coat, and blanket — half-choked with a stiff leather girdle about the throat, and as many cross buff belts as would harness a donkey.'

Colours

Each battalion of the infantry of the Line, except Rifles, carried two Colours: the King's Colour and the Regimental Colour. They were large, being 'six feet six inches flying and six feet deep on the pike'. The King's Colour was the Union flag with in the centre the regimental number within a wreath of roses, thistles, and (after 1800) shamrocks. Regiments which had a badge, however, bore this in the centre of the Colour and the number appeared in the canton (the upper corner next to the pike). The Regimental Colour was of the facing colour of the regiment and was emblazoned with the same devices as the King's Colour, except that any secondary badges were placed in the other three corners. Regiments of the Foot Guards also carried two Colours in each battalion, but these followed an earlier tradition. In brief, the King's Colour was crimson and the Regimental Colour was the Union flag with one of the company badges in the centre. Rifle regiments did not carry Colours because they normally fought in too extended an order for the Colours to serve as a rallying point.

The Colours not only symbolised the soul of an infantry regiment; they were the rallying point to which men looked when the tides of battle severed the unity of a battalion. Their retention was a matter of honour; the carriage and guarding of them a dangerous privilege. They were carried by ensigns, and sergeants were detailed as their escort. Their large size made them conspicuous aiming marks, and casualties were consequently heavy amongst those close to them. At Waterloo Sergeant William

Lawrence of the 40th Foot was at 4pm ordered on duty with the Colours of his regiment. He disliked this intensely because 14 sergeants of the Colour party had already been killed or wounded, in addition to heavy casualties amongst the officers. The Colours themselves and their pikes had been nearly cut to pieces.[32] At the crisis of the battle Sir Colin Halkett, commanding the 5th Brigade, took the Regimental Colour of the 33rd Foot from the hands of the mortally wounded Lieutenant Cameron, and, resting the pike on his stirrup, took post in front of the Brigade. Soon he was shot through both cheeks and carried to the rear.[33] When the strength of the 5th Brigade had sunk below 800 men the Colours of all the regiments were ordered to the rear; and Lieutenant Macready in the Light Company of the 30th was overjoyed to see their safety assured. In the 73rd, also in the 5th Brigade, the commanding officer ordered the Colours, which had been completely riddled, to be removed from their pikes and rolled round the body of a trusty sergeant who was to take them to Brussels, there being no officer left to carry them.[34]

During the campaign of 1812 in the Peninsula the rank of colour sergeant was introduced. There was one in each company, and from them were drawn the escort to the Colours. They received extra pay for this dangerous duty and wore a special badge above their chevrons.[35]

Bands

Most infantry regiments had their bands with them during the Peninsular War, but they differed vastly in quality. Most of the bandmasters in peacetime had been hired civilians, many of them foreigners, and they were not therefore obliged to accompany the regiments on active service. As a result, some of the bands in regiments overseas were in charge of the drum-major or fife-major, or indeed bandsmen NCOs. Bands tended to diminish in strength, for casualties amongst bandsmen were rarely replaced. In many regiments the bandsmen had additional duties and, after playing the regiment into action, would be required to assist in evacuating the wounded or provide a baggage guard. At Talavera the band of the 48th Regiment laid aside their instruments and fought in the ranks.

When the regiment was in line the band normally formed in rear and played during the action — probably a more exacting demand on courage than standing in the ranks with a musket. When a battalion formed square the band moved to the centre, taking post near the Colours — a particularly dangerous position as already noted. In the Peninsular War such tunes as 'The British Grenadiers' and 'Rule Britannia' were popular; but favourite melodies of the French bands, such as 'Ça Ira' and the 'Marche des Marseillois' were also played, to amuse our own troops and tease those of the enemy.[36] Regiments, proud of themselves, liked to swank a bit, marching into their battle positions. On 18 June 1815 the 4th King's Own, a battalion of Peninsular veterans, marched on to the field of Waterloo with their band playing and Colours flying.[37]

Tactics and Training

The drill adopted for light infantry at Sir John Moore's Shorncliffe camp seems to have originated with Kenneth Mackenzie, for the *Royal Military Calendar* of 1820 says;

'Lieut-Colonel Mackenzie commenced with the 52nd a plan of movement and exercise in which Sir John Moore at first acquiesced with reluctance, the style of drill, march, and platoon-exercise being entirely new; but when he saw the effect of the whole in a more advanced stage, he was not only highly pleased, but became its warmest supporter. The other light corps were ordered to be formed on the same plan, and the 43rd and 95th

Regiments were moved to Shorncliffe camp to be with the 52nd. Letters from Sir John Moore corroborate the assertion that the improved system of marching, platoon-exercise, and drill were entirely Lieutenant-Colonel (afterwards Major-General) Mackenzie's.'[38]

As Moore pointed out, the resultant light infantry of the British Army were different from the light troops of other armies, for these latter were seldom required to fight in the rigid line, and were not even armed with bayonets. British light infantry, on the other hand, were expected to be able to fight either in the line or as skirmishers, and were also regarded as picked troops who could be called upon to undertake attacks or other enterprises where initiative, activity, and boldness were needed.[39]

The formation in two ranks to make maximum use of firepower soon became universal in the British Army. The battle discipline of the British Regular soldier compensated for the lack of depth which made generals in the conscript armies of other nations so reluctant to adopt a thin line.

In accordance with Dundas's *Rules and Regulations*, heavy infantry in line formed up shoulder to shoulder, whilst battalions of light infantry were normally drawn up in 'Close Order of Light Infantry', which allowed six inches from elbow to elbow. Moore introduced this more open formation into battalion companies of heavy infantry regiments under his command. To cover a wide front, Dundas's 'Extended Order' was used, which allowed two paces between files; and if necessary this could be lengthened to any given number of paces.

Moore taught light infantry to function in pairs. In each file the front rank man was the file leader, and he chose his coverer in the rear rank. Moore laid down that the two men of a file were never to be separated in the field or on any duty, or in their quarters. Volley firing was not practised by light infantry. Once the order to 'Present' was given, each man fired as soon as he had covered his target, and then went on firing as quickly as he could, without sacrificing good aiming. When in extended order, the two men of a file were never to be unloaded at the same time. These instructions were based on de Rottenberg's *Regulations*.[40]

A large part of the Shorncliffe training was devoted to target practice. In addition to the old long-shaped target, there was a new circular one which was white and four feet in diameter with a bull's eye and three concentric circles. The firing points were respectively, 90 yards, 140 yards, 200 yards, and 300 yards from the targets.[41] Moore also introduced a new musketry drill, in which the musket was raised to the 'present' position from the 'rest', instead of being brought down from the shoulder. The 52nd believed that this led to more accurate shooting.[42]

In the field, it was seldom that more than one half of a company or battalion of light infantry was sent forward to skirmish; the other half was retained in reserve in a formed body. The skirmishing element was also divided into two; half of it provided a chain of files, covering the front, while the other half was held back in support.[43]

As a result of the attention paid to light infantry and rifle units, Wellington had, as has been down, a considerable body of light troops at his disposal, and they played a big part in his tactics, particularly in defence. He generally concealed his main infantry line behind the crest of a hill, with the men lying down. In front of the crest would be a line of skirmishers, probably stronger than the *tirailleurs* covering the advance of the French columns. The skirmishers prevented the *tirailleurs* from achieving their object of reaching and disrupting the main line of defence, and it was not till the approach of the main body of the enemy that the skirmishers would retire slowly. The infantry in the main position then rose to their feet, waited till the enemy were at a vulnerable distance, and then fired one volley, followed by a charge with the bayonet. If this charge was successful the skirmishers followed the enemy in pursuit while the line took up its former position.[44]

An example of a light infantry regiment forming line is provided by the 52nd at the battle of Vittoria. The regiment in column of march came under fire from six enemy guns and formed line. Observers remarked with admiration on the precision with which the manoeuvre was carried out, and the steadiness and accuracy with which the alignment was completed; the pivots taking up their dressing under the direction of the second-in-command with the regularity of the parade ground. Captain John Dodds, then a Lieutenant in the 52nd, relates: 'This alignment was taken up with the same precision as on a field day, and a beautiful line was formed, the enemy's balls knocking a file out of it at every discharge, the sergeants in rear calling out, "Who got that?" and entering their names on their list of casualties.'[45]

When threatened by a cavalry attack, a battalion normally formed square. It was not a manoeuvre to be lightly undertaken because the square presented such a good target for artillery. The possibility of cavalry charges often resulted in battalions taking up formations from which a square could be formed rapidly. During one day's march in the retreat from Madrid in 1812, when enemy cavalry were riding in the rear and on the flanks of the Light Division, the 52nd marched in columns at quarter distance (ie close column of companies) and had to form square frequently.[46]

Each side of a square was normally four deep, both to give adequate depth against shock and to prevent gaps from casualties. A line of four ranks deep was also used as a compromise formation against an attack by both infantry and cavalry. Lieutenant-General Sir P. Maitland wrote that when he was commanding the 1st Infantry Brigade (Guards) at Waterloo: 'About seven o'clock pm the Duke of Wellington, aware of the Enemy's preparations for a new attack, desired me to form the 1st Brigade of Guards into line four files deep, His Grace expecting that the French Cavalry would take part in the affair.'[47] The Brigade consisted of the 2nd and 3rd Battalions of the 1st Foot Guards and they were in square at the time this order was given. They formed line by simply wheeling up the sides of the square — opening from the centre of the rear face.[48] In the 3rd (Light) Infantry Brigade the 52nd and the 95th formed a line of four ranks from their normal two ranks by moving the left wing of the battalion behind the right wing.[49]

What happened when a regiment was caught by cavalry out of square was shown at Quatre Bras in 1815. The 33rd were charged by French cuirassiers but formed square in time to repel them. The cuirassiers then swung round against the 69th Regiment, which had just been ordered out of square into line by the Prince of Orange. The regiment was cut to pieces and lost their King's Colour. Two French batteries then opened fire at point blank range on the 33rd square, causing casualties of about 10 officers and 100 men. The 33rd Regiment fell back rapidly into the Bois du Bossu, where they were reformed.[50]

At the battle of Waterloo the 5th Brigade deployed into 'contiguous column of companies at quarter distance,' with the 30th and 73rd Regiments in front and the 33rd and 60th in second line and echeloned to the right.[51] In other words, the 30th and 73rd were side by side, each with their companies in line, one behind the other and at very close distance. The 33rd and 69th were in similar formation, but staggered to the right to cover the intervals between the battalions in front of them. This was a handy formation from which to form line or square comparatively quickly.

A tribute to the efficiency of the 95th as skirmishers was paid by a spectator, who wrote in his book *Twelve Years of Military Adventure:*

'Our rifles were immediately sent to dislodge the French from the hills on our left, and our battalion was ordered to support them. Nothing could exceed the manner in which the ninety-fifth set about their business ... Certainly I never saw such skirmishers as the ninety-fifth, now the rifle brigade. They could do the work much better and with infinitely less loss than any other of our best light troops. They possessed an individual boldness, a mutual understanding, and a quickness of eye, in taking advantage of ground, which, taken all together, I never saw equalled.'[52]

That the 95th could carry out a normal attack is shown by the account, related by Kincaid, as follows:

'The action commenced by five companies of our third battalion advancing, under Colonel Ross, to dislodge the enemy from a hill which they occupied in front of their intrenchments; and there never was a movement more beautifully executed, for they walked quietly and steadily up, and swept them regularly off without firing a single shot until the enemy had turned their backs, when they then served them out with a most destructive discharge.'[53]

This account shows how the slow but accurate fire of the rifle could be retained until it should have the most telling effect.

As regards an attack by heavy infantry in line, nothing can surpass Napier's description as follows of the charge by the Fusilier Brigade (the 1st and 2nd Battalions 7th Royal Fusiliers and the 1st Battalion 23rd Royal Welch Fusiliers) at the battle of Albuera:

'Such a gallant line, issuing from the midst of the smoke and rapidly separating itself from the confused and broken multitude, startled the enemy's masses, which were increasing and pressing onwards as to an assured victory; they wavered, hesitated, and then vomiting forth a storm of fire, hastily endeavoured to enlarge their front, while a fearful discharge of grape from all their artillery whistled through the British ranks. Myers was killed, Cole and the three colonels, Ellis, Blakeney, and Hawkshaw, fell wounded, and the fuzileer battalions, struck by the iron tempest, reeled and staggered like sinking ships; but suddenly and sternly recovering they closed on their terrible enemies, and then was seen with what a strength and majesty the British soldier fights. In vain did Soult with voice and gesture animate his Frenchmen, in vain did the hardiest veterans break from the crowded columns and sacrifice their lives to gain time for the mass to open out on such a fair field; in vain did the mass itself bear up, and fiercely striving, fire indiscriminately upon friends and foes, while the horsemen hovering on the flank threatened to charge the advancing line. Nothing could stop that astonishing infantry. No sudden burst of undisciplined valour, no nervous enthusiasm weakened the stability of their order, their flashing eyes were bent on the dark columns in their front, their measured tread shook the ground, their dreadful volleys swept away the head of every formation, their deafening shouts overpowered the dissonant cries that broke from all parts of the tumultous crowd, as slowly and with a horrid carnage it was pushed by the incessant vigour of the attack to the farthest edge of the hill. In vain did the French reserves mix with the struggling multitude to sustain the fight, their efforts only increased the irremediable confusion, and the mighty mass, breaking off like a loosened cliff, went headlong down the steep: the rain flowed after in streams discoloured with blood, and eighteen hundred unwounded men, the remnant of six thousand unconquerable British soldiers, stood triumphant on the fatal hill!'[54]

Notes

1 *Cornwallis Correspondence*, vol I p212; quoted by The Hon J. W. Fortescue, *A History of the British Army*, vol III (London, Macmillan, 1902), p531

2 Colonel J. F. C. Fuller, *British Light Infantry of the Eighteenth Century* (London, Hutchinson, 1925), pp193-4

3 ibid, pp215f
  'Sir John Moore's Light Infantry Instructions of 1798-1799', ed Major-General J. F. C. Fuller, *The Journal of the Society for Army Historical Research*, vol XXX (1952)

4 Fuller, op cit, pp230f

5 Carola Oman, *Sir John Moore* (London, Hodder & Stoughton, 1953) p242
  H. M. Chichester and G. Burgess-Short, *The Records and Badges of the British Army*, 2nd edn (London, Gale & Polden, 1900), p385

6 Carola Oman, op cit, pp308-10
  W. S. Moorsom, *Historical Record of the Fifty-Second Regiment* (London, Richard Bentley, 1860), pp60-62

7 Chichester & Burgess-Short, op cit, p858

8 Colonel L. I. Cowper, *The King's Own* vol I (Oxford, 1939), pp318-27

9 Moorsom, op cit, pp63-73

10 Cowper, op cit, pp318-27

11 *Selections from the Dispatches and General Orders of Field Marshal the Duke of Wellington*, ed Lieutenant-Colonel Gurwood (London, John Murray, 1861), p668

12 Colonel H. C. B. Rogers, *Weapons of the British Soldier* (London, Seeley Service), pp85, 90-5

13 ibid, pp143-46

14 Moorsom, op cit, p72

15 Rogers, op cit, pp147-51

16 Major-General Sir George Bell, *Soldier's Glory*, ed Brian Stuart (London, G. Bell & Sons, 1956), p32

17 Rogers, op cit, p156

18 Bell, op cit, p169

19 ibid, p72

20 Moorsom, op cit, p137

21 ibid

22 Cowper, op cit, pp490-94

23 Lieutenant-Colonel R. M. Grazebrook, 'The Wearing of Equipment, 1801', *Journal of the Society for Army Historical Research*, vol XXIV (1946)

24 Cowper, op cit, p495

25 ibid, pp339-40

26 Moorsom, op cit, p38

27 Cowper, op cit, pp361, 365, 370

28 Moorsom, op cit, p120

29 Cowper, op cit, p370

30 'A Subaltern in the Peninsular War, ed A. S. White, *Journal of the Society for Army Historical Research*, vol XIII (1934)

31 Bell, op cit, p58

32 Major-General G. Surtees, 'British Colours in the Waterloo Campaign' *Journal of the Society for Army Historical Research*, vol XLIII (1965)

33 'A Line Regiment at Waterloo', ed Brigadier B. W. Webb-Carter, *Journal of the Society for Army Historical Research*, vol XLIII (1965)

34 Surtees, op cit

35 Cowper, op cit p246

36 H. G. Farmer, 'Our Bands in the Napoleonic Wars', *Journal of the Society for Army Historical Research*, vol VL (1962)

37 Major-General H. T. Siborne, *Waterloo Letters* (London, Cassell, 1891), p393

38 Moorsom, op cit, p68

39 'Sir John Moore's Light Infantry Instructions', op cit

40 ibid
    Captain T. H. Cooper, *A Practical Guide for the Light Infantry Officer* (London, 1806; facsimile, London, Frederick Muller, 1970), pp14, 16

41 Cowper, op cit, pp318-27

42 Moorsom, op cit, pp137-38

43 Cooper, op cit, pp75, 76

44 Cowper, op cit, p378

45 Moorsom, op cit, pp185-86

46 ibid, p178

47 Siborne, op cit, p244

48 ibid, pp254, 256-57

49 ibid, pp290, 302

50 'A Line Regiment at Waterloo', op cit

51 ibid

52 Captain J. Kincaid, *Adventures in the Rifle Brigade* (London, Peter Davies, 1929), p215

53 ibid, pp187-88

54 Major-General Sir W. F. P. Napier, *History of the War in the Peninsula and in the South of France*, vol III (London, Frederick Warne), p170

Cavalry

General

Unlike the infantry, the cavalry garnered little experience from the American War of Independence. Only two regiments of light dragoons served with the Army in America, and the bulk of the cavalry had fought in no more recent campaign than the operations in Germany during the Seven Years War. The usefulness of light cavalry had inded been noted, but it was the glamour of the 'set-piece' charge which appealed most to cavalry officers, and the mounted attack to break and pursue the enemy was given the primary emphasis in training. Too little attention was paid to the important duties of reconnaissance and protection. In 1778 Captain Hinde had published his *The Discipline of the Light Horse*, in which he described the primary tasks of light cavalry as reconnoitring the enemy, providing advanced posts to protect the army against surprise, sending out patrols, and harassing the enemy;[1] but this admirable counsel was largely ignored. The cavalry could certainly charge, as was demonstrated in 1794 by the three brilliant actions mentioned in Chapter 1; but there was often a failure to control, which exasperated Wellington, and, according to Fortescue[2], they were so useless for outpost work at the opening of the Duke of York's campaign in Flanders, that a Prussian hussar accompanied every British vedette, and a Prussian NCO every officer's post, to teach these duties.

Before the start of the war a great improvement had been made in the Household Cavalry. On 26 July 1788 the Duke of York wrote to Earl Cornwallis:

'... I have no doubt Your Lordship will not regret the reduction of the four Troops of Horse Guards and Horse Grenadiers, as they were the most useless and the most unmilitary Troops that ever were seen. I confess that I was a little sorry for the Horse Grenadiers because they were to a degree Soldiers, but the Horse Guards were nothing but a collection of London Tradespeople. If the two new Regiments keep exactly to the standard they have settled they will be the finest body of men that were seen, the tallest not to exceed six foot one, the shortest five foot eleven ... '[3]

The Duke's letter referred to a Royal Proclamation of 8 June 1788. This announced the transformation of the First and Second Troops of Horse Guards into Regiments of Life Guards. The First Troop was to become the First Regiment of Life Guards and the Second Troops was to be the Second Regiment. The intention to carry out this reorganisation had been notified by an Order of 14 March 1788. Each regiment was to consist of 230 all ranks. The Private Gentlemen (ie the non-commissioned ranks) of the First and Second Troops were to be discharged. The new regiments were to be recruited by transferring other ranks and horses from the Troops of Horse Grenadiers (which were being disbanded), together with such men of the Troops of Horse Guards who were acceptable and willing to re-engage under the new conditions.[4] The practical effect was that the Life Guards consisted almost entirely of the officers of the Troops of Horse Guards and the other ranks of the Horse Grenadiers.

The Life Guards were 'Horse', the heaviest form of cavalry. There was one other regiment of horse, the Royal Regiment of Horse Guards (Blue). Although it had many special privileges, and its status was gradually assimilated to that of the Life Guards, it did not officially become part of the Household Cavalry until 1 March 1820, when a letter notifying the dignity was written to its Colonel, the Duke of Wellington.[5]

There had been seven other regiments of horse, but three had been reformed in 1746 into the more generally useful dragoons, with a greater emphasis on musketry, and the remaining four had been similarly reformed in 1788. In recognition of their previous dignity as horse, they were given the designation of Dragoon Guards, and continued to carry the square Standard of the Horse instead of the slit-tailed Guidon of the Dragoons.

Dragoons had by this time become heavy cavalry. A movement towards a lighter cavalry had begun with the formation of a regiment during the Jacobite rebellion of 1745-6, and in 1756 a troop of light cavalry was added to the establishment of each regiment of dragoon guards and dragoons. These proved so useful that in 1759 it was decided to raise complete regiments of light dragoons, and five numbered 15 to 19 were raised in that year. In 1760 two more were formed, the 20th and 21st, but these only lasted a few years. In 1763 the light troops in the regiments of dragoon guards and dragoons were disbanded, and the men transferred to the regiments of light dragoons. In the following years a number of dragoon regiments were transformed into light dragoons: in 1768 the 12th, in 1775 the 8th, in 1776 the 14th, and in 1783 the 7th, 8th, 10th, 11th, and 13th. New regiments of light dragoons were raised during the war years after 1793, but all these had been disbanded by 1820.

The last innovation was the introduction of hussars. In 1806 the 10th Light Dragoons became hussars, and shortly afterwards the 7th, 15th, and 18th Light Dragoons were similarly converted. The change, however, was only in dress, for their role as light cavalry remained the same. Indeed, they were still officially described as light dragoons.

Organisation

In 1783, when the Army was reduced after the end of the War of American Independence, the establishment of a regiment of dragoons was fixed at six troops, each with a strength of a captain, a lieutenant, a cornet, a quartermaster (warrant officer), two corporals, a hautbois, a trumpeter, and 28 privates — or 36 all ranks. This would provide a regimental strength, including the headquarters, of some 220 all ranks. With the approach of fresh war clouds in 1792, the troop strength was increased by 10 privates. The following year, when war actually broke out, three more troops were added to each regiment and the establishment of a troop of dragoons became 'three sergeants, three corporals, and a trumpeter, 47 private men and horses with the usual number of commissioned officers'.[6] This about doubled the strength of a regiment, making it about 530 all ranks. However, when regiments of cavalry were sent overseas to Flanders in 1794 all except the 1st King's Dragoon Guards (which had the authorised nine troops) were still on the six-troop establishment; and as two troops were always left at home to form a depot squadron, all regiments (except the 1st Dragoon Guards, which had six troops organised in three squadrons) had four troops, or two squadrons.

The Life Guards at the beginning of 1799 had the rather unusual establishment for each regiment of five troops, but a troop of Life Guards was unusually strong (see below), and one probably sufficed to provide a depot unit. The officers in a regiment of Life Guards comprised a colonel, a lieutenant-colonel commanding, a supernumary lieutenant-colonel, a major, five captains, six lieutenants, a lieutenant and adjutant, five cornets and sub-lieutenants, a surgeon, and a veterinary surgeon. According to regimental standing orders, lieutenant-colonels commanding were responsible for the discipline and internal economy; the major, assisted by the adjutant, was responsible for training, horses, and the regimental books and papers; captains were concerned with the appearance, clothing and equipment, and subsistence of their troops; and subalterns had to attend troop parades and carry out weekly inspections of the troops to which they belonged.[7]

A sixth troop was added to each regiment in September 1799, but this addition does not seem to have lasted long, for the *Royal Military Chronicle* of 1810[8] says: 'There are five troops in each Regiment, each troop having a Captain, a Lieutenant, a Cornet, a Quarter Master, and three companies of Fifty Privates each, inclusive of the Trumpeter. The arms are firelocks with bayonets, pistol, and sabre.' The division of a troop into three companies was a relic of the original division of a Troop of Horse Guards in 1660 into three squadrons. The term 'squadron' was replaced at a later date by 'company' to avoid confusion with the later squadron, composed of two troops. A troop of the Life Guards was considerably stronger than the average squadron in the Cavalry of the Line.

In the Troops of Horse Guards the rank of Troop Quartermaster was introduced in 1756. Up till then there had been no NCOs or warrant officers; the duties of such being entrusted to 'right hand men'. At Christmas 1756 it was ordered that the four senior right hand men of each troop should be warrant officers bearing the title of quartermasters and that the four junior right hand men should be NCOs styled corporals-of-horse. The Horse Grenadier Guards, however, had always been regarded as mounted infantry, like dragoons, and therefore had sergeants and corporals.[9]

The position of troop quartermaster offered one of the outlets for promotion from the ranks, and the adjutant was frequently a lieutenant promoted from troop quartermaster. There was a noteworthy example in the Blues when Troop Quartermaster John Elley was detailed to act as Adjutant to the detachment of the Blues sent to Flanders in 1794. Elley had enlisted in the Blues on 5 November 1789. His father, who ran an 'eating house', helped him to buy a troop quartermastership in the Regiment in 1790, and to purchases each of his subsequent steps in rank. Elley distinguished himself in the cavalry actions of 1794 and was promoted Cornet in that year. Two years later he became a lieutenant and in 1801 he was a captain, commanding a troop of the Blues. In 1804 he was promoted Major and in 1808 he was Lieutenant-Colonel of the Blues. During 1808 and 1809 he served in the Peninsula as Assistant Adjutant-General of Cavalry under Moore, and from 1809 to 1814 he served in the same capacity throughout Wellington's Peninsular campaign. At Salamanca he was wounded and had two horses shot under him. At the battle of Waterloo he was Adjutant-General of the Cavalry. He was made a KCB and promoted Major-General. In 1820 Sir John Elley was Governor of Galway, and from 1829 till his death he was Colonel of the 17th Lancers. In 1835 he became MP for Windsor, and two years later was promoted Lieutenant-General. He died in 1839 and was buried in St George's Chapel, Windsor.[10]

In 1804 a regimental corporal-major was added to the establishment of the Life Guards and the Blues. In 1806 the commission of lieutenant and adjutant was abolished, and replaced by the non-saleable appointment as adjutant of an existing officer.[11] The rank of troop quartermaster was abolished throughout the cavalry in 1810 and replaced by a troop corporal-major in the horse and a troop sergeant-major in the dragoons. There was now a single quartermaster on the headquarters of a regiment who was promoted from the ranks and whose commission could not be purchased. A trumpet-major, with the pay of a sergeant, was also added to the establishment. He was borne on the strength of one troop, whilst each of the other troops had a trumpeter.[12]

In 1800 the establishment of cavalry regiments of the line was increased to 10 troops, each of 90 rank and file. This was reduced by two troops during the short-lived Peace of Amiens, but increased again when hostilities were resumed.[13] Out of the 10, two were to provide a depot squadron, whilst the remaining eight formed four service squadrons, each commanded by a field officer or by the senior of the two troop commanders. From 1803 field officers no longer commanded troops, extra captains being added to the establishment in consequence.[14] Establishments varied, however, during the course of the war. In 1811 the number of troops serving overseas with a regiment was reduced from eight to six, and on 5 December of that year two troops of the 14th Hussars left the Peninsula to join the regimental depot at Weymouth.[15]

When the 7th Hussars embarked for active service in 1813 the regiment had 10 troops lettered from A to K. These were organised into squadrons, each of two troops, as follows: The Right Squadron commanded by the second lieutenant-colonel, the Second Squadron commanded by the senior of its two troop commanders, the Third Squadron commanded by the senior of its two troop commanders, the Fourth Squadron commanded by a major, and the Depot Squadron commanded by a major. The Depot Squadron was to remain at Hyde Park Barracks until further orders.[16] In September 1813 the establishment of a light cavalry regiment was increased to 12 troops, the additional ones being lettered L and M.[17]

Command of a cavalry regiment could produce some peculiar complexities. The Colonel of the 14th Light Dragoons (Hussars) from 1797 to 1823 was General J. W. Egerton, later Earl of Bridgwater. The senior Lieutenant-Colonel, S. Hawker, was in rank a Colonel, and, although nominally in command of the Regiment, held a staff appointment in the Peninsula till in 1811 he was promoted Major-General on the staff in the United Kingdom. Lieutenant-Colonel Hervey then succeeded to the command of the regiment, which he had virtually held since his promotion the previous year on the death of the second Lieutenant-Colonel, Talbot. But it was not till 1816 that Hervey's name appeared in the Army List as the senior Lieutenant-Colonel, because up till then Hawker's name had continud to appear in that appointment, even though he held the rank of Major-General.[18] Hawker no doubt, did not wish to sell his Lieutenant-Colonelcy because, if the war came to an end and he was no longer employed as a major-general, he would get no pay for that rank and would depend on his lieutenant-colonel's pay. However, after the war he did continue in employment, was promoted successively Lieutenant-General and General, and in 1831 was appointed Colonel of the 3rd Dragoon Guards, which assured him a considerable income until his death in 1839.[19]

In 1812 it was decided to send out to the Peninsula two squadrons each from the 1st and 2nd Life Guards and the Blues, or nearly half the total strength of these regiments. As a result of a dispute with the Duke of Northumberland, Colonel of the Blues, over the privileges of his regiment, he was replaced as Colonel by Wellington. It is said that in the Peninsula, on the first occasion after his pasing the Foot Guards after his appointment, Wellington remarked: 'Thank God, I have got a "present" out of the Guards at last!' (ie a present arms salute).[20]

As regards the higher organisation of the cavalry in the Peninsula; from 1810 there was a cavalry divsion, composed of a varying number of brigades in which regiments were normally of the same type. The commander of the Cavalry Division from 1810 till the end of the war in the Peninsula was Sir Stapleton Cotton (later Lord Combermere). The final divisional order of battle in 1814 is of some interest as showing the distribution of the different types of cavalry[21]:

Brigade	Regiments	Type
B	3rd Dragoon Guards, 1st Dragoons	Dragoons
C	12th and 16th Light Dragoons	Light Cavalry
D	13th and 14th Light Dragoons	Light Cavalry
E	18th Hussars and 1st KGL Hussars	Light Cavalry
F	5th Dragoon Guards, 3rd and 4th Dragoons	Dragoons
G	1st and 2nd KGL Dragoons	Dragoons
H	7th, 10th, and 15th Hussars	Light Cavalry
I	1st and 2nd Life Guards, Blues	Horse

Horses

At the start of the French Revolutionary War it was the general custom for horse, dragoon guards, and dragoons to be mounted on black horses with long tails; and the cavalry regulations of 1795 fixed the length of a horse's tail as to reach 'half way between the hoof and the fetterlock'. However, the large expansion of the cavalry during the the war led to difficulty in purchasing horses of the accepted colour and type, particularly as it was now the custom in civilian circles to dock horses' tails. In 1796 the Adjutant-General wrote to the Board of General Officers, set up by the Duke of York to enquire into cavalry matters, asking whether, on account of the scarcity and exorbitant price of long-tailed chargers, they might consider recommending the use of 'nag-tailed' (ie docked) chargers for officers of heavy cavalry instead. The Board agreed, and indeed went further. They pointed out that black horse suitable for riding were almost extinct in the civil market, and those obtainable were only of use for draught. They noted, however, that there was a new breed of horses intended for gentlemen's carriages, but well adapted for heavy cavalry, and they recommended that, without discontinuing the blacks, horses of other colours should be accepted.[22]

The Board's recommendations were approved and were put into effect by an Army General Order of 10 August 1799. Only the heavy cavalry were affected as light cavalry already rode nag-tailed horses of various colours. Its main provisions were:

1 The heavy cavalry, with the exception of the Life Guards and the Blues, were to be mounted on nag-tailed horses.
2 The 1st (or King's) Regiment of Dragoon Guards, the 1st (or Royal) Regiment of Dragoons, and the 3rd (or King's Own) Regiment of Dragoons were to be mounted on black nag-tailed horses.
3 The 2nd (Queen's) Regiment of Dragoon Guards were to be mounted on bay or brown nag-tailed horses.
4 The 2nd (or Royal North British) Regiment of Dragoons were to be mounted on grey nag-tailed horses.
5 All other regiments of heavy cavalry were to be mounted on nag-tailed bay, brown, or chestnut horses.[23]

That the officers' horses, at least, of the Household Cavalry were not necessarily black is shown by the standing orders of the 2nd Life Guards, dated 11 November 1798, which stated that:

'His Majesty has given repeated and particular orders that the Regimental Horses of the Commissioned Officers of the Second Regiment are to continue long tail'd Bays, and His Majesty having remarked at Reviews that Officers were not Regimentally Mounted, one horse at least of each Officer must be of this description.'[24]

The care of horses was regarded as of considerable importance, and in the Standing Orders of the 2nd Life Guards, dated November 1799, it was ordered that the utmost gentleness was to be used to all horses, especially young horses; and any man misusing horses or terrifying young horses was to be confined immediately to the stable guard.[25]

The care of horses was of concern to Wellington in the Peninsula. On 27 January 1810 he wrote to Lieutenant-General Payne, at that time commanding the Cavalry Division:

'Considering that the cavalry do no work, and that they are all in stables, and adverting to the very excellent condition in which the horses of the hussars [1st Hussars, King's German Legion] are, which have been most worked, and which I am sorry to say are now frequently fed upon rye, I cannot but be apprehensive that there is some deficiency of attention to stable duties. I should recommend to you, therefore, to call the attention of commanding officers of regiments to this subject.'

On 27 May 1811 he wrote to Brigadier-General Peacocke, Commandant of Lisbon, about the 11th Light Dragoons, which regiment was about to disembark. He asked Peacocke to point out to the commanding officer how much the condition of the horses would depend on the attention paid to them on their arrival, and to the care with which they were first moved. Great attention was to be paid to the mode of feeding and watering the horses.[26]

Feeding was a constant problem. Captain Lovel Badcock of the 14th Light Dragoons said that the Royal Dragoons, when they arrived in Portugal, were a fine regiment, but as their horses had not yet been fed on barley they might not keep their good condition if it was given to them. The horses of the 14th were being fed on green barley with some Indian corn; they were doing well on it and were 'quite fat'.[27]

An officer of the same Regiment, Captain (later General Sir) T. W. Brotherton writes the following amusing story about feeding:

'When the 14th Light Dragoons were cantoned in Portugal in 1812 at Fundao, a large proportion of the troop horses were turned out to grass more than five miles from the town. They had previously been groomed and fed at particular hours in the great square. The day after they were turned out they all came galloping in at the accustomed hour of feeding, and placed themselves in the square as if they had been led there!'[28]

On 3 July 1809 Captain Thomas Fenton of the 4th Dragoons wrote from Castelo-Branco: 'I have had to go out to procure forage for the horses, which in this part of the country is difficult to get. The poor horses frequently go without for a day.'[29]

The movement of the Army depended largely on forage. Major (later Colonel Sir) Augustus Frazer, commanding Wellington's Horse Artillery, wrote on 9 February 1813: 'There is a kind of rainy season yet to be expected, and the green forage, which in the spring is the chief support of the cavalry, will not be fit to eat for four or five weeks. In the meantime the want of long forage, that is of straw, is felt a great deal.'[30]

Neither the climate nor the food suited British horses or, indeed, French ones. The diet was all to frequently green maize and chopped straw. Wellington sometimes imported hay and oats from England, but due to transport difficulties this ideal forage could not be moved far inland.[31] Fenton, on 31 May 1809 at Abrantes, wrote that the country did not agree with the horses: 'We have more than eighty unfit for service, and should we march immediately that number will be doubled.'[32] In October 1813 Frazer commented: 'Forage now is exceedingly scarce; our troops and brigades near Urogre are reduced to grazing their horses, which must soon lose their condition.' And in January 1814: 'Our horses are eating chopped furze, of which, in the absence of hay or straw, they seem vastly fond ... The horses keep their condition surprisingly, the chopped and braized furze has proved invaluable; hay and straw they have none.' The furze was very likely the plant which Commissary Schaumann calls 'prickly thistles'. He says that in the French town of Hasparen, in January 1814, a local rustic pointed out to him the prickly thistles that flourished on the neighbouring heaths and said that if these were chopped up and mixed with corn and hay they made very good fodder for the horses. Schaumann reported this and the suggestion was adopted immediately. The thistles had to be crushed before the horses would touch them, and soldiers did this by lifting a barn door off its hinges, laying it on the ground, and beating the thistles on it with clubs. Long afterwards Schaumann learned that this method had been known to the Romans, and that Fabricius and Quintilius Varus, cavalry generals, received the thanks of the Roman senate for having discovered it at a time when forage was scarce.[33]

Shoeing was another problem with the horses. During Moore's retreat to Corunna many horses were lost for want of shoes and nails. One morning over 60 horses had to be left behind, most of which were shot, for lack of shoes. The 7th Hussars, for instance, took 640 horses to the Peninsula and brought back only about 60. The trouble was that, in the disorganisation of the retreat, the stocks of horse shoes were not where they were needed. As a result of this experience, each man was in future provided with a set of spare shoes and a supply of nails which he carried on his saddle.[34] In the regimental orders of the 7th Hussars in 1813 it was laid down that each man on active service was to carry a set of horse shoes and 40 nails on the peak of his saddle, and that each farrier was to take 45 sets of horse shoes, and 10,000 nails for his troop.[35]

Farriers were not always popular. Captain Brotherton says that at the battle of Vittoria the men of his regiment were too busily employed in following the enemy to be able to stop and pick up the rich plunder, so that all the valuables were acquired by the 'non-combatants' and the civilians attached to the Army. Amongst the former were the farriers, who did not fight in the ranks and who frequently stopped behind to plunder, under the pretence of shoeing horses. On this occasion the farriers of the 14th Hussars took advantage of this trick to stop behind and plunder the French carriages which the Regiment had passed and not touched. All farriers carried containers called 'churns' — large leather cases carried on the horse in the place where the dragoon's pistol holsters were located. Into these they crammed all the jewellery and other valuables that they had rifled from the carriages. Also they secured some of the mules abandoned by the French Pay Department drivers, which were loaded with boxes of money. The Commanding Officer of the 14th Hussars, Lieutenant-Colonel Sir F. B. Hervey Bart, was well aware of what the farriers had been up to, and he suddenly ordered the 'Rouse and Assembly' to be sounded. He then ordered a square to be formed, brought the farriers into the middle and, ordering them to dismount, 'had their churns taken off, and the plunder disgorged from them, to the joy and glee of the whole corps.'[36]

Practically all remounts for the cavalry came from England. Portuguese and Spanish horses were tried many times but were found unsatisfactory.[37] Nevertheless the horses sent out from England were not always satisfactory. A note in the diary of Captain Henry Neville of the 14th Light Dragoons on 1 July 1809 says: 'We received today a remount of 61 (I may almost say Cart) Horses from the *Irish Commissariat Corps!* What makes this most ridiculous is that they are chiefly Horses that have been *cast* in *England* as being unserviceable for the *Heavy Dragoons!*'[38] On the other hand, Fenton of the 4th Dragoons was able to write on 1 May 1812: 'I am also particularly fortunate in having the best Troop in the Regiment, for with all our marching I have only two horses unfit for duty, and the remainder are in most excellent condition.' He added: 'We are going to have a strong remount of 90 horses from the Depot, and between 80 and 90 from the Light Dragoons.'[39]

Brotherton had a rather pathetic story about a horse in 1811, as follows:

'I had my charger shot under me, and got on a troop-horse, which was also shot under me, through the head, by the pistol of a French officer, so closely that my own face was singed. The animal fell, and a sergeant behind me dismounted and gave me his own horse, and I thought no more of the animal that was shot through the head, supposing that he never rose again; but on rejoining the main body of the regiment I found that the poor animal had risen by an effort, gone back to where the regiment was formed, placed himself in the ranks in his own squadron, and then fell down dead! This fact, almost incredible, can be vouched for by any officer of private belonging to the 14th Light Dragoons at the time.'[40]

Weapons

The swords with which the cavalry were equipped in the Peninsular War were all of patterns introduced in 1796. Before that there had been no official pattern, but they had to be the same in each regiment and to be approved by the Horse Guards. There were two types of sword issued in 1796, one for heavy cavalry and one for light. The former was extremely bad, whilst the latter was outstandingly good.

This light dragoon sword was a short sabre with a blade measuring about 33 inches in a straight line. The blade was broad and heavily curved, and a stirrup hilt gave good protection for the hand. The weight and balance of this weapon gave it tremendous cutting power and made it probably the finest cutting sword ever produced for general military use. It is said that during the Peninsular War a French commander made an official complaint about the fearful wounds it inflicted. It was also a good thrusting sword, and was generally used as such against infantry.

The sword for the heavy cavalry had a straight 35 inch blade with a hatchet point. It could not therefore be used for thrusting and its poor balance made it a bad cutting weapon. Furthermore, the design of the hilt afforded very little protection for the hand.[41]

The cavalry firearms were also selected in 1796. The Board of General Officers had criticised the existing 'Brown Bess' type carbines and pistols of the heavy cavalry as useless, inconvenient, and cumbersome, and had recommended a carbine with a 26 inch long barrel of musket bore. Until this could be provided, they recommended cutting the existing firelock in length and adding a swivel bar to enable it to be carried butt downwards. The bayonet, they added, should be reduced to a length of 15 inches, and each man should carry one pistol with a nine-inch barrel, also of musket bore, and an iron ramrod fixed to the holster pipe. These recommendations were all put into effect in 1796.[42]

A much more remarkable carbine was issued to the light cavalry in about 1800. This was the so-called 'Paget' carbine, supposed to have been invented by Lord Paget. The barrel, of carbine bore (16 nominal and 20 actual balls to the pound) was, with its length of 16 inches, the shortest that had ever been designed for a British carbine, which made it a particularly light and handy weapon for a horseman. Of particular benefit to the mounted soldier, however, was the permanent attachment of the ramrod to the carbine, by means of a link, known as a 'stirrup' fitted near the muzzle. This cured one of the main troubles in loading a flintlock weapon on horseback — the accidental dropping of the ramrod. A pistol of carbine bore was brought out at the same time as the carbine with a similarly attached ramrod. Both these Paget firearms were successful and they continued until flintlocks disappeared from the Army — indeed, some survived to be fitted with percussion locks in the 1830s.[43]

In 1803 there was an issue of rifled carbines to light cavalry. The relevant War Office Order said: '9th August 1803. Rifle carbines to be supplied, one hundred to a regiment, to the several regiments of Light Dragoons.' There were at least two patterns; those issued to the 7th Light Dragoons, for instance, differed from the ones received by the 10th.[44] The 10th Light Dragoons were actually the first to get them. Ezechiel Baker wrote: 'In the year 1803 a target was fired at 200 yards distance by command of his present Majesty, then Prince of Wales, with a rifle barrel 22 inches in length; and from its accuracy was adopted for the use of the 10th Light Dragoons.'[45] (The Prince of Wales was Colonel of the 10th Light Dragoons.)

Uniform and Equipment

The Life Guards, the Dragoon Guards and the Dragoons wore red, whilst the Royal Horse Guards, the Light Dragoons, and the Hussars were clad in blue. At the start of the war in the Peninsula the heavy cavalry were still wearing the heavy bicorne cocked hats, crossways on the head, and jack boots up to the knee. The cocked hat had the disadvantage that it soon became sodden in heavy rain and lost its shape. In 1812, therefore, it was replaced by a brass helmet, and at the same time the jack boots and breeches were replaced by overalls and short boots. On 1 May 1812 Captain Fenton of the 4th Dragoons wrote: 'We have just got our new clothing and according to the new regulations we now only want the new helmet.'[46] The Light dragoons started the war wearing a black leather helmet topped by a bearskin crest, and buckskin breeches with Hessian boots. In 1812 they too had a change in dress; the helmet giving way to a slightly bell-topped shako, and the existing jacket being replaced with one having a broad plastron front in the facing colour of the regiment. Later, overalls and short boots were taken into wear.

The rather exotic hussar dress consisted of jacket (or dolman), pelisse (or over-jacket and normally worn slung from the shoulder), 'barrel' sash, overalls, and busby. The busby did not please Captain Badcock of the 14th Light Dragoons (Hussars) as, compared with the old helmet, there was no defence for the head. The early busby was very high in the crown and very unwieldy. The men of the 15th Hussars complained that at the charge at Sahagun on 21 December 1808 the fur caps either tumbled off in the charge or were cut down by the heavy French cavalry swords like so much cartridge paper. One Member of Parliament called them 'monstrous muffs'. In 1812 they were withdrawn from the 15th and replaced by shakos of red cloth.[47]

Apart from the uniform, the following 'necessaries' were carried by each man in the 7th Hussars during 1813 in the Peninsula: three shirts, two pairs of trousers, two pairs of flannel drawers, two flannel jackets, three pairs of stockings, two towels, three shoe brushes, a clothes brush, a pair of braces, a stock and clasp, a mane comb and sponge, a pipe clay sponge, a pair of scissors and case, a lock case, a hair comb, a button brush, a foraging cap, a corn bag, a large feather, a turn screw, a horse picker, two stable jackets, a pair of 'high-lows' (laced boots, reaching up over the ankle), and a pair of low shoes.[48] When compared with the infantryman's kit, the advantage or riding a horse will be apparent!

One may finish this section with Colonel Vivian's five points for his Regiment, the 7th Hussars, going on active service in 1813. They were:

1 The horse should be treated with kindness and attention.
2 The soldier's person should be the object of care, and attention was to be paid to neatness and cleaniness. Wet clothes, particularly stockings and linen, were to be changed the first moment possible after a march.
3 The pack (carried on the horse) was always to be complete and in good order.
4 A portion of provisions should always be kept in the haversack and canteen. A spoonful of spirits would support a man under great fatigue.
5 Swords were to be kept sharp, and carbines and pistols clean and well flinted.[49]

With adjustments suited to changed weapons and mounts, there could be many worse precepts for the cavalry regiment of today!

Tactics and Training

Dundas produced a training manual for the cavalry which followed the same lines as his regulations for the infantry. Such a book was badly needed because cavalry officers on the whole were too concerned with display and with rapid troop and squadron evolutions, and many regarded the charge at the gallop as the only operation in war to which training should be directed.[50] The Duke of York directed all colonels of cavalry to see that Dundas's drill should be taken into use. Presumably the results were considered satisfactory, for when in 1796 the Duke of York appointed his board of general officers to enquire into and make recommendations on the cavalry, their report did not comment on their tactical competence.

That famous cavalryman Lord Paget, Colonel of the the 7th Hussars, played a prominent part in the training of the cavalry. In 1805 William Verner was commissioned into the 7th Hussars, then stationed at Ipswich, with Vivian as its Lieutenant-Colonel in command and Kerrison as the second Lieutenant-Colonel. Verner says: 'Ipswich was looked upon as a kind of drill for the Cavalry. There were two regiments of Cavalry always quartered there, and one at Woodbridge. All the regiments in England were sent in rotation to be drilled under Lord Paget, in consequence of which the 7th remained there for six years, for the last three of which I was with it.'[51] This means that the 7th Hussars constituted the training regiment at Ipswich from 1802 to 1808, and it appears that Paget ran something of a cavalry equivalent of Moore's infantry camp at Shorncliffe.

Rather strangely, it was by no means the universal practice at the beginning of the nineteenth century to train horses of the heavy cavalry to jump. Light cavalry, on the other hand, were expected to cross any normal country. In a book written by 'A Field Officer' in 1809, entitled *Strictures in the Army*, the author emphasises the importance of teaching cavalry horses to jump. General George Warde, Colonel of the 4th Royal Irish Dragoon Guards from 1778 to 1803, insisted on his regiment being able to jump, and when he was commanding the troops in Ireland at the age of about 70 he often led the 4th Dragoon Guards across country.[52] Captain Badcock and four men of the 14th Light Dragoons were once cut off by French cavalry in the Peninsula, but escaped by jumping several fences which the French were unable to do.[53]

Wellington's views on his cavalry were somewhat mixed. In an often quoted letter to Lord John Russell on 31 July 1826, well after the end of the war, he wrote:

'I considered our cavalry so inferior to the French from want of order, that although I considered one of our squadrons a match for two French, yet I did not care to see four British opposed to four French, and still more so as the numbers increased, and order (of course) became more necessary. They could gallop, but they could not preserve their order.'

Wellington was referring, of course, to the charge, and to the loss of control once it had started. The British cavalry always pressed home their charge with dash and gallantry, but too often they failed to rally afterwards, and were unable to meet the French cavalry's counter-attack. One squadron was obviously a very effective unit in the attack indeed, if it was equal to two French.

An instance of the behaviour to which Wellington objected is provided by Major-General John Slade's action at Maquilla. In June 1812, Lieutenant-General Sir Rowland Hill, seeking to cut off General Lallemande with two regiments of French dragoons, ordered Slade, with the 3rd Dragoon Guards and the 1st Royal Dragoons to enter a wood and await further orders. Slade, hearing that Lallemande was not superior in numbers, disobeyed orders and attacked the French cavalry, driving them back with loss. He then galloped after them beyond the defile of Maquilla for a distance of eight miles, and allowed his supporting squadrons to join in the pursuit. Lallemande, however, had by this time rallied his regiments, and awaited the British cavalry in the plain beyond the defile with his reserves well in hand. As Slade's now disorderly mass of horsemen approached, Lallemande counter-attacked and pursued in his turn for some six miles, recovering his own men taken prisoner and capturing more than 100 of his opponents.[54]

Wellington wrote to Hill:

'I have never been more annoyed than by Slade's affair, and I entirely concur with you on the necessity of inquiring into it. It is occasioned entirely by the trick our officers of cavalry have acquired of galloping at everything, and their galloping back as fast as they gallop on the enemy. They never consider the situation, never think of manoeuvring before an enemy — so little that one would think they cannot manoeuvre, excepting on Wimbledon Common; and when they use their arm as it ought to be used, viz, offensively, they never keep nor provide for a reserve.

'All cavalry should charge in two lines, of which one should be in reserve; if obliged to charge in one line, part of the line, at least one-third, should be ordered before hand to pull up, and form a second line as soon as the charge should be given, and the enemy has been broken and has retired. The Royals and the 3rd Dragoon Guards were the best regiments in the cavalry in this country, and it annoys me particularly that the misfortune has happened to them. I do not wonder at the French boasting of it; it is the greatest blow they have struck.'[55]

Yet a month later, at the Battle of Salamanca, Wellington, after witnessing the brilliant charge of the Dragoons, turned to Sir Stapleton Cotton (later Lord Combermere), commanding the cavalry, and exclaimed: 'By God, Cotton, I never saw anything so beautiful in my life; the day is *yours*.'[56] He subsequently wrote to Earl Bathurst, Secretary of State for War,

'I am very anxious that a mark of His Royal Highness's favor should be conferred upon Sir S. Cotton. I believe he would be much gratified to receive the Red Riband. No cavalry could act better than ours did in the action; and I must say for Sir Stapleton that I do not know where we should find an officer that would command our cavalry in this country half so well as he does.'[57]

At Espeja in the Peninsula, in September 1811, there occurred an affair between troopers armed respectively with sabres and lances. The 14th and 15th Light Dragoons (or Hussars) were brigaded with the 1st Hussars, KGL, under General Count Arenschildt. The Polish Lancers of the French Army being observed drawn up on rising ground, Arenschildt rode up to the Commanding Officer of the 14th and said, 'Sir, you will charge them'. Two squadrons of the 14th immediately advanced to the attack, the Lancers awaiting them with lances 'advanced', doubtless thinking that the 14th, with sabres, would never get inside them. However, the 14th charged, broke the Lancers' ranks, and cut down more than 60 of them. It is said that the 14th were offered lances as a compliment on their return home after the war, but refused them.[58]

The very successful cavalry action at Sahagun in December 1808 is well described by Lord Paget, commanding the light cavalry and horse artillery in the Army of Sir John Moore. Paget planned a surprise attack at Sahagun, with the object of destroying its garrison, the French 16th Dragoons of the Guard. He wrote the following account, in a letter of 22 December 1808 to his brother Arthur, which illustrates well the strengths and weaknesses of the cavalry under Moore and Wellington:

'You will be pleased to hear that I have had an affair with the French cavalry, and have given them a good licking. It was those lucky rogues the 15th, who always happen to be under my hand when there is anything to be done.

'The following is the history:- Hearing that a French General with 700 or 800 cavalry was at this place, I determined upon trying to catch them, and for this purpose ordered Gl. Slade [commanding the Hussar Brigade of the 7th, 10th, and 15th Hussars] to march with the 10th and 7 Guns on our side of the River, to make a Show and if possible push into the town, whilst I marched at 1 o'clock am to get round the town with about 400 of the 15th and about 12 men of the 7th. In the night my advanced guard fell in with a Patrole of the Enemy, from whom 5 Prisoners were taken, but as the others escaped, I was obliged to push very fast, lest they should take the alarm and escape. I judged right, for having come to my point before daylight, I found the Enemy formed without the town. I judged them to be between 600 and 700 Men, but from the reports of Prisoners they must have amounted to 750. As soon as they could distinguish us they made off in good order. I marched in column Parallel, but a good deal behind them, gaining however upon them. At length seeing they must be caught, they halted and formed; I pursued a little further to secure them, halted, wheeled into Line and charged, just as you have seen us do at Ipswich. The French fired at us and stood firm to receive us. We broke them and the result was several killed, 19 wounded, 2 Lt Cols., 1 Capt., 10 Lieuts., between 150 and 160 Men and 125 Horses and some Mules made prisoners. — Col. Grant, Ajt. Jones and 22 Men of the 15th wounded. The March and the Attack were beautiful, nothing could exceed it, but the pursuit was sadly disorderly. I gave the Regiment a good scolding for it after the affair was over, and the answer they gave me was three cheers, and a request that I would accept as a token of their regard the two best Officers' Horses that were taken.'[59]

Paget's orders to Brigadier-General Slade were as follows:

'The 10th Hussars with 4 guns will march from the Monasteries so as to arrive at the Bridge of Sahagun at half-past six in the morning . . . The object of the movement is to surprise Sahagun. The piquet at the Bridge will be driven in briskly, If serious resistance is shown, a squadron or more may be dismounted, who, followed by a mounted squadron, will enter the town, make for the General's and principal officers' quarters to make them prisoners. The grand object is to drive the enemy through the town, on the other side of which Lt-General Lord Paget will be posted with the 15th Hussars. The moment this object is in way of being accomplished two squadrons of the Tenth must be detached to the left, where the enemy has a piquet of from 60 to 100 men. These must be briskly attacked, and made prisoners. This done they will return to Sahagun.'[60]

The detail in this order shows Paget's assessment of Slade's abilities.

Notes

1 Captain Hinde, *The Discipline of the Light Horse* (London, W. Owen, 1778), pp147-8
2 The Hon J. W. Fortescue, *The British Army 1783-1802* (London, Macmillan, 1905), pp93-4
3 *Correspondence of Charles, 1st Marquis Cornwallis,* ed Charles Ross (London, J. Murray, 1859), vol I, p402
4 Captain Sir George Arthur, Bart, *The Story of the Household Cavalry* (London Archibald Constable, 1909), vol II pp480-82
5 ibid, p629
6 Colonel R. S. Liddell, *The Memoirs of the Tenth Royal Hussars* (London, Longmans, Green, & Co, 1891), pp59f
7 Arthur, op cit, pp498-99
8 ibid, p529
9 ibid, p428
10 ibid, pp526-7
11 ibid, p529
12 Liddell, op cit, pp96-7
    Colonel Henry Blackburne Hamilton, *Historical Record of the 14th (King's) Hussars* (London, Longmans, Green & Co, 1901), p77
13 ibid, pp48f
14 Liddell, op cit, pp59f
15 Hamilton, op cit pp48f
16 T. H. McGuffie, 'The 7th Hussars in 1813', *Journal of the Society for Army Historical Research*, vol XLII (1964)
17 Liddell, op cit, p118
18 Hamilton, op cit, p91

19 N. B. Leslie, 'The Succession of Colonels of the British Army from 1660 to the Present Day', *The Society for Army Historical Research* Special Publication No 11, 1974

20 Arthur, op cit, pp545, 557

21 C. W. C. Oman, *Wellington's Army* (London, Edward Arnold, 1912), p371

22 Fortescue, op cit, pp108-10
Colonel H. C. B. Rogers, *The Mounted Troops of the British Army* (London, Seeley Service 2nd edn, 1967), p148

23 ibid, p149

24 Arthur, p149

25 ibid, p509

26 *Selections from the Dispatches and General Orders of Field Marshal the Duke of Wellington*, ed Lieutenant-Colonel Gurwood (London, John Murray, 1861), pp343-44, 491

27 C. T. Atkinson, 'A Light Dragoon in the Peninsula', *Journal of the Society for Army Historical Research*, vol XXXIV (1956)

28 Hamilton, op cit, pp116-7

29 'The Peninsula and Waterloo Letters of Captain Thomas Charles Fenton', ed Major C. W. de L. Froude, *Journal of the Society for Army Historical Research*, vol LIII (1975)

30 Major-General Edward Sabine, *Letters of Colonel Sir Augustus Simon Frazer, KCB* (London, Longman, Brown, etc, 1859), p67

31 Oman, op cit, pp112-13

32 Froude, op cit

33 A. L. F. Schaumann, *On the Road with Wellington*, ex & tr Anthony M. Ludovici (London, William Heinemann, 1924), p440

34 Ruth W. Verner, 'Reminiscences of William Verner', *Society for Army Historical Research*, Special Publication No 8, 1965

35 McGuffie, op cit

36 Hamilton, op cit, pp123-24

37 Oman, op cit, pp112-13

38 Rogers, op cit, pp165-66

39 Froude, op cit

40 Hamilton, op cit, p86

41 Rogers, op cit, pp 151-52
R. Scurfield, 'The Weapons of Wellington's Army', *Journal of the Society for Army Historical Research*, vol XXXVI (1958)
Colonel H. C. B. Rogers, *Weapons of the British Soldier* (London, Seeley Service, 1960), pp138-9

42 Rogers, *Mounted Troops*, op cit, pp163-64
Rogers, *Weapons*, op cit, p146

43 ibid, pp146-7
Scurfield, op cit

44 Rogers, *Mounted Troops*, op cit, pp163-64
Scurfield, op cit

45 Ezechiel Baker, *Twenty-two Years Practice and Observations with Rifle-Barrelled Guns*, p85

46 Froude, op cit

47 Rogers, *Mounted Troops*, op cit, p162
   C. T. Atkinson, op cit
   Oman, op cit, p298
   T. H. McGuffie, 'The Life of a Light Cavalry Regiment', *Journal of the Society for Army Historical Research*, vol XXXVIII (1960)
48 McGuffie, 'The 7th Hussars in 1813', op cit
49 ibid
50 The Hon. J. W. Fortescue, *A History of the British Army*, vol III (London, Macmillan, 1902), p538
51 Verner, op cit
52 Rogers, *Mounted Troops*, op cit, pp149-51
53 Atkinson, op cit
54 Major-General Sir W. F. P. Napier, *History of the War in the Peninsula and in the South of France*, vol IV (London, Frederick Warne), p193
55 *Selections from the Dispatches*, op cit
56 Rogers, *Mounted Troops*, op cit pp 168-69
57 *Selections from the Dispatches*, op cit, p601
58 Hamilton, op cit, pp90-1
59 'Sahagun' (from 'The Paget Papers' (Heinemann, 1896), vol II app I, pp388-9). quoted *Journal of the Society for Army Historical Research*, vol XXV (1947)
60 Liddell, op cit, p84

Artillery

General

The Royal Artillery, like the Royal Engineers, did not come under the Horse Guards (the headquarters of the Commander-in-Chief in the United Kingdom) but under the Master-General of the Ordnance, and was not, therefore, properly considered part of the Army. The career structure of its officers was vastly different because promotion was by seniority and not, as in the cavalry and infantry, by purchase.

At the start of the war with the French Republic the artillery for field service had been formed into a field train, comprising all the pieces of ordnance, gun carriages, specialist vehicles, and personnel (artillerymen, artificers, and others). The train was normally divided into 'brigades of guns' with about 12 pieces in each; but these pieces were distributed amongst the infantry, two being allocated to each infantry battalion. The train was drawn by horses with civilian drivers, purchased or hired for the campaign, and temporarily employed 'conductors' were responsible for the management of drivers and horses.

In January 1793 there was a revolution in the tactical organisation of the artillery with the formation of two bodies of horse artillery. Each of these was called a troop and was equipped with four (later six) pieces. Two more troops were raised the following November. As these troops were completely mobile, all gunners being either mounted or carried on carriages and waggons, civilian drivers and their horses were clearly inadequate, and a new Driver Corps was raised, composed of soldiers and army horses. The improvement was so marked that in 1794 sections of the Driver Corps were allotted to the field artillery as required, and the civilian drivers and hired horses gradually disappeared.

The artillerymen in the train were concerned solely with the service of their pieces, and one artillery company of 100 gunners was about sufficient to man a brigade of 12 pieces. This train organisation was retained for the field artillery (but not of course for the horse artillery) during the first period of the war up till 1802. In that year the field artillery was reorganised into brigades of six pieces each. Throughout the Peninsular and Waterloo campaigns the field artillery unit of six pieces was officially styled a brigade, but it was often referred to as a battery, after the emplacement which such a unit would normally occupy. The brigade or battery became the tactical unit of field artillery as the troop was of horse artillery. Gunners of the field brigades normally marched on foot but they were sometimes lifted on vehicles if circumstances required part of the field artillery to move at a quicker pace than a walk. Although the tactical unit of horse artillery was the troop, the whole of the Royal Horse Artillery was paradoxically known as the Royal Horse Brigade. In 1806 the Driver Corps was renamed the Corps of Royal Artillery Drivers.[1]

Artillery Equipments and Ammunition

The British field equipment most constantly in use throughout the French War was the light 6-pounder gun, a brass (or more properly bronze) piece five feet in length. The brass 9-pounder gun was introduced in 1808 and became the very effective weapon of the field artillery in the Peninsular War, and some troops of horse artillery were later equipped, or partially equipped, with it. There were two types of field howitzer, one light and one heavy, and both of 5½-inch calibre. The light version was a very short piece and consequently erratic, but it had a high trajectory and fired a powerful common shell for its size. The heavy pattern was a very good and accurate howitzer. It was the practice in the Peninsula to include one or two light howitzers in every troop of horse artillery and one or two of either type in every field battery.

The heavier equipments were primarily in the siege trains. During the Peninsular War the 42-pounder gun was occasionally included in the siege train, but the heaviest pieces was generally the 32-pounder gun, which was of great use at long ranges. There were a number of different types of 24-pounder gun, but the 50-cwt version, used in the Peninsula, proved the best of all British ordnance for breaching defensive works. With round shot it could pierce 12 feet of rammed earth, and General Sir Alexander Dickson, who, as a Lieutenant-Colonel, was Wellington's Commander Royal Artillery in the Peninsula, thought it the most efficient breaching weapon in the world. It was used in all Wellington's successful sieges. The 18-pounder gun figured in the siege train as the complement to the 24-pounder; its principal role being to neutralise the enemy artillery while the 24-pounder breaching batteries were being established. Two types of mortar, the 10-inch and the 8-inch, were normally included in the siege train. The 10 inch was predominantly a siege weapon and was at one time much used for ricochet fire. The 8-inch was a very popular mortar and during the latter part of the Peninsular War it was often used as in a counter-battery role instead of the 18-pounder gun.[2]

It was the sieges of the Peninsular War that brought out a weakness in brass ordnance. At the start of the war, siege trains were composed entirely of brass ordnance, but the heat of rapid fire so softened the metal that muzzles began to droop. As a result, brass pieces had to be limited to 120 rounds in 24 hours. Iron guns, being unlimited, could fire three times this number in the same period, or one round every four minutes. Because this drawback seriously reduced the volume of fire, from 1811 onwards only iron guns were allowed in the siege trains.[3]

Up till the time of the outbreak of war against France, all gun carriages were of the so-called 'bracket' type; that is to say, the tail was formed of two wooden planks called 'cheeks' or 'brackets', which were placed on edge parallel to each other and connected by four transoms. These transoms, or cross-pieces, were called, respectively from rear to front, the trail transom, the centre transom, the bed transom, and the breast transom. The axle-tree was just behind the foremost of these, the breast transom. The bed and centre transoms were close together and over them was a board called a bed. On the top of the trail, and over the forepart of the axle-tree, were the trunnion holes (semi-circular holes cut in the cheek) and the capsquares, which were curved iron straps secured over the trunnions of the piece to hold them in the trunnion holes. On top of the bed there was a vertical elevating screw on which the knob behind the breech of the piece rested. In the trail transom was the pintle hole into which went the pintle, or vertical spike, on the end of the limber, usually above the limber axle-tree. At this stage the limber still consisted only of axle-tree, wheels, and shafts.[4]

A disadvantage of the bracket trail was that the weight and length combined to shift the point of balance so far to the rear that moving the trail to traverse the piece entailed very hard work. In 1792 General Sir William Congreve introduced a much lighter and shorter block trail, which was a solid piece of narrow rectangular section. The centre of gravity with this trail was further forward and traversing became a much easier task. This block trail was used in the Peninsular War for the 6-pounder and 9-pounder guns. Bracket trails were retained for the heavier guns and for howitzers.

The 8-inch and 10-inch howitzers had carriages of quite different design. The piece was supported in front by two long brackets and at the rear by a short trail called a perch, under the end of which were two small truck wheels. On either side of the brackets and hinged to them at one end were two long brake levers, the free ends of which could be lashed down to bear on the naves of the truck wheels and thus control the recoil.[5]

All the mortars were mounted on a bed which had no wheels and rested flat on the ground; bed and mortar being transported in a cart.[6]

The limber of horse and field artillery developed into a platform on which, by 1800, were permanently mounted wooden boxes containing such items as were normally needed close to the gun. These boxes, and those fitted also to the limbers and bodies of the ammunition waggons, provided seats which could be used for men of the gun detachments. In a field battery two men could be carried on the limber and six on the waggon body and its limber, but to save the horses they were not allowed to be used except in an emergency. The iron strapping at the end of the block trail was extended to form a 'trail eye' into which fitted a hook at the back of the limber.[7]

In 1813, when Wellington's advance through Spain had reached the Pyrenees, the first mountain battery was formed by Lieutenant W. L. Robe, RA. It was equipped with six 3-pounder guns, each of which weighed 252 pounds and could be carried on a mule. The gun carriage could be easily dismantled and loaded on to two other mules.[8]

Cartridges came into increasing use during the eighteenth century, the powder charge being wrapped in paper. Loose powder, however, was retained for mortars, because, their elevation being fixed, the range depended on the weight of the powder charge. The principal artillery projectile was the round shot, and this accounted for some three-quarters of the ammunition. A round shot was fastened to a wooden circular plate called a sabot, the purpose of which was to seal the bore behind the shot and so prevent the escape of gas. Case, or canister, shot, in which a number of bullets were contained in, and blasted widespread from, a metal canister, was normally used for defence and had an effective range of about 300 yards. In 1784 Lieutenant Henry Shrapnel of the Royal Artillery invented what he called a 'Spherical Case Shot', which was a hollow iron sphere containing a number of bullets, together with a bursting charge and a fuse to fire it. The invention was demonstrated before the General Officer Commanding Gibraltar in 1797 and was finally approved for service in 1803-04. Its first recorded use in action was the battle of Rolica in 1808. Common (ie explosive) shell was normally fired from howitzers or mortars. The 'windage' in a piece was sufficient to allow the flash from the charge to ignite a fuse inserted in a hole in the shell casing. The fuse was made of quick match, enclosed in a wooden tube which had rings cut round the outside and spaced half-a-second's burning time apart, so that the fuse could be cut to the required length.[9]

Rockets were first added officially to the armament of the Royal Artillery in 1813, and responsibility for the new equipment was allocated to the Royal Horse Artillery, in which Rocket Detachments were formed. The following year the rocket detachments at home and overseas were organised respectively into the 1st and 2nd Rocket Troops.

The rocket adopted in the British Army had been designed by Colonel William

Congreve, son of the inventor of the block trail. The weapon consisted of a rocket, a stick, and a cradle for discharge. Rockets were classified as heavy, medium, or light, of which the last was by far the most extensively used. There were four types of light rocket: the 18-pounder armed either with shell or 9-pound solid shot, the 12-pounder armed with 6-pound shot, the 9-pounder armed with a grenade, and the 6-pounder armed with either shell or 3-pound shot. The maximum range and the height of the trajectory depended on the length of the stick; the full-length stick giving the longest range and the highest trajectory. Sticks were jointed together by iron ferrules, and the complete stick was attached to the rocket by three metal bands.[10]

Organisation and Uniform

As we have seen, the modern organisation of the Royal Artillery into self-contained units with a standard scale of equipments started with the formation of the Royal Horse Artillery. Up till then officers and men of the Royal Artillery were organised in companies and apportioned as required to serve the guns and howitzers of the field train; and these pieces were grouped according to calibre and tactical requirements into brigades. The company was a purely administrative unit. There was originally no tactical unit, but the brigade and its derivative, the battery, eventually became so.

The Royal Horse Artillery Troop, in contradistinction to the field brigade, was a tactical unit from the start. It was first equipped with two light 12-pounder guns, two light 6-pounder guns, and two light 5½-inch howitzers. At the start of the Peninsular campaign the two 12-pounders were replaced by 6-pounders, because it was thought that the terrain might prove too difficult for the heavier gun. The 6-pounder also became the standard piece for the field artillery. However, Napoleon, when he became First Consul in 1799, ordered the equipment of the field artillery with 6-pounder and 12-pounder guns and 24-pounder howitzers, thus giving them a considerable advantage in weight of metal over their British opponents. The Royal Artillery's answer was the 9-pounder brass gun, which appeared first in the Peninsula in 1808 as the equipment of a reserve field brigade. This piece was so successful in action that it became the standard equipment of the field artillery.

In 1810 Wellington, short of British artillery, attached Portuguese batteries to several of his infantry divisions. In 1811, when he formed the last two infantry divisions, it would not have been possible to provide even one field battery for each division without making use of the Portuguese artillery. When in May 1811 the battles of Fuentes de Onoro and Albuera were fought, Wellington had, of British artillery, only three troops of Royal Horse Artillery (attached to the Cavalry and the Light Division) and five Royal Artillery field batteries (attached to the infantry divisions). However, he had eight batteries of Portuguese artillery, which enabled him to allot two field batteries each to the 2nd, 3rd, 5th 6th British Divisions and to Hamilton's Portuguese Division, and one field battery each to the 1st, 4th, and 7th Divisions. In 1812, due to fresh artillery units arriving from the United Kingdom, every division, except the Light (which was left with its solitary troop of horse artillery), had a complement of two field batteries, and there was sufficient left over to provide a small reserve of field artillery as well.[11]

When the Army first arrived in the Peninsula it was short, not only of artillery, but of horses to pull such equipment and carriages as it had. For instance, on 16 August 1808, before the battle of Rolica, Wellington (then of course still Wellesley) wrote to Lord Castlereagh: 'Our artillery horses are not what we ought to have. They have great merit in their way as cast horses for dragoons, and Irish cart horses, bought at £12 each! but not fit for an army, that, to be successful, and carry things with a high hand, ought to be able to move.'[12]

In April 1813 Major (later Colonel Sir) Augustus Frazer was appointed to command the Royal Horse Artillery in the Peninsula. Of his horse artillery troops, he says that one was with Hill's Corps, one was on the march to Sabugal, one was at Oporto with the cavalry, and one was attached to the Light Division. He adds: 'All have 6-pounders, except the troop lately arrived from England, which have 9-pounders; that troop is yet unattached. I hope to see two others unattached also, and, should any opportunity offer, shall endeavour to have it so arranged. Our arm, in high and unequivocal efficiency, should be kept like greyhounds on the slip; its value is yet but little known.'[13]

The troop with 9-pounders, under Webber-Smith, was eventually posted to the Hussar Brigade. But on 1 June Frazer removed it from the Hussars and replaced it with Gardiner's Troop. He then divided up Webber-Smith's 9-pounders between the Troops commanded by Webber-Smith, Gardiner, and Bull. Frazer says that Webber-Smith was very annoyed.'[14] The 9-pounders were so successful as horse artillery equipments that, before the Waterloo campaign, Wellington, persuaded by Frazer, directed the replacement of the 6-pounders by 9-pounders in more than half the horse artillery troops. Events justified the decision, for the case shot of the 9-pounders, stationed in front of the British lines, caused far heavier casualties than did that of the 6-pounders. Each of these re-equipped troops had five 9-pounder guns and one 5½-inch howitzer. However, the neavier guns needed teams of eight horses instead of six to maintain their original mobility.[15]

Frazer has some interesting comments on the organisation of the artillery for the Waterloo campaign, during which he commanded the horse artillery. On 22 May 1815 he writes: 'Three batteries of 18-pounders (four guns each) will be ordered up immediately . . . We are waiting for more companies of artillery from England, and daily expect dismounted cavalry to act as drivers for the artillery.' Three days later he says: 'As Ross, Bull, Mercer, and Macdonald all have guns of a heavier nature [ie Bull had heavy 5½-inch howitzers and the others had 9-pounder guns] than the other troops [ie Ramsay, Bean, Webber-Smith, and Whinyates], I have been puzzled to find horses to increase their numbers [ie increase the number of horses to eight per team], but . . . I have been able to promise Lord Uxbridge that the six troops (Ross's not having arrived) shall be new armed and equipped.'[16]

Frazer gives the Royal Horse Artillery troops and their equipment at Waterloo as follows:

A Troop, Lieutenant-Colonel Ross, 9-pounder
D Troop, Major Bean, light 6-pounder
E Troop, Lieutenant-Colonel Gardiner, 9-pounder
F Troop, Lieutenant-Colonel Webber-Smith, light 6-pounder
G Troop, Captain Mercer, 9-pounder
H Troop, Major Ramsay, light 6-pounder
I Troop, Major Bull, heavy 5½-inch howitzer
2nd Rocket Troop, Captain Whinyates, light 6-pounder and rocket.[17]

All these troops were under Frazer's command. Six of them (E, F, G, H, and I, and the 2nd Rocket) were attached to the Cavalry and were under the command of Lieutenant-Colonel Macdonald, while the remaining two (A and D) were with the Reserve Artillery.[18] The mixture of officers' ranks looks odd, but many of them were brevet ranks, conferring

Right: Lieutenant-General Sir John Moore (by Sir Thomas Lawrence). / *National Army Museum*

Below: Field Marshal the Duke of Wellington (by P. E. Stroehling). / *National Army Museum*

Above left: The Brigade of Guards under General Lake repulsing a French attack on Wilhelmstadt, 6 March 1793 — the first British land engagement of the war. The view is from the French position. / *National Army Museum*

Left: The British 15th Light Dragoons (on the left) attacking French cavalry in Flanders in 1793. / *National Army Museum*

Above: The Duke of York with his troops in action during the siege of Valenciennes in 1793. / *National Army Museum*

Right: Uniform worn by the Light Infantry of the Foot Guards in Flanders during 1973. / *National Army Museum*   *1793*

Above: The 15th Light Dragoons charging French infantry during the action at Villers-en-Cauchies, 24 April 1794. / *National Army Museum*

Below: The Battle of Beaumont, 26 April 1794. Cavalry charging French infantry. The horsemen in the right foreground are British light dragoons. / *National Army Museum*

Above: The Duke of York during the Battle of Beaumont, Three guns are firing to the right of the cottage. The infantry at the bottom right are Austrians. / *National Army Museum*

Below: Volunteer infantry being presented with their Colours at Carisbrooke Castle, 24 June 1798. / *Parker Gallery*

Left: Major-General Francis D'Oyly's Brigade, of the two battalions of the 1st Guards, landing in Holland, 27 August 1799, together with the first two pieces of artillery which are being mounted on their carriages in the left foreground. The brigades already landed (those of Coote and Macdonald) are in action on the sandhills in the background. / *National Army Museum*

Below left: The campaign in North Holland 1799. British infantry (on the right) being attacked by French and Dutch troops / *National Army Museum*

Above: The 3rd Worcestershire Militia being reviewed at Southsea at the beginning of the nineteenth century. The battalion is at the salute; the commanding officer, with the Colours behind him, is on foot in front of the centre of the line; the band, on the right of the line, is playing a General Salute; the second in command and the adjutant are mounted on the right and left of the line respectively. / *G. N. Hopcraft*

Below: Major-General George Ludlow's Brigade of the Coldstream and 3rd Guards landing in Aboukir Bay, 8 March 1801, and being charged by French Cavalry. The boats shown are the cutters carrying the second line of the attack, the first line were in flat boats. The flag and pennant are those of the captain, Royal Navy, commanding the division of boats carrying this brigade. / *National Army Museum*

Above: The Battle of Alexandria, 21 March 1804, showing the attack by General Lanusse's Division against the British right, where Moore was in command. On the right are the ruins ('the Roman Camp') which were manned by the 58th Foot, with the 28th on their left. The 42nd Royal Highlanders (the Black Watch) have arrived to cover the left flank of the 28th. / *National Army Museum*

Below: The 28th Foot (later the 1st Battalion The Gloucestershire Regiment) at the Battle of Alexandria. The French got behind the 28th and the rear rank of the regiment turned about to face attacks from that direction as well as from the front. This was the incident that earned the regiment the right (still exercised) to wear their badge on the back as well as the front of their headdress. / *National Army Museum*

Above: The 95th Rifles (later The Rifle Brigade) in 1804, showing the tapered shako with green plume, the ornate black braid embellishment to the green uniform, and the long sword bayonet. This aquatint by Rowlandson depicts the disposition of a piquet to resist a cavalry attack. / *Parker Gallery*

Below: Another Rowlandson illustration of the 95th in 1804. Various methods of firing the Baker rifle are shown. There are two officers, one of them wearing a sabretache and with a pistol stuck in his waist sash, and a bugler is sounding a call. / *Parker Gallery*

Above: The magnificent Benedictine convent in
Catania, Sicily, which was so admired by Sir John
Moore in 1806. It was the headquarters of Major-
General William Wynyard, commanding the
Guards Brigade, and there are British sentries at the
door of the convent, and various British officers
and other ranks in the foreground.
/ *National Army Museum*

Below: The Battle of Maida 1806. The illustration
shows the Light Infantry Brigade, commanded by
Lieutenant-Colonel Kempt, engaging the French
1st Light Regiment of three battalions, commanded
by General Compère. The British light infantry are
wearing shakos with a green plume on the left, and
in rear is an officer wearing a hat 'fore-and-aft'.
/ *National Army Museum*

Above: On 5 September 1807 Copenhagen capitulated to the British force commanded by General Lord Cathcart. The illustration shows British troops forming up and marching into the city with bayonets fixed and uncased Colours to take possession. / *National Army Museum*

Below: At the Battle of Vimiero the 71st Highlanders were ordered to charge. One of their pipers was wounded severely, but, seated on the ground, he continued to play the regiment into action. / *National Army Museum*

Above: The 10th Hussars in rearguard action during the retreat to Corunna. The Hussar Brigade in Moore's army consisted of the 7th, 10th and 15th Hussars. On active service the 10th Hussars preferred to wear their undress red shako, rather than the very tall pattern of fur cap, or busby, then issued. / *National Army Museum*

Left: During the retreat to Corunna, the 95th Rifles formed part of the Reserve under Major-General Sir Edward Paget, which provided the rearguard to the army after the Light Brigades left the main body and marched to Vigo. / *National Army Museum*

Above right: The 20th Regiment were also part of Paget's Reserve. Here they are at the tail of the long column crossing the bridge on the road to Corunna. The picture gives a vivid impression of the type of country through which the retreat was conducted. / *National Army Museum*

Right: At a critical point during the Battle of Corunna, Sir John Moore placed himself at the head of the 42nd and ordered them to advance, calling out: 'My brave Highlanders! Remember Egypt!' The regiment fired one volley and charged. / *Parker Gallery*

Left: On 12 May 1809 Sir Arthur Wellesley forced the passage of the River Douro, seizing Oporto and defeating Soult. The illustration shows Sir Edward Paget, second in command to Wellesley, organising the crossing, and the capture of the Seminary — the large building high above the far bank, which was the key to the French position. Paget was severely wounded whilst standing on the roof of the Seminary, losing an arm. / *National Army Museum*

Below left: Talavera; the decisive attack by the 48th Foot (later the 1st Battalion The Northamtonshire Regiment), led by their commanding officer, Lieutenant-Colonel Donellan, who has fallen from his horse, severely wounded. / *National Army Museum*

Right: Major-General Robert Craufurd, commander of the famous Light Division. / *National Army Museum*

Below: The bridge over the River Coa, looking upstream. On the left is the junction of two roads approaching the bridge from Almeida. That on the left came down a hill too steep for vehicles, and all used the road on the right. Between the two roads, a short way to the left of the picture, is the knoll held by the 43rd and 95th to cover the retreat to the bridge. The difficult country over which the action of 24 July 1810 was fought will be noted. / *National Army Museum*

Above: At the Battle of Busaco the 43rd and 52nd Light Infantry were lying in a hollow road (seen running from the fir trees along to the left) which was parallel to the ravine at the foot of the hill, from which the French were advancing. As the latter prepared for their final rush, Craufurd waved his hat and shouted: 'Now 52nd, revenge the death of Sir John Moore!' (the regiment's Colonel). Both battalions rose to their feet, delivered a volley at 10 paces distance, and charged.
/ *National Army Museum*

Below: The 5th Battalion 60th (later the King's Royal Rifle Corps) at the Battle of Busaco on 27 September 1810 was split up; one company being allotted to each brigade (except in the Light Division). However, battalion headquarters and three companies were with Lightburne's Brigade of the 3rd Division, and were extended in front of the British line as skirmishing troops. Here they are carrying out a fighting withdrawal before the heavy French columns. / *National Army Museum*

seniority in the Army but not in the Royal Artillery. Brevet rank was awarded for distinguished service, but until 1813 the Board of Ordnance had refused to allow brevet promotions to 'second captains' (ie seconds-in-command of troops and batteries). However, 14 second captains successfully petitioned the Prince Regent, with Wellington's strong support, and hence the big proportion of apparently senior troop commanders in 1815.

All except one of the infantry divisions at Waterloo had two batteries (the exception having only one), though one of the two might actually be a troop of horse artillery from the King's German Legion. The divisional artillery was commanded by a field officer, generally a lieutenant-colonel. The Reserve Artillery consisted of Bean's and Ross's Troops, RHA, together with a field battery, and it was commanded by Major Drummond, who in regimental rank was senior to Brevet Lieutenant-Colonel Ross.[19]

Except that their coats were blue instead of red, field artillery were uniforms that were almost exactly similar to those of the infantry of the line. The Royal Horse Artillery also wore blue coats, but they were dressed in similar fashion to the light dragoons, before the latters' uniform was changed in 1812.

Operations

Napier's classic description of the charge by Ramsay's Troop of the Royal Horse Artillery at the battle of Fuentes do Onoro is worth quoting as illustrating the spirit that animated that famous and latest branch of the Royal Artillery. Napier wrote as follows:

'The French . . . cut off Ramsay's battery of horse artillery, and came sweeping in upon the reserves of cavalry and upon the seventh division. Their leading squadrons, approaching in a disorderly manner, were partially checked by fire, but a great commotion was observed in their main body; men and horses were seen to close with confusion and tumult towards one point, where a thick dust and loud cries, and the sparkling of blades, and flashing of pistols indicated some extraordinary occurrence. Suddenly the multitude became violently agitated, an English shout pealed high and clear, the mass was rent asunder, and Norman Ramsay burst forth sword in hand at the head of his battery, his horses, breathing fire, stretched like greyhounds along the plain, the guns bounded behind them like things of no weight, and the mounted gunners followed close, with heads bent low and pointed weapons in desperate career.'[20]

As far as possible the heavy siege artillery was moved by sea. As Frazer put it, 'We re-embark our guns as a matter of necessity. Our means of transport are limited, and our heavy guns can readily be carried coastways and landed where we want hereafter.'[21] Frazer, indeed, was himself removed temporarily from his duties with the horse artillery to play a prominent part in the transport and emplacement of siege artillery. On 25 June he was sent to Santander to bring up the siege train for the investment of the fortress of Pampeluna. He was to meet the ordnance transports at that port and transfer the heavy equipment and stores needed for the siege to smaller vessels. He was then to convey them by sea to the small port of Deba a little west of San Sebastian, which could not accept the bigger ships. From there he would have to arrange land transport. On 30 June, the reloading having been completed, Frazer embarked in a frigate and sailed with the craft carrying the ordnance to Deba. However, on 3 July the disembarkation of stores was stopped and their re-embarkation ordered because it had been decided to blockade Pampeluna rather than to try and reduce it. Frazer was ordered back to Headquarters;

but not for long, because the siege train was to be used against San Sebastian and on 16 July he was ordered to go there and make the arrangements. The main breaching battery consisted of twelve 24-pounder guns, of which three were of the shorter type, borrowed from HMS *Surveillante*. Another breaching battery had six 24-pounders. Apart from these there were other batteries in which were, respectively, two 24-pounder guns and four howitzers, four 68-pounder carronades, six 18-pounder guns, two 8-inch howitzers, and four 10-inch mortars.[22]

Two days after the battle of Waterloo Frazer wrote his comments on the part played by the horse artillery, as follows:

'I find my late troop (G) has lost ninety horses, but it behaved so well, so steadily, that I am highly and justly pleased. The English horse artillery did great execution, and I must be allowed to express my satisfaction, that, contrary to the opinion of most, I ventured to change (and under discouraging circumstances of partial want of means) the ordnance of the horse artillery. Had the troops continued with light guns, I do not hesitate to say the day had been lost. The earlier hours of the battle were chiefly affairs of artillery; but kept down by the admirable and steadily-continued fire of our guns, the enemy's infantry could not come on *en masse*, and his cavalry, though bold, impetuous and daring, was forced to try the flanks rather than the front of our position.'[23]

Bull's troop was, as has been said, equipped with the heavy type of 5½-inch howitzer. At one stage of the battle, Frazer learned that Wellington was determined not to lose Hugoumont Wood. Frazer had visited this wood on the previous day and decided that the heavy-howitzer troop should be brought into it. Uxbridge had offered Frazer the free use of the horse artillery which had been attached to the cavalry, and Frazer accordingly ordered up Bull's Troop, reporting his action to Wellington. On the arrival of the Troop, Wellington said: 'Colonel Frazer, you are going to do a delicate thing; can you depend upon the force of your howitzers? Part of the wood is held by our troops and part by the enemy.' Frazer replied that he could depend on the Troop and talked to Bull and his officers. Ten minutes after the Troop opened fire the enemy was driven from the wood.'[24]

One serious problem during the battle was that the guns in recoiling lost their original position, and Frazer said that it was not possible in the deep stiff soil to move them back to the creast without horses, and horses, if they had been used, would have been killed.[25]

One more comment from Frazer, of September 1813, is worth quoting: 'The British Artillery have never lost a single piece of artillery in the Peninsular War. The Portuguese have occasionally.'[26]

Notes

1 Colonel H. C. B. Rogers, *Artillery through the Ages* (London, Seeley Service, 1971), pp75-6
2 ibid, pp78-84
  Major-General B. P. Hughes, *British Smooth-Bore Artillery* (London, Arms & Armour Press, 1969), p90
3 Rogers, op cit, pp78-84
4 ibid, pp69-70
5 ibid, pp84-6
6 Hughes, op cit, p97

7 ibid, p66
8 Rogers, op cit, p86
9 ibid, pp72, 88-9
10 ibid, pp194f
11 C. W. C. Oman, *Wellington's Army* (London, Edward Arnold, 1912), pp176-7
12 *Selections from the Dispatches and General Orders of Field Marshal the Duke of Wellington*, ed Lieutenant-Colonel Gurwood (London, John Murray, 1861), p207
13 *Letters of Colonel Sir Augustus Simon Frazer, KCB*, ed Major-General Edward Sabine (London, Longman, Brown, etc, 1859), p96
14 ibid, p131
15 Hughes, op cit, pp71f
    Frazer, op cit, pix
16 ibid, pp515f
17 Major P. E. Abbott, 'A Waterloo Letter: The Royal Artillery and its Casualties', *Journal of the Society for Army Historical Research*, vol XLII (1964)
18 Frazer, op cit, pp515f
19 ibid
20 Major-General Sir W. F. P. Napier, *History of the War in the Peninsula and in the South of France*, vol III (London, Frederick Warne), pp50-51
21 Frazer, op cit, p308
22 ibid, pp167f
23 ibid, pp515f
24 ibid
25 ibid
26 ibid, p254

Engineers

General

The Royal Engineers, as previously mentioned, came under the direction of the Master-General of the Ordnance. The Corps was comparatively young when war broke out in 1792, and it was unique in being composed entirely of officers — there were no other ranks. Although the organisation of the Engineers as part of the military branch of the Ordnance was directed by an Order in Council of August 1717, it was not till 1757 that commissions were issued to officers of Engineers. In 1788 the military officers of the Department of Engineers were constituted the Corps of Royal Engineers in recognition of their past services.

Meanwhile, the inconvenience attending the employment of civilians on the defensive works at Gibraltar led to the formation there in 1772 of a local company of Military Artificers under the command of Engineer officers. In 1788 further companies of the new Royal Military Artificers were raised at home, consisting almost entirely of mechanics and commanded by 'doing duty' officers of the Royal Engineers.

Both the Royal Engineers and the Royal Military Artificers wore at first a dark blue uniform, but it is said that this blue dress led to mistakes in the trenches during the campaign in Flanders in 1793, and so the colour was changed from dark blue to scarlet. In 1812 a new corps, the Corps of Royal Military Artificers and Royal Sappers and Miners, began to replace the old companies of Royal Military Artificers, but the following year the term 'Military Artificers' was dropped from the title, and from then until after the Crimean War there was the Corps of Royal Sappers and Miners, officered by the Corps of Royal Engineers.[1]

These changes reflected the inadequacy of the Engineer establishment to fulfil the tasks required of it in the Peninsular War. In April 1809 the Corps of Royal Engineers consisted of 179 officers. Of these, nine were colonels and 12 were lieutenant-colonels, all of them at least fairly elderly because, as in the Royal Artillery, promotion was by seniority and commissions could not be sold to provide a comfortable sum for retirement. By the end of 1809 17 of these officers were in the Peninsula, under the command of 41 year old Brevet Major Richard Fletcher, RE. The companies of Military Artificers were completely static organisations, and the men in them rarely moved from the location, to which they had been posted, throughout their service. At the end of 1809 only two sergeants and 27 rank and file were in Portugal, and even two years later there were still less than 100 other ranks of the corps in the Peninsula.[2]

Engineers in Operations

Napier puts the Engineers troubles well in the following extract from his history:

'The engineer officers were zealous; and notwithstanding some defects in the constitution and customs of their corps, tending rather to make regimental than practical scientific officers, many of them were well versed in the theory of their business: yet the ablest trembled at their destitution of all things necessary to real service. Without a corps of sappers and miners, without a private soldier who knew how to carry on an operation under fire, they were compelled to attack fortresses defended by the most warlike, practised, and scientific troops of the age ... The sieges carried on by the British in Spain were a succession of butcheries, because the commonest materials and means necessary for their art were denied to the engineers.'

And of the second siege of Badajoz in May 1811, Napier writes:

'The regular engineer officers were twenty-one in number; eleven volunteers from the line were joined as assistant engineers; and a draft of three hundred intelligent infantry, including twenty-four artificers of the staff corps, strengthened the force immediately under their command. It is not strange that the siege failed. It was strange and culpable that the British Government ... should have sent an engineer corps into the field so ill-organised and equipped that all the officers' bravery and zeal could not render it efficient.'[3]

Wellington blamed the fearful loss of life in the capture of Badajoz on the lack of trained sappers available to the engineer officers, but also on the latters' inadequate knowledge of siegecraft. Sir Charles Oman,[4] unlike Napier, held that the shortage of sappers and miners was the fault of the professional advisers to the administration, who should have drawn attention to the need of such a corps. Once the Government did appreciate the need, a warrant was issued by which the Military Artificers were to be converted into sappers through instruction in military field works. This was soon followed by an order for the despatch of six companies to the Peninsula as soon as they had finished their training. Late in 1812 the first company arrived in the Peninsula and by the spring of 1813 Wellington had about 300 men of the new corps.

The request for sappers and miners came, indeed, from Wellington himself. On 11 February 1812 he wrote to the Earl of Liverpool:

'While on the subject of artillery, I would beg to suggest to your Lordship the expediency of adding to the Engineers' establishment a corps of sappers and miners. It is inconceivable with what disadvantage we undertake any thing like a siege for want of assistance of this description. There is no French corps d'armée which has not a battalion of sappers and a company of miners. But we are obliged to depend for assistance of this description upon the regiments of the line.'[5]

Richard Fletcher, who became a Brevet Lieutenant-Colonel shortly after his arrival in Portugal, was the Commanding Royal Engineer in the Peninsula until he was killed at the siege of San Sebastian in September 1813. He earned fame as the designer of the Lines of Torres Vedras. On his death he was succeeded by Lieutenant-Colonel Elphinstone, who was responsible for the celebrated bridge of boats across the River Adour in 1814, which made the siege of Bayonne possible.[6]

Engineer Responsibilities
Wellington's method of dealing with the CRE is shown by his memorandum of 20

October 1809,[7] giving Fletcher his instructions for the preparation of the Lines of Torres Vedras. The memorandum begins:

'In the existing relative state of the Allied and French armies in the Peninsula, it does not appear probable that the enemy have it in their power to make an attack upon Portugal. They must wait for their reinforcements; and as the arrival of these may be expected, it remains to be considered what plan of defence shall be adopted for this country. The great object in Portugal is the possession of Lisbon and the Tagus, and all our measures must be directed to this object. There is another also connected with that first object, to which we must likewise attend, viz. — the embarkation of the British troops in case of reverse.'

Having stated the object, the memorandum examines the likely enemy lines of attack, and the methods which would have to be used both in summer and winter to counter them. The French would probably advance by two routes, one north and the other south of the Tagus. In winter the level of the Tagus would be high and provide a barrier, but in summer it would be low and fordable in many places. In summer, therefore, the enemy would use his corps south of the Tagus to turn the British positions taken up on the north side of the river. This could only be avoided by a retreat to a line beyond which the Tagus was unfordable.

Wellington then dealt with the positions which the Army should occupy on his selected line of defence, and followed this with the positions to which it should withdraw should this line be forced.

The memorandum continues: 'In order to strengthen these several positions, it is necessary that different works should be constructed immediately, and that arrangements and preparations should be made for the construction of others. Accordingly, I beg Colonel Fletcher, as soon as possible, to review these several positions.' Then follow 21 numbered instructions on what Fletcher was to do. They included entrenching posts, examining positions to determine lines of defence and works to be constructed, constructing redoubts, damming the mouths of rivers to create obstacles, fixing spots for semaphore signal posts to communicate from one point on the position to another, improving roads and constructing new ones, and calculating the time and labour required for all these. Each of the sites on which defensive works were required is specified in the memorandum.

From an engineer's point of view this must have been an ideal instruction; for the Commander-in-Chief gives his appreciation of the situation, his plan, and the engineer tasks required for the plan. His CRE, therefore, is in a position to do his detailed planning and so site his defences as to best meet the possible movements of our own and enemy forces.

The Royal Staff Corps

The Royal Staff Corps was formed by the Duke of York in order that there should be a body of engineers under the direct control of the Horse Guards, able to deal with such matters as field defences and survey, whilst leaving the more technical tasks to the Royal Engineers. The new corps was under a Lieutenant-Colonel Commandant, and its establishment made provision for officers and staff of all the ranks and categories required in a battalion sized unit. The other ranks were limited, however, to the following: sergeant-majors, quartermaster-sergeants, sergeant-overseers, buglers, and privates 1st, 2nd, and 3rd class. Each company had a warrant officer who was either a sergeant-major or a quartermaster-sergeant.[8] But the primary importance of the Royal Staff Corps was to lie in the extra-regimental employment of its officers; and this is demonstrated by the story of one of its officers, William Staveley.[9]

Staveley had held a commission in a local regiment disbanded at the peace of 1802. On the resumption of hostilities, he was anxious to obtain a regular commission and, thanks to his having studied surveying, he was granted an ensigncy in the Royal Staff Corps in July 1804. He was then employed at home for four years in a company of the Corps on coast defences and siege works. In 1808 he was promoted Lieutenant, and in April 1809 he was sent to the Peninsula and attached to Army Headquarters.

Officers of the Royal Staff Corps serving at Headquarters, came under the Quartermaster-General's branch of the staff, and were employed on such duties as surveying, road reconnaissance, bridging, demolition, laying out field defences, etc. Staveley was employed more on survey than anything else. Working at first under Major Dundas of the Royal Staff Corps, he assisted him to report on the fords of the River Alberche before the battle of Talavera, and they had the task of guiding British columns across the river. The night before the battle Wellington (or Wellesley as he was then) sent for an officer of the Staff Corps. Staveley went in response to this summons and was ordered by the Commander-in-Chief to look for the Reserve Artillery, which could not be found. Staveley was equally unsuccessful. Later in the battle, so Staveley reports, 'The Chief soon after observed shot and shell falling thick among the 87th regiment, immediately in our front, when turning sharp round, he said, "Look at those d--d fools!" and ordered me to go and tell them to form in rear of the 88th.'

Of the battle of Fuentes de Onoro, Staveley writes: 'During the battle I superintended the constuction of the entrenchments thrown up on the right of the enemy to cover our flank.' Before the siege of Ciudad Rodrigo Staveley spent some time sketching the River Coa area and various positions. He then joined the besieging troops. In the trenches he met General Crauford, who was killed soon after, and, says Staveley, 'He demanded if I was an officer of the Engineers. In replied, "No, of the Staff Corps", and offered my services. He told me to show the breaches to the storming party which I had just passed through.'

Wellington's use of the officers of the Staff Corps is interesting, and his trust in Staveley is remarkable. At Burgos, during the siege, Wellington ordered Staveley to go to Corunna and bring up the 1st Guards. During the retreat from Burgos he sent for Staveley one evening, when he and his staff were at dinner, and asked him how many marches the 91st Regiment were from Headquarters. Staveley replied that he did not know how many marches they were away, but he did know where they were. Wellington said that was sufficient and ordered Staveley to go and bring them up, adding: 'And you will act according to circumstances and your own judgement, if you find those d--d fellows have driven me across the Tagus.'

Before and during the battle of Vittoria, Staveley was busy carrying orders to the troops and after it was over he had to find quarters for Wellington and the staff in the town of Vittoria. That evening Wellington arrived, and Staveley says: 'On going into an inner room where the dinner was being prepared, he said, "Tell Murray I shall march the army off myself in the morning." I asked, "At what hour?" "When I get up", was the short reply.' (Major-General Sir George Murray was Wellington's Quartermaster-General.)

It is apparent that officers of the Royal Staff Corps were used both on the less technical engineer tasks as well as on route reconnaissance and guide duties which were also carried out by staff officers of the Quartermaster-General's branch; their functions thus overlapped those of two separate departments, but in areas where there was a common interest. The quotation from Napier relating to the second siege of Badajoz shows how other ranks of the Royal Staff Corps could be placed under the command of Royal Engineer officers.

Notes

1 H. M. Chichester & G. Burges-Short, *The Records and Badges of the British Army* (London, Gale & Polden, 1900), pp152-53

2 Michael Glover, *Wellington as a Military Commander* (London, Batsford, 1968), pp17f, 171-3

3 Major-General Sir W. F. P. Napier, *History of the War in the Peninsula and in the South of France*, vol III (London, Frederick Warne), pp159-60, 304, 310

4 C. W. C. Oman, *Wellington's Army* (London, Edward Arnold, 1912) pp281, 284

5 *Selections from the Dispatches and General Orders of Field Marshal the Duke of Wellington*, ed Lieutenant-Colonel Gurwood (London, John Murray, 1861), p574

6 Oman, op cit, p158

7 *Dispatches*, op cit, pp300-03

8 *A Collection of Orders, Regulations, and Instructions for the Army*, Published by Order of the Secretary at War (War Office, 25 April 1807), p54

9 Major-General Sir Louis Jackson, 'One of Wellington's Staff Officers', *Journal of the Society for Army Historical Research*, vol XIV (1935)

Auxiliaries

From the beginning of the war with Revolutionary France, a large number of foreign regiments had served under British command and as an integral part of the British Army. In the early years they had been largely composed of French Royalist *emigrés* or Swiss, but by 1809 most of these regiments had been broken up, and the few that remained were serving in garrison stations overseas. However, a considerable proportion of foreign troops served under Wellington's command in the Peninsula. By far the largest body of these consisted of Portuguese regiments and brigades, which, largely commanded by British officers, formed some two-fifths of Wellington's forces through much of the Peninsular War. The next most numerous element was provided by the King's German Legion, which, because it was originally formed from the Hanoverian Army, owed allegiance to George III as the Elector of their country, and thus for practical purposes officers and men were British troops. The remaining foreign troops were two infantry regiments, the Brunswick Oels Jägers and the *Chasseurs Britanniques*.

The Portuguese Army

When the Portuguese Government asked in 1809 for a British general to reorganise their army, Major-General William Carr Beresford was selected. Two prime factors in that selection were that he was a stern disciplinarian and could speak Portuguese. On his appointment, he was made a local Lieutenant-General in the British Army, and the Portuguese gave him the rank of Marshal in their army. Beresford found the Portuguese Army in very poor condition; badly commanded and inefficient. But within a year had had transformed it into a well-disciplined force, capable of taking a creditable part alongside the British regiments. Indeed, it won praise from Wellington for its performance at the battle of Busaco, its first engagement after reorganisation. To get his results, Beresford had been completely ruthless in cashiering officers and in shooting deserters and marauders amongst the rank and file, without regard either to the personal or court influences of the officers concerned, or to the adverse public opinion aroused by the execution of the men.[1]

Beresford's most improtant step was to bring in a large number of British officers. He sacked all the really incompetent regimental commanders and replaced them by British officers. As a sop to national pride, Beresford left a number of the less inefficient Portuguese in command of regiments and brigades, but each had British officers immediately above or below them. Where a Portuguese colonel commanded a brigade, his two regimental commanders were British. If the officer commander was Portuguese, the senior major was British. In addition, there were from two to four British captains in each regiment. To encourage good British officers to volunteer for service in the Portuguese Army, each of those accepted for service was given one step in rank above that which he held in the British Service.[2]

The Portuguese Regular Army, when Beresford took over command, consisted of 24 infantry regiments of the line, each of two battalions, six Caçador (light infantry) battalions (which had been raised the previous year), 12 regiments of dragoons, and four regiments of artillery. These last were of unequal strength; they could together provide nine or ten field batteries and garrison companies to man the guns of fortresses.[3] Six more battalions of Caçadores were formed in 1811, and these were the only further additions to the Portuguese Regular Army during the remainder of the war. Three of these battalions were formed from an irregular formation, the Loyal Lusitanian Legion, which had been raised by Sir Robert Wilson at Oporto in 1808, and which consisted of two light infantry battalions, a squadron of cavalry, and an incomplete battery of artillery. The Loyal Lusitanian Legion was dissolved on 4 May 1811. Its two battalions became the 7th and 8th Caçadores, and the 9th Caçadores was formed from the remainder. The Caçadores wore a uniform of similar pattern to that of the Rifle Brigade; in nine of the battalions it was dark brown, but the battalions late of the Loyal Lustianian Legion retained their individuality by wearing ivy green. The uniform of the infantry of the line was bright blue and white. Caçadores were supposed to be armed with rifles, but owing to a shortage of these weapons a large proportion of the men had smoothbore muskets.[4]

The first six Caçador battalions were originally organised in three brigades each of two battalions; but they were never tactically so employed. From March 1810 the 1st and 2nd Battalions were attached to the Light Division; but two months later the 2nd was replaced by the 3rd, and the 1st and 3rd Caçadores from then on became an integral part of the Light Division.

The line regiments were organised into brigades, and after Beresford's reorganisation in September 1809 there were 12, each of two two-battalion regiments. To most of these were added in the following year one battalion of Caçadores. Two of the brigades were organised into a Portuguese Division, which, until February 1813 (when he had to give up owing to ill health), was commanded by Major-General John Hamilton, and formed with the 2nd Division a Corps under the command of Lieutenant-General Sir Rowland Hill. All the British divisions, except the 1st, had a Portuguese brigade attached to them in due course. On 13 August 1813 the Portuguese brigades were numbered, and the ten then existing were disposed as follows: 3rd Brigade in the 5th Division, 5th Brigade in the 2nd Division, 6th Brigade in the 7th Division, 7th Brigade in the 6th Division, 8th Brigade in the Portuguese Division, 1st and 10th Brigades independent. Brigades attached to British divisions were supplied by the British Commissariat, whilst the others were the responsibility of the Portuguese Commissary-General. The Caçador battalions in the Light Division were an integral part of it, and not just attached. The 2nd Brigade was the only one which was always under Portuguese command, and two brigades, the 1st and 4th, never had a Portuguese commander.[5]

The Portuguese cavalry were by no means up to the standard of the infantry and were very under strength; 300 men being the most that any regiment ever had in the field. Three regiments were dismounted and served as garrison troops. Of the remaining nine, some were mere skeletons. Two regiments served in the Fuentes do Onoro campaign, but they only mustered 450 effectives between them. The Portuguese artillery, on the other hand, became very efficient, and after 1820 Portuguese field batteries constituted a large part of Wellington's divisional artillery.[6]

On 24 May 1813 Lieutenant-Colonel Frazer attended Wellington's Review of the Portuguese Division in Hill's Corps. There were eight line battalions, one Caçador battalion, three squadrons of dragoons, and three field batteries on parade, with a total strength, excluding the artillery, of about 5,000 all ranks. Frazer wrote:

'The men looked healthy, cheerful and well . . . the whole in most creditable and efficient order, both as to equipment and appearance and facility of movement. The division is commanded by the Conde de Amarante, a lieutenant-general. The infantry were 4480, caçadores 220, cavalry 230, and artillery twelve field pieces. I never saw finer troops. I hope tomorrow to see the British division of Hill's corps; it is in our front. The Spanish regiments of Hibernia and Mallorca left Ciudad Rodrigo yesterday to join Castaños: they are well-looking troops, but inferior to the Portuguese. Each regiment had something under 500 on parade.'[7]

In the earlier days the Portuguese troops did not meet with Wellington's uncritical approval. A General Order of 10 April 1811 said:

'The Commander of the Forces desires that the commanding officers of regiments of Portuguese troops may be directed to oblige their men to keep themselves clean, and to have their clothes and shoes mended. The Commander of the Forces particularly observed the shameful state in which the --d and --th regts are; and he now gives notice that unless there shall be an immediate amendment in the discipline, as well as appearance of these two regiments, the Commander of the Forces will turn them out of the army as being unfit to do duty with the other troops.'[8]

On the other hand, a month later, Wellington wrote to his brother, Henry; 'What a pity it is that the Spaniards will not set to work to discipline their troops! We do what we please now with the Portuguese troops; we manoeuvre them under fire equally with our own, and we have some dependence on them; but these Spaniards can do nothing, but stand still, and we consider ourselves fortunate if they do not run away.'[9]

When Wellington was appointed Commander-in-Chief of the Armies of Spain, he wrote on 4 December 1812 a letter to Don J. de Carrajal, Spanish Minister at War, which is perhaps the most damning indictment of troops under his command ever penned by a commander in the field. The following is an extract:

' . . . Not only are your armies undisciplined and inefficient, and both officers and soldiers insubordinate from want of pay, pensions, clothing, and necessaries, and the consequent endurance of misery for a long period of time, but the habits of indiscipline and insubordinatiion are such, that even those corps which have been well clothed and regularly paid by my directions, and have, to my knowledge, seldom, if ever, felt any privations for more than a year, are in as bad a state, and as little to be depended upon as soldiers, as the others. The desertion is immense, even from the troops last adverted to.'[10]

It is probable that Wellington's strictures had some effect, for Spanish troops performed much better in the later battles. On 31 August 1813 18,000 Spaniards under General Freyre, holding the heights of San Marcial and covering the fords over the Bidassoa, were attacked by two French divisions under Count Reille. Wellington narrated what happened to Baron de Ros, as follows:

'I was sitting upon a rock observing the affair with my glass, about four or five miles from the position upon the road, when a Spanish aide-de-camp came galloping to the rear and earnestly entreated I would direct the English division of General Cole, placed in reserve about a mile behind the Spanish position, to advance, for they were so hard pressed they could no longer answer for repelling the French attacks. It was curious that at this instant I observed the French commencing a retreat, and, desiring him to satisfy himself by my glass that such was really the fact, I strongly urged him to withdraw his request on the part of his Genreral, and thus enable him to claim the whole honour of the success without any aid from us. He looked through the glass, became in a moment as much elated as he had before been downcast, took my advice with thanks, and galloped off to be in time for his share of glory and boasting.'[11]

The King's German Legion

The history of the King's German Legion starts from the invasion of Hanover by a French army under Mortier in May 1803. The Hanoverian Army of the Electorate was in no position to offer any resistance and the country was occupied without a struggle. By the Convention of Elbe, on 4 July 1803, the Hanoverian Army was to surrender all its arms, ammunition, and horses, and officers and men were to go to their homes on parole. It was also stipulated that all ranks were prohibited from taking arms against France, but Mortier agreed to keep this section of the Convention secret.[12]

The Electorate of Hanover had been administered by Adolphus Frederick, Duke of Cambridge, on behalf of his father, George III, and he now originated plans to raise a contingent for service with the British Army from the officers and other ranks of his disbanded army. He persuaded his brother the Duke of York, Commander-in-Chief, to have a Warrant issued for the formation of a regiment of 4,000 all ranks. To implement the terms of the Warrant, which was dated 18 July 1803, he selected Major Johann Friedrich von der Decken, his Adjutant and former tutor. Decken had left Hanover before the capitulation and had been granted a commission in the 60th Regiment. Under the terms of the Warrant he was promoted Colonel and was to receive 15 guineas for each recruit who satisfied the physical conditions required. Rather strangely, a Scottish officer, Major (late Lieutenant-General Sir) Colin Halkett was also given a Warrant on the same date to raise a battalion 459 strong. [13]

Recruiting was slow at first, and an appeal to his Hanoverian subjects was made by George III on 10 August 1803. Decken was authorised to raise a corps of light infantry, to be entitled 'The King's Germans' (all reference to Hanover being omitted for fear of French reprisals), and all foreigners, though preferably German, were invited to take service in the regiment. As soon as it had recruited to its establishment, it was to be under the immediate command of the Duke of Cambridge.[14]

Enlistments now picked up rapidly, and by the end of September 1803 the regiment's depot at Lynmington was so full that some of the men were moved to Parkhurst in the Isle of Wight. Meanwhile, competition between Decken and Halkett had become absurd, and on 3 October 1803 the two signed an agreement to amalgamate their contingents of recruits, the whole being under the command of the Duke of Cambridge. Decken was to organise recruiting on the Continent whilst Halkett was to be responsible for it in England.[15]

By November the strength of the Corps had reached 1,000, and separate branches for cavalry and artillery were organised. On 19 December 1803 the Duke of Cambridge was given a letter of service authorising him to form a force of all arms 5,000 strong. At the same time Decken was appointed its Adjutant-General and Chief Recruiting Officer, and given command of the artillery and Engineers. Recruiting of all European nationalities was permitted, except citizens of France, Italy, and Spain; but no British subjects were to be enlisted.

After the transfer of men, selected from those already enlisted, to the Cavalry and Artillery, two battalions of light infantry, dressed in green, were formed from those remaining. The King's German Legion was now rapidly taking shape. A line battalion, a heavy dragoon regiment, a light dragoon regiment, an artillery company, and a horse artillery troop were all started, and a corps of Engineers, consisting entirely of officers, was formed. These various arms were composed mostly of officers and men from similar arms in the old Hanoverian Army. By June 1805 there were two light battalions and four line battalions of infantry, each of eight or ten companies, one heavy dragoon and two light dragoon regiments, each of three two-troop squadrons, two horse artillery troops, and three artillery companies. The infantry were organised in three brigades, each of two battalions.[16]

The Legion, 6,000 strong, sailed with the British force which disembarked in the Elbe in October 1805. It had to be re-embarked in February 1806, after Napoleon's victory at Austerlitz freed French troops for employment elsewhere; but during this short occupation of Hanover, local enthusiasm increased the number of volunteers considerably. Though 1,442 men seized the opportunity to desert, thousands more were enlisted. On return to England the Legion was increased by a second regiment of heavy dragoons, a third regiment of light dragoons, three more line battalions of infantry, the cadre of a fourth line battalion (to make a total of eight infantry battalions), and a fourth artillery company.[17]

Recruiting depots had been left in the towns of Hanover and Stade, and Decken remained in the Electorate to take charge of them. However, this arrangement did not last long, for the Prussians marched into the country and stopped all recruiting for the Legion. Decken had to leave, but the Prussian triumph was short-lived, for a few months later Napoleon broke their military power at the battles of Jena and Auerstadt. Following the cessation of recruiting in the Electorate, the establishment of the Legion was fixed at 14,000.[18]

Organisation of the King's German Legion

The King's German Legion, like a British infantry regiment of two battalions or more, was never organised in the field as a formation under its own commander. Only the two light battalions and the two heavy dragoon regiments had a permanent brigade organisation. Indeed, the Legion was treated much like a British regiment. The Duke of Cambridge was the Legion's Colonel-in-Chief, and he was responsible for recruiting, promotion, and supply; and in these duties he was assisted by von der Decken as Adjutant-General. General officers of the King's German Legion (who had normally inherited their ranks from the Hanoverian Army) were usually employed as 'Colonels-in-Command' of a regiment or battalion; but they could be appointed to the command of a brigade or a division, which of course included British and often Portuguese troops.[19]

Most of the officers were Hanoverian, but British applicants could obtain commissions in the KGL, and that without purchase — an attraction to those of limited means. Edmund Wheatley, for instance, was commissioned as an Ensign in the 5th Line Battalion in November 1812. There was only one other British officer (other than the Paymaster) in the battalion, but amongst Wheatley's friends were three British officers in the 1st Line Battalion and one in the Artillery. After the peace of 1814, whilst all non-German other ranks were discharged, British officers retained their commissions.[20] In August 1812, in recognition of the distinguished conduct of the King's German Legion, particularly in the battle of Salamanca, its officers were granted permanent rank in the British Army.[21]

The order of precedence of arms in the Legion differed from that in the British Army. The Engineers were the senior arm, followed by the Artillery, and then came the Cavalry and Infantry, in that order. The Corps of Engineers was a very small unit, for only 13 officers served in it and there were no other ranks. The Artillery was able to produce two horse troops or batteries and four field batteries, and in each of these there was a captain in command, a second captain, and four subalterns. In action the senior captain commanded the battery, whilst the second captain had charge of the wagon line. Battery establishments varied according to the types of equipment, and these were the same as those of the Royal Artillery. Each battery normally had eight ammunition wagons, two baggage wagons, a forge cart, and a wagon for small arms ammunition. There were no appointments for field officers, but to compensate for this the more senior battery commanders were promoted to major and subsequently lieutenant-colonel when they reached the requisite seniority.

In a cavalry regiment there were four squadrons, each of two troops. The number of squadrons was increased to five in 1812, but reduced again in 1814. In 1813 the three light dragoon regiments were officially redesignated hussars, though they had been unofficially known as such and had worn hussar uniforms since their formation. At the same time, the two heavy dragoon regiments became light dragoons, and their uniform and equipment were changed to that customary in the British Army for light cavalry.

Infantry battalions were organised as in the British Army. The light battalions were supposed to be armed with rifles, as were also the platoons of sharpshooters, one of which was included in each line battalion. But owing to a shortage of rifles a large number of the men who should have had them were armed with smoothbore muskets.[22]

Uniforms of the King's German Legion were basically the same as in the British Army, in fact at a casual glance it would be difficult to detect any difference.

The King's German Legion in the Peninsula

In 1808 the 3rd Hussars, the 1st and 2nd Light Battalions, the 1st 2nd, 5th, and 7th Line Battalions, and two batteries of Artillery of the King's German Legion were sent to Portugal. Of these, the 3rd Hussars and the 1st and 2nd Light Battalions marched under Sir John Moore into Spain, and were eventually evacuated after the battle of Corunna. The line battalions and the batteries remained in Portugal and eventually formed a permanent part of the Peninsular Army. In the spring of 1809 the 1st Hussars landed in Portugal; and in the spring of 1811 the two light battalions returned from England to the Peninsula, together with the 2nd Hussars. In the winter of 1811-12 the 1st and 2nd Heavy Dragoons joined the Peninsular Army; but the 7th Line Battalion had been so reduced by casualties that the remaining rank and file were distributed amongst the other line battalions, whilst the officers, sergeants, and band returned to England to recruit. Wellington, who regretted the loss of the 7th Battalion, wrote to the Duke of York: 'It is impossible to have better soldiers than the real Hanoverians; and it would be very desirable that the 1st, 2nd, and 5th Line Battalions of the Legion should be reinforced by any man of that description who may be in the depots'. At the end of 1812 the 2nd Hussars, in their turn, were sent back to England owing to the drop in their strength.[23]

By the time the Army was on the Bidassoa, in November 1813, the five battalions of the King's German Legion were organised into two brigades; one consisting of the 1st and

2nd Light Battalions under Colonel Halkett (known as 'Halkett's Green Germans' from the colour of their uniform), and the other composed of the 1st, 2nd, and 5th Line Battalions commanded by Major-General Heinrich von Hinuber.[24]

The two regiments of heavy dragoons achieved fame as being the only cavalry recorded to have broken properly formed squares of well-disciplined infantry. The morning after the battle of Salamanca the two regiments attacked Marmont's rearguard of fresh infantry at Garcia-Hernandez in what the French General Foy described as the finest cavalry charge he had ever seen. Two squares, each composed of a battalion of the 6th Léger, were broken. At the first square a mortally wounded horse carrying a dead rider leaped on to kneeling front rank, bringing down half a dozen men in its struggles. A KGL officer, Captain Gleichen, spurred his horse into the gap, and, the troopers following him, a wedge was driven into the square, breaking it up. Most of the battalion, attacked front and back, then surrendered. The men of the second square were apparently shaken by the disaster to their sister battalion and, when they were charged a few minutes later, they fired a rather wild volley at the oncoming cavalry, wavered, gave ground, and broke. Some 1,400 prisoners were taken and about 200 French were killed and wounded. The dragoons, whose combined strength was only 700, lost four officers and 50 men killed, and two officers and 60 men wounded. (The high proportion of killed to wounded reflects the lethal effect of the smoothbore musket at very short range.)[25]

Of all the KGL units, probably the greatest reputation was enjoyed by the 1st Hussars under their noted commanding officer, Lieutenant-Colonel Friedrich von Arentschildt, particularly for their performance on outpost and reconnaissance. The infantry of the Light Division placed implicit reliance on them. John Kincaid of the 95th wrote: 'If we saw a British dragoon at any time approaching in full speed, it excited no great curiosity among us, but whenever we saw one of the first hussars coming on at a gallop, it was high time to gird on our swords and bundle up.'[26]

From March to May 1801 the Regiment held an outpost line, 40 miles in length, along the Rivers Agueda and Azava, in face of French cavalry four times more numerous, without allowing any enemy reconnaissance to penetrate their screen, and without losing a single man or horse. Nor did they ever send back wrong information to the headquarters of the Light Division, whose front they were covering.[27]

The Brunswick Oels Jägers

In 1809 Frederick William, Duke of Brunswick and George III's nephew, raised a force in his Duchy and attacked the Kingdom of Westphalia, ruled over by Napoleon's brother Jerome, and created from Hesse Cassel and all Prussian possessions west of the Elbe. The attack was a failure and the remnants of his army were embarked in British ships and brought to England. Two regiments, dressed in black uniform, were formed from them — the Brunswick Oels Jägers and the Brunswick Oels Hussars, of which the former served in the Peninsula. Officers and men were originally North Germans, the former mainly Prussians. Because recruits to replace losses could not be obtained from Germany, a large proportion of the rank and file soon consisted of volunteers from the prisoners of war and of all nationalities. Inevitably, standards soon deteriorated, particularly as the King's German Legion had the first call on suitable prisoners. However, the Regiment, under its Prussian officers, fought well in the Peninsula, but it could not be trusted on outpost duty because the men were so prone to desertion. There were many excellent shots in the ranks, and companies of the Regiment were attached to different brigades to strengthen the Army's skirmishing lines.[28]

Chasseurs Britanniques

This regiment was formed in 1794, early in the war with Revolutionary France, from Royalist officers and men.The officers remained of the same category, though by the time of the Peninsular War many were sons and nephews of the original Emigré officers. The men by this time, however, were entirely different. They were mostly French and Italian prisoners of war and only too anxious to return to the enemy ranks. Desertion amongst them was far worse even than in the Brunswick Oels. Wellington issued an order that the Regiment was never to be employed on the outposts. Yet it fought well, mainly owing to the iron discipline exercised by its officers.

Notes

1 C. W. C. Oman, *Wellington's Army* (London, Edward Arnold, 1912), pp119-20
2 ibid, pp228-223
3 ibid
  S. G. P. Ward, 'The Portuguese Infantry Brigades', *Journal of the Society for Army Historical Research*, vol LIII (1975)
4 ibid
  Oman, op cit, pp228-233
  Christopher Hibbert, *The Wheatley Diary* (London, Longmans, 1964), p8
5 Ward, op cit
6 Oman, op cit, pp113, 228-33
7 *Letters of Colonel Sir Augustus Simon Frazer*, ed Major-General Edward Sabine (London, Longman, Brown, etc, 1859), pp115-18
8 *Selections from the Dispatches and General Orders of Field Marshal the Duke of Wellington*, ed Lieutenant-Colonel Gurwood (London, John Murray, 1861), p468
9 ibid, p483
10 ibid, pp648-49
11 *De Ros MS*, quoted Sir Herbert Maxwell, *The Life of Wellington* vol I (London, Sampson Low, 1900), p344
12 Daniel Savage Gray, 'Prisoners, Wanderers, and Deserters: Recruiting for the King's German Legion, 1803-1815', *Journal of the Society for Army Historical Research*, vol LIII (1975)
13 ibid
  Lieutenant-Colonel R. E. F. G. North, 'The Raising and Organising of the King's German Legion', *Journal of the Society for Army Historical Research*, vol XXXIX (1961)
14 'ibid
  Gray, op cit
15 ibid
  North, op cit
16 ibid
17 ibid
  Gray, op cit
18 ibid
19 North, op cit
20 Hibbert, op cit, ppxi, 55
21 ibid, pxi

22 ibid, p8
    North, op cit
23 Gray, op cit
    Oman, op cit, pp222-23
24 Wheatley, op cit, p14
25 Oman, op cit, p101
26 Captain John Kincaid, *Random Shots of a Rifleman*, 2nd edn (1847), quoted Michael
    Glover, *Wellington as a Military Commander* (London, Batsford, 1968), p225
27 Oman, op cit, pp110-11
28 ibid, pp224-25

Command and Staff

General

In the field force which landed in the Netherlands in 1793, 'every department of the staff was more or less deficient, particularly the commissariat and medical branches[1]; and in the early campaigns the work of commanders in active operations were circumscribed by Government interference. For instance, the Government appointed the Duke of York to command the combined British and Russian expeditionary force to Holland in 1799, but instructed him that before taking action on any occasion of importance he was to convene a Council of War, composed of himself, Lieutenant-General David Dundas, Lieutenant-General Sir Ralph Abercromby, Lieutenant-General J. M. Pulteney, the Russian Commander, and Major-General Lord Chatham (a member of the Cabinet with no military experience).[2] It is hardly surprising that British operations during the last years of the eighteenth century were not conspicuously successful.

The staff in the field consisted of the personal staff of commanders of formations, the departments of the Quartermaster-General and the Adjutant-General, the headquarters of the Artillery and Engineers, the Medical Department, the Paymaster-General's Department, the Commissariat, the Purveyor's Department, and the Department of the Storekeeper-General.

In the earlier years of the war with Revolutionary and Napoleonic France, these various branches of the staff owed their allegiance firstly to their departmental chiefs in London and only secondly to the commander on whose headquarters they served. For instance, a commissary-general in the field could, and often did, refuse to obey an order from the general officer commanding the field force on the grounds that it conflicted with his instructions from home. This impossible state of affairs changed, of course, in due course. The double allegiance remained, but it was established that a staff officer had no authority other than that in which he was vested by his commander.[3] The status of the staff officer was eventually established by Wellington in the following minute:

'Every staff officer must be considered as acting under the direct orders and superintendence of the superior officer for whose assistance he is employed, and who is responsible for his acts. To consider the relative situation of the general officer and the staff officer in any other light would tend to alter the nature of the Service, and, in fact, might give the command of the troops to a subaltern staff officer instead of their general officer.'[4]

The effect of this was that although correspondence on departmental matters was carried on directly between, for instance, the Quartermaster-General on Wellington's Headquarters and an Assistant Quartermaster-General at a divisional headquarters, the divisional commander's instructions to his AQMG took precedence. Furthermore, if the

QMG wished to send this AQMG on some particular duty, he would in courtesy write to the latter's commander first.[5]

At the start of the French war, it had been the normal practice for the head of a staff branch in the field to be accompanied by a number of assistants to whom he allotted various duties as the needs arose. However, when in June 1809 the brigades in the Peninsula were grouped into divisions, the opportunity was taken to allocate to each divisional headquarters an officer from both the QMG and the AG branches, and this allocation was eventually increased to an assistant and a deputy assistant from these two branches (ie AMG, DAQMG, AAG, and DAAG).[6]

The term 'General Staff' was used officially to distinguish the staff on the headquarters of a brigade and upwards, from the officers on the headquarters of a regiment. However, Wellington, when he referred to the General Staff, always meant only the QMG and AG branches.[7]

The Quartermaster-General

The Quartermaster-General's branch of the staff was responsible, not only for many of the matters which would be dealt with by that staff today, but also for most of those which are the province of the modern General Staff.

In theory the main responsibilities of the QMG were the quartering and movement of the troops, and the provision of certain categories of stores; though movement only became the exclusive concern of the QMG after a reorganisation of this department in 1803. Previously a commander had often issued movement orders through the Adjutant-General. In practice movement became the most important 'Q' task, because it soon embraced, not only administrative movement from one point to another, but also tactical movement and the disposition of troops on the battlefield. Reconnaisance was an indispensible prelude to a movement order, because it was necessary to assess the suitability of roads, bridges, etc for infantry, guns and vehicles; and so it gradually became a 'Q' duty to reconnoitre and evaluate possible lines of defence, attack, withdrawal, etc. Thus, by a logical progression, the QMG staff became responsible for drawing up operation orders, as well as movement orders.

All administrative movements were carried out under the authority of 'routes' issued by the QMG's department, and without such authority no body of troops could move. Routes were entered in the Distribution Book at Headquarters, and copies were sent to the unit concerned in the march, the commander of each post through which the troops would pass and of that at which the march would terminate, and the Commissary-General. The Distribution Books, in addition to recording the routes issued, provided the information from which a return was drawn up periodically, showing the distribution and location of all units and detachments of the Army.[8]

Although there were only certain stores that the QMG was responsible for providing, it was his duty to see that the Army was complete in all items, for authorising the issue of various stores, and, when necessary, drawing up a scale for such articles as did not figure in standard scales. The allocation of quarters for the troops was his affair. During the campaigning season their selection might be governed by the availability of forage and rations, and, therefore, whether billeting was feasible or whether troops would have to be housed in tents or bivouacs to be near these sources of supply. In such matters he would be guided by the advice of the Commissary-General.[9]

The original lack of clarity as to the duties of the two principal staff officers is illustrated by Sir Ralph Abercromby's use of them during the campaign in Egypt in 1801.

The QMG, Colonel Anstruther, drew up, under Abercromby's instructions, and in conjunction with the naval officer concerned, the order for the landing of the troops. He also wrote the orders for the administration of the forces being landed. These included the formation the troops were to adopt after landing; ammunition to be carried by each man; the scale of rations to be carried by officers and men and the amount to be landed separately in charge of regimental quartermasters, as well as the forage to be loaded on each horse; entrenching tools, scale of necessaries in the packs, camp kettles, and blankets; and medical arrangements.[10]

When the fleet entered Aboukir Bay, Abercromby, taking Major-General John Moore and some staff officers, carried out a reconnaissance of the beach in a cutter. Later he despatched Moore, accompanied by Anstruther, to examine the beach more closely. After the landing had been successfully accomplished. Anstruther rode forward with Moore and a strong escort to reconnoitre the area beyond the beachhead. However, later on Abercromby sent his Adjutant-General, Brigadier-General John Hope, to examine the ground and the strength of the French position in front of Major-General the Hon John Hely Hutchinson's Brigade.[11]

A good instance of a QMG using his own initiative when his commander failed to take action is provided by Bunbury himself. In 1805 Bunbury was appointed QMG to the British force in the Mediterranean, commanded by Lieutenant-General Sir James Craig. At the end of the year Craig was invalided home and succeeded by Lieutenant-General Sir John Stuart.

Stuart commanded the force which landed in Calabria from Sicily and which defeated the French at the battle of Maida on 4 July 1806. Once battle had been joined, Stuart, says Bunbury,

'seemed to be rather a spectator than a person much, or *the* person *most*, interested in the result of the conflict. He formed no plan; declared no intention, and scarcely did he trouble himself to give an order . . . As I found that I could get no orders from him, I made it my business to go round to the leaders of our several brigades, to give them what information I could, and try to supply their wants.'

Bunbury adds that there was great difficulty in getting up ammunition supplies, and as the enemy were fresher than the British and well posted, the issue of the battle seemed far from certain. He continues:

'As I was riding along the rear of Cole's brigade, anxiously watching the French sharp-shooters, who were stealing further and further round his left, and were backed by their horsemen, one of my assistants came galloping to me from the beach with the welcome tidings that the 20th regiment had landed and was coming through the brushwood at double quick time. I rode instantly to meet them and explained to Ross how matters stood. He caught the spirit of the affair in an instant, pressed onward, drove the swarm of sharp-shooters before him; gave the French cavalry such a volley as sent them off in confusion to the rear; and passing beyond the left of Cole's brigade, wheeled the 20th to their right, and opened a shattering fire on the enemy's battalions. The effect was decisive.'[12]

Action by a trained 'Q' staff officer in a theatre of war is demonstrated by the eminent Lieutenant-Colonel (later Major-General Sir) Benjamin D'Urban, who in 1808 was appointed Assistant Quartermaster-General to the army assembling in Falmouth for the Peninsula. He had studied at the Royal Military College at High Wycombe in 1800, and, after a period of regimental duty, had joined the staff of the Quartermaster-General's Department in Ireland in 1806. Sailing with the force under Sir David Baird, he arrived at Corunna to find, to his disappointment, that he had been appointed to that part of the army left behind in Portugal when Moore advanced into Spain. He decided to travel by land in the hope of meeting Sir John Moore's Headquarters and obtaining permission to remain with the active army. During this trip the daily entries in his journal include lengthy comments on the provisions available in the country through which he was passing, the roads and their practicability or otherwise for artillery on account of structure and gradients, suitable defence positions for troops, bridges over rivers and the suitability of the latter as obstacles in defence, the supply of horses to provide replacements, and the accommodation afforded by towns and villages for billeting troops.

D'Urban met Moore with Colonel Murray, his Quartermaster-General, between Salamanca and Ciudad Rodrigo. But Murray told him that nothing could be done to alter his posting because it had been arranged in London. At Almeida D'Urban met Anstruther, now a Brigadier-General commanding a brigade and laterly Deputy Quartermaster-General at the Horse Guards. D'Urban knew him well and had written to him from Corunna, in the hopes that he could arrange for his retention with Moore's army. This Anstruther had tried unsuccessfully to do, and D'Urban assumed that he would have to continue his journey and report at Lisbon. However, Anstruther persuaded him to stay for a few days, and then sent him off to reconnoitre the country on either side of the River Coa, as the area might become the winter quarters of the army and he wanted to know its resources, its road communications with Spain and Portugal, and its natural features for defence. D'Urban went off, accompanied by a Captain Pierrepoint, who was a DAQMG and happened to be in Almeida. After a reconnaissance lasting about a fortnight, D'Urban handed to Anstruther a report and a sketch, which pleased him and presumably Murray, for D'Urban was retained temporarily with the Army and sent off on another reconnaissance which Moore wanted carried out. The subsequent report he was directed to submit both to Colonel Murray and to the Commander of the Forces at Lisbon.[13]

However D'Urban was determined not to remain in Lisbon and persuaded Colonel Donkin, DQMG of the Army in Portugal, to send him on a reconnaissance of the River Tagus. Later he got himself attached as staff officer to Sir Robert Wilson, commander of the Loyal Lusitanian Legion. By the beginning of March he was giving tactical advice to Portuguese and Spanish generals!

On 10 April 1809 D'Urban, at Marshal Beresford's request, was made Quartermaster-General of the Portuguese Army, which Beresford had just started reorganising, and was granted the rank of Colonel in that Army. In May D'Urban met Major (later Field-Marshal Lord) Hardinge, one of the officers Beresford had brought out to organise and discipline the Portuguese troops. Impressed with Hardinge's ability, D'Urban got Beresford to appoint him DQMG.

On 22 July 1809 D'Urban, with two junior members of his staff, reconnoitred a river line to determine its suitability for defence. Satisfying himself on this score, he prepared a plan for the occupation of the position, showing the detailed disposition of the available Portuguese units. Beresford approved this, and orders were despatched to the commanders concerned.[14]

As QMG, D'Urban was intimately concerned with the activities of the Commissariat.

On 5 August he commented: 'The want of food, notwithstanding the exertions of the Brigadiers and the British officers attached to the Regiments, as well as of the officers of my Staff who have acted as Commissaries, is shocking.' He says that in Lisbon he had remonstrated against having a Portuguese Commissary-General and had been continually remonstrating since to no effect. Spanish obstruction also infuriated him. Ciudad Rodrigo was stocked with supplies of British biscuit, yet, with the Portuguese troops almost starving, the Duke of Parque, Spanish commander of the town, evaded all requests for its issue. D'Urban wrote in his journal: 'I shall advise their helping themselves.'[15]

Beresford had so much trust in D'Urban, that the latter was able to correct errors made by his somewhat impetuous chief. On 11 August 1809 Beresford told D'Urban, to his 'utter astonishment', that he had ordered a Loyal Lusitanian Legion detachment of 300 men to march to Placentia. D'Urban commented: 'These people will be cut off. I have sent Capt. Harvey to stop and turn them (if possible) to Herelaga, where they will form the advance of Wilson.[16]

George Murray of the 3rd Guards, mentioned by D'Urban, had been DQMG to Anstruther in the Egyptian campaign of 1801, QMG in the Stralsund and Copenhagen operations, and QMG to Moore on the expedition to Sweden in 1808. For this last he had been specially chosen by Lord Castlereagh as suitable in character to go ahead of the expedition and negotiate with the reputedly difficult King of Sweden. He continued as QMG when Moore's force had been sent on to Portugal, and then became QMG of the whole British Army in that country. Under instructions from Sir Hew Dalrymple, he had negotiated with General Kellermann, representing Junot, the terms of the Convention of Cintra. From April 1809 to December 1811 he was QMG to Wellington. Having been promoted Major-General, he returned home and was replaced by Colonel James Gordon. However, Gordon went home early in 1813 and Murray returned to resume his old appointment. He was appointed QMG again for the Waterloo campaign, but he was in Canada, where, now a Lieutenant-General, he was Governor, and contrary winds prevented him arriving in time. Murray, one of the most famous of British staff officers, had a most distinguished career, and, as General Sir George Murray, he was Master-General of the Ordnance in 1841. Whilst Murray was his QMG, Wellington normally only gave him verbal instructions from which Murray drew up the written operation orders.

Staveley of the Royal Staff Corps had been on the QMG staff in Canada during the latter stages of the war with the United States of America; but with hostilities at an end and the possibility looming of a campaign in Europe, he resigned his appointment and in due course embarked with a detachment of the Royal Staff Corps for the Netherlands. With his staff experience and being personally known to Wellington, he was not allowed to remain long with his Corps, but was appointed to Headquarters as an extra AQMG.

During the battle of Waterloo, Wellington received a message from Blücher, timed at 1pm, saying that he would attack in half an hour. At 4pm Wellington sent Staveley off to see what Blücher was doing and to 'tell him how well we are getting on'. Staveley says that he rode off at a gallop and about two miles beyond the Allied left he found Blücher. The Prussian commander asked him to tell Wellington that he would attack as soon as he could form up his troops, which would probably be in an hour or less. (This proved unduly optimistic, for Staveley comments that in fact, 'Blücher did not come up with the enemy until they were fairly driven from the field.') On his return to Headquarters he asked Lord Fitzroy Somerset to give Wellington Blücher's message; to which Fitzroy replied, 'The Chief is in a damned bad temper this morning', and added that Staveley had better make his report himself. This Staveley tried to do, but Wellington, who was looking through his telescope, interrupted him with, 'Damn it, Sir, get out of my way.' Staveley thereupon again asked Fitzroy to tell the Duke; but the latter told him to wait a bit and try again. This Staveley did, and, managing to make his report, Wellington said, 'Thank you.'[17]

The Adjutant-General

The Adjutant-General's branch was concerned primarily with personnel, discipline and statistics. It was responsible for collecting and compiling morning states showing the total strength of men and horses, the numbers fit for duty, and the numbers of sick, casualties, prisoners of war, etc. Until Wellington assumed responsibility for intelligence himself, this was an additional duty of the Adjutant-General, and it included the interrogation of prisoners, reconnaissance missions to obtain information of enemy strengths and movements, and the organisation and payment of spies. Where reconnaissance revealed opportunites, officers of the 'A' branch were expected to take them. For instance, it was due to the intitiative of Lieutenant-Colonel J. Waters, an AAG, that the Army was able to cross the Douro in 1809, as recorded in Chapter 1. The French had removed all boats to the north bank of the river, and Napier describes the occurrence: 'Colonel Waters, a quick daring man, discovered a poor barber who had come over the river with a small skiff the previous night; and these two being joined by the prior of Aramante, who gallantly offered his services, crossed the water unperceived and returned in half an hour with three large barges.'[18]

During the campaign in Egypt in 1801 General Hutchinson employed his Adjutant-General, Brigadier-General John Hope, to meet the French negotiators and settle the terms for the surrender of Cairo;[19] and in 1810 in Sicily, on the alarm of the approach of French invasion boats, it was Brigadier-General James Campbell, the Adjutant-General, who galloped to assume command of the British troops in the threatened quarter.[20]

Wellington's Adjutant-General from April 1809 to April 1813 was Major-General the Hon Charles Stewart (later Lord Londonderry), half-brother of Lord Castlereagh. Moore had described Charles Stewart as 'a very silly fellow',[21] and certainly his initial behaviour as Wellington's AG seems to support this view. Stewart tried to assert his supposed rights as Adjutant-General to deal exclusively with the examination of prisoners of war. This was a claim that Wellington (or Sir Arthur Wellesley, as he then was) would not tolerate, and the violence with which he reacted reduced Stewart to tears.[22]

In 1809 the AG had eight AAGs and six DAAGs, but these numbers were soon increased and officers of the Adjutant-General's branch were allocated on approximately the same scale as those of the QMG's staff.

Personal Staff

The Military Secretary, ADCs, and Brigade-Majors were all considered as personal staff. The official duty of the Military Secretary was, as the title of his appointment implies, the drawing up of all the official correspondence of the Commander of the Forces; but a good military secretary had an influence and a responsibility far beyond his purely secretarial tasks. One of the most famous military secretaries of all time was Lord Fitzroy Somerset who, as a captain and one of Wellington's ADCs, was made acting Secretary in September 1810, and confirmed in the appointment on 1 January 1811. He remained Wellington's Military Secretary till the end of the war, by which time he had reached the rank of Colonel. Many years later he was Field-Marshal Lord Raglan, Commander-in-

Chief of the British Army in the Crimea. Napier has this to say of him as Military Secretary:

'Lord Fitzroy Somerset, military secretary, had established such an intercourse between the head-quarters and the battalion chiefs, that the latter had, so to speak, direct communication with the general-in-chief upon all the business of their regiments, a privilege which stimulated the enthusiasm and zeal of all. For the regimental commanders being generally very young men, the distinctions of rank were not rigidly enfored, and the merit of each officer was consequently better known and more earnestly suported when promotion and honours were to be obtained. By this method Lord Fitzroy acquired an exact knowledge of the moral state of each regiment, rendered his own office important and gracious with the army, and with such discretion and judgement that the military hierarchy was in no manner weakened: all the daring young men were excited, and, being unacquainted with the political difficulties of their general, anticipated noble triumphs which were happily realised.'[23]

At least one ADC was authorised for every general officer; a lieutenant-general was allowed two, and the commander of the forces in the field could have as many as he wished. Wellington had six, headed by his chief ADC, Colonel Alexander Gordon. There was a brigade major on the staff of each infantry and cavalry brigade, who could be, and frequently was, a captain in rank. He dealt with the 'A' and 'Q' staff officers on divisional headquarters and with the adjutants of regiments. He might previously have been an ADC, but was more likely to have served as a regimental adjutant.[24]

A fine example of a personal association between a commander and a staff officer is provided by Paul (later Lieutenant-General) Anderson, who served Sir John Moore for many years in this capacity. Anderson's family lived near Waterford, and he joined the 51st Regiment in Ireland as a Lieutenant in 1791, when Moore was commanding it. In 1796, having transferred to the 31st Regiment, he was in the West Indies when Moore arrived there as a brigade commander. Moore promptly selected Captain Anderson as his Brigade Major, and, when Moore was nearly dying from yellow fever, it was Anderson's care and devotion that saved his life. He went home with Moore and accompanied him to Ireland in 1797 as Brigade Major, when Moore was appointed to a brigade command in that country; subsequently serving in that capacity throughout the 1798 rebellion. In 1799 he was again with Moore as Brigade Major during the campaign in Holland. Moore took him on the expedition to Egypt in 1801, but this time as ADC, for Moore was a Major-General, assistant to Sir Ralph Abercromby, with no specific command. Anderson was wounded at the battle of Alexandria, and had to go home on half pay. But he was well enough again to go out to Sicily on Moore's staff when the latter was appointed second-in-command of the British forces in the Mediterranean in 1806. The Commander of the Forces, Lieutenant-General the Hon Henry Fox, had two daughters. Bunbury married the elder; Moore fell in love with the younger, but she was only 17, and he confided to Anderson: 'She is so young, that her judgment may be overpowered. My present feelings must therefore be suppressed, that she may not have to suppress hers hereafter, with loss of happiness.'[25] When Moore was given command of the force sent to Sweden in 1808, Anderson was an AQMG on his headquarters, with George Murray as his chief, and continued as such when the force was sent on to Portugal. By the time that Moore's army fought the battle of Corunna, Anderson was Adjutant-General, and he supported Moore as he lay dying.[26]

ADCs were employed on a number of duties, including the carriage of orders from their generals to subordinate commanders, and any other missions that might be required of them. Two ADCs have left accounts of their activities during the battle of Waterloo. Captain (later Colonel Sir) Horace Seymour of the 60th Rifles was one of Lord Uxbridge's ADCs, and was sent by him with numerous orders. Other commanders, seeing an ADC, would often seek to use him in an emergency. Seymour says:

'At the moment Sir Thomas Picton received the shot in the forehead which killed him, he was calling to me to rally the Highlanders, who were for the instant overpowered by the masses of French infantry who were moving up to the right of the high road. Late in the day of the 18th, I was called to by some Officers of the 3rd Guards defending Hougoumont, to use my best endeavours to send them musket ammunition. Soon afterwards I fell in with a private of the Waggon Train in charge of a tumbril on the crest of the position. I merely pointed out to him where he was wanted, when he gallantly started his horses, and drove straight down the hill to the Farm, to the gate of which I saw him arrive. He must have lost his horses, as there was a severe fire kept on him. I feel convinced to that man's service the Guards owe their ammunition.

'Still later in the day, when delivering the order for Sir Hussey Vivian's Brigade to move towards the centre, we saw the advance of the Prussians. Sir H. Vivian sent me with an Officer and a patrol to assure myself that it was the Prussians who were advancing on our left, which, in proving, I made the best of my way to Lord Anglesey, whom I found with the Duke of Wellington, to whom I reported what I had seen. Sir Alexander Gordon questioned me as to my certainty of it being the Prussians with whom I had communicated, I assuring that it was so.

'I was desired by the Duke of Wellington to tell General Bülow that the Duke wished him immediately to send Prussian Infantry to fill up the loss that had taken place in his lines. On starting to deliver this message my horse was killed, and I believe Colonel Freemantle delivered it to the Prussian General.'[27]

Major-General J. Freemantle (then Lieutenant-Colonel 2nd Foot Guards and ADC to the Duke of Wellington) confirms this. He writes:

'I am very glad to state to you the occurrence which took place with the Prussian Army on the 18th June. Many officers were sent in the morning in search of the Army. Towards six o'clock Sir Horace Seymour came and reported to the Duke of Wellington that he had seen the Prussian column. The Duke called upon me to go to the head of their Column, and ask for the 3,000 men to supply our losses. Bücher had not arrived, but Generals Ziethen and Bülow were at the head of the Column, who gave me for answer — that the whole Army was coming up, and that they could not make a detachment. I said I would return to the Duke with such a message. On my way back I found a Prussian Battery of eight guns firing between our first and second lines, and desired the officer to cease fire . . .'[28]

Intelligence

Wellington had a well organised intelligence system composed of civilian men and women in many walks of life — mostly Portuguese, Spaniards, and French Royalists — who were referred to as 'correspondents'. His Army intelligence resources included a number of junior officers, extremely well mounted and sometimes accompanied by a party of other ranks on especially good horses, who carried out reconnaissances of the French Army. They were often visible to the irritated French, but cavalry sent out to intercept them never had horses with sufficient speed and cross-country ability to do so. Apart from such 'picketing' of the French Army, some of these officers carried out deep reconnaissance into enemy occupied territory during the winter of 1812-13, some 200 miles ahead of the British forces to ascertain the practicability of the roads passing north and west of Burgos. Captured French despatches were another source of information. Many of these were encyphered, but Captain George Scovell of Wellington's staff took up the study of cryptography and was soon able to decypher the bulk of the information contained in them.[29] An example of such decyphering is referred to by Wellington in a letter of 29 January 1813 to a deputy in the Cortes, as follows: 'I enclose you the extract of a letter from King Joseph to Napoleon, which was in cipher, and which we have deciphered, which is well deserving of your attention and that of your friends in the Cortez.'[30]

Wellington's Headquarters

In battle the headquarters of the Army was either mobile or housed in some building from which Wellington had adequate communications and observation. At the battle of Busaco, for instance, Schaumann says: 'The monastery, with its beautiful garden, had a rich and imposing appearance. As, however, Lord Wellington's headquarters were here, we did not dare to enter to inspect the inside of the building.' But Wellington was not tied to this building. Schaumann writes: 'After the first attack had been repulsed, Wellington galloped past with a numerous staff, and shouted only the following orders to General Hill. "If they attempt this point again, Hill, you will give them a volley, and charge bayonets; but don't let your people follow them too far down the hill."' Of Wellington's dress in the field, Schaumann says: 'He wears no befeathered hat, no gold lace, no stars, no orders — simply a plain low hat, a white collar, a grey overcoat, and a light sword.'[31]

Under static conditions Army Headquarters were housed in suitable buildings allocated by the Headquarters Commandant, Colonel Colin Campbell. One building would be occupied by Wellington and his personal staff, the QMG and his staff would have another, and the AG with his staff would be in a third. In addition, buildings were needed by the commanders and staffs of the Arms and Services. These included the Commander Royal Artillery, the Commanding Royal Engineer, the Inspector-General of Hospitals, and the Commissary-General. The CRA had a general supervisory charge of batteries attached to divisions and a more direct command of the siege train and the reserve artillery. The Inspector-General of Hospitals (Sir James McGrigor from 1812 to 1814) was in general charge of the physicians, surgeons, assistants, etc, attached to the various units of the Army.

The Deputy Postmaster-General was often sent for by Wellington. The money which the Deputy PMG sent to regimental paymasters for the troops' pay was all too often in arrears, due to the difficulty experienced in converting sterling into acceptable local currency.[32]

The Commissary-General, the head of the Commissariat, also had his officers at the Headquarters, and Schaumann is scathing about the occupant of the post and the accommodation often provided. He writes: 'Our Commissary General, Sir Robert Hugh Kennedy, was ... such a pitiably stoical or feeble man, that I have often seen him, together with his whole staff of twenty-four clerks, install himself and his office in a broken down hovel without any windows, writing by artificial light in the day time.'[33] In

90

descending order, the ranks in the Commissariat were Commissary-General, Deputy Commissary-General, Assistant Commissary-General, Deputy Assistant Commissary-General, Commissary, Assistant Commissary, and Commissariat Clerk. The Commissariat was divided into two branches, Stores and Accounts. An assistant commissary was attached to each infantry brigade and each cavalry regiment, and Army Headquarters and the headquarters of the Artillery each had one. Sometimes these duties were performed by a commissariat clerk, earmarked for promotion to assistant commissary. (Schaumann, who finished his service as a DACG, is an example.) The duties and organisation of the Commissariat are dealt with in more detail in the next chapter.

Schaumann, in August 1811, gives the following description of Wellington's Headquarters in a town:

'In addition to the excursions connected with my duties, I often had to got to headquarters. At these headquarters of Lord Wellington, as in Villar Formoso and Fuente Guinaldo, everything was strikingly quiet and unostentatious. Had it not been known for a fact, no one would have suspected he was quartered in the town. There was no throng of scented staff officers with plumed hats, orders ansd stars, no main guard, no crowd of contractors, actors, valets, cooks, mistresses, equipages, horses, dogs, forage and baggage wagons, as there is at a French or Russian headquarters! Just a few aides-de-camp, who went about the streets alone and in their overcoats, a few guides, and a small staff guard; that was all! About a dozen bullock carts were to be seen in the large square of Fuente Guinaldo, which were used for bringing up straw to headquarters; but apart from these no equipages or baggage trains were visible.'[34]

Wellington's day during the more static periods followed a set routine. At 6am he got out of bed, and at 6.30am sat down at his desk, where he worked at papers till 9am, when he had breakfast. From 9.30am until about 3pm he sent in turn for various members of his staff, such as the Adjutant-General, the Quartermaster-General, the Inspector of Hospitals, the Commissary-General, the CRA, the CRE, and the Deputy Paymaster-General. As regards the last, Wellington once said: 'There is no part of the service to which I have at all times paid so much attention as to the settlement of the soldiers' accounts; I account early settlement to be essential to discipline.'

As soon as he had finished his staff interviews, Wellington went off for a ride, often joining in a hunt with his pack of hounds. At about 6pm he returned to his headquarters and dined at 7pm. From after dinner until midnight he dealt with correspondence and then went to bed. He said, 'When I throw off my clothes, I throw off my cares, and when I turn in my bed it is time to turn out.'[35]

In the Waterloo campaign Wellington's 'A' and 'Q' staffs were made up almost entirely from officers who had served with him in the Peninsula. He had first, however, to get rid of a number of unknown officers who had been foisted on him by the Horse Guards. He wrote to the Military Secretary there: 'I enclose a list of officers I should prefer to all others', and added that he had turned off all the subalterns employed as DAA & QMGs. His Adjutant-General, Major-General Sir Edward Barnes, had commanded a brigade in the Peninsula. The Deputy Adjutant-General, Sir George Berkely, had served in the same capacity in the Peninsula in 1820 and had been an AAG before that. There were 10 assistant adjutant-generals for the various divisions, and of these, five had served as such in the Peninsula, two had been ADCs there, one had commanded a Portuguese Brigade, and two had served in the Peninsula in non-staff appointments. It is worth remarking that two of the AAGs, Sir John Elley and Major G. Evatt, had risen from the ranks.

Colonel Sir William Delancey, the acting Quartermaster-General (who was mortally wounded at Waterloo) had been DQMG in the Peninsula from 1810 to 1814. One DQMG, Lieutenant-Colonel Sir George Scovell, had been a DAQMG under Moore at Corunna, and subsequently an AQMG under Wellington, and the other, Lieutenant-Colonel R. Torrens, had been an AQMG in the Peninsula and then DQMG in Flanders from November 1814. There were 17 AQMGs and DAQMGs, of whom 12 had served in similar appointments in the Peninsula. Two, Lieutenant-Colonel C. Grant and Colonel F. B. Hervey, were intelligence officers in the Peninsula. Grant used to ride deep into the enemy lines; on one occasion he was taken prisoner, but escaped within four months. Hervey also penetrated the enemy lines, but, mounted on a very fast hunter, he always escaped capture. Lieutenant-Colonel J. Waters was an AAG in the Peninsula, and his exploits have already been mentioned. Of the remainder, Colonel the Hon Alexander Abercromby had been ADC to Moore in Portugal and Spain.[36]

Command Organisation

Until 1809 the British Army normally had no fixed echelon of command between Force headquarters in the field and the infantry and cavalry brigades into which regiments and battalions were grouped. Properly formed divisions were first used in the Danish campaign of 1807. In the following year, Sir John Moore formed the column under his immediate command for the advance into Spain into a cavalry brigade and four divisions, each of two infantry brigades. Each division had a quota of light troops (light infantry or rifles), but the 4th Division was almost entirely composed of them, and this division formed the advanced guard for the advance into Spain. On arrival at Salamanca, Moore regrouped his army and replaced the 4th Division by two flank brigades, mostly composed of light troops. At this stage neither Hope's column of the artillery, with escorting infantry and cavalry, nor Sir David Baird's column from Corunna, had as yet joined him. By 20 December the whole army was united and Moore carried out further reorganisation. There were now three divisions, each with an artillery brigade of six pieces; two flank brigades of light troops; a 'Reserve', composed of three battalions of heavy infantry and two of light, with a brigade of artillery; and a Cavalry Division of five regiments and two troops of horse artillery, each with six pieces. In addition there was the artillery park and artillery reserve of five brigades.[37]

Wellington did not adopt a divisional organisation until after his 1809 campaign on the Douro. By the end of the Peninsular War the Army consisted of a cavalry division of eight British and one Portuguese brigade (though this last under D'Urban was really unattached), and two troops of horse artillery; seven infantry divisions, each of two British and one Portuguese brigade (except the 1st Division, which had one British Guards Brigade and one KGL Brigade), each brigade having one or more companies of light troops and a battery of field artillery; the Light Division with two brigades of light troops and a troop of horse artillery; a Portuguese division of two brigades and two Portuguese field batteries; and the reserve artillery.

D'Urban says of this organisation:

'Lord Wellington now organised the Anglo-Portuguese Army after a manner peculiarly his own, different from the formation of any modern army . . . He distributed it into divisions of about 6,000 men respectively, each having all the component parts of an army, and thus becoming independent and capable of taking care of itself. One of these

Divisions, usually commanded by a Lt-General, consisted of Artillery (Cavalry where the country admitted of its use), Riflemen, Light and Heavy Infantry and an Engineer's Commissariat, Medical, Quartermaster-General and Adjutant-General's staff, and was thus an Army in miniature . . . It afforded great facility of action, and may be considered the mainspring of the admirable movements which distinguished the Campaign of this Great Captain.'[38]

Notes

1 Sir Henry Bunbury, *Narratives of some Passages in the Great War with France* (London, Peter Davies, 1927 (original edn 1854)), pxxi
2 ibid, p28
3 S. G. P. Ward, *Wellington's Headquarters* (London, Oxford University Press, 1957), pp36-40
4 Minute on p572 of the *Collected General Orders* (quoted by Oman in *Wellington's Army*)
5 S. G. P. Ward, 'The Quartermaster-General's Department in the Peninsula 1809-1814', *Journal of the Society for Army Historical Research*, vol XXIII (1945)
6 ibid
7 ibid
8 ibid
  Ward, *Wellington's Headquarters*, op cit, pp130-52
9 Ward, QMG Dept, op cit
10 Bunbury, op cit, pp105-6
11 ibid, pp58-61, 68
12 ibid, pp164-5
13 *The Peninsular Journal of Manor-General Sir Benjamin D'Urban*, ed I. J. Rousseau (London, Longmans, Green & Co, 1930), pp1-17
14 ibid, pp50f
15 ibid, pp68-9
16 ibid, p70
17 Major-General Sir Louis Jackson, 'One of Wellington's Staff Officers', *Journal of the Society for Army Historical Research*, vol XIV (1935)
18 Major-General Sir W. F. P. Napier, *History of the War in the Peninsula and in the South of France*, vol II (London, Frederick Warne), p105
19 Bunbury, op cit, p92
20 ibid, pp264-5
21 Carola Oman, *Sir John Moore*, (London, Hodder and Stoughton, 1953), p513
22 J. W. Croker, *Correspondence and Diaries*, ed L. J. Jennings (London, John Murray, 1884 vol I p346
23 Napier, op cit, vol IV, p80
24 Ward, *Wellington's Headquarters*, op cit, pp36-40
25 Carola Oman, op cit, p423
26 ibid, pp591-602
27 *Waterloo Letters*, ed Major-General H. T. Siborne (London, Cassell, 1891), pp19-20
28 ibid, pp21-22
29 Jac Weller, 'Wellington's Asset', *Military Review*, June 1962
30 *Selections from the Dispatches and General Orders of Field Marshal the Duke of*

Wellington, ed Lieutenant-Colonel Gurwood (London, John Murray, 1861), p659

31 A. J. F. Schaumann, *On the Road with Wellington*, ed and tr Anthony M. Ludovici (London, William Heinemann, 1924), pp249-51

32 Ward, *Wellington's Headquarters*, op cit, pp36-40
    C. W. C. Oman, *Wellington's Army* (London, Edward Arnold, 1912), pp153f

33 Schaumann, op cit, p238

34 ibid, p317

35 Sayings of the Duke of Wellington', ed Major-General H. Essame, *Army Quarterly*

36 Brigadier General Sir James Edmonds, 'Wellington's Staff at Waterloo', *Journal of the Society for Army Historical Research*, vol XII (1933-4)

37 Napier, op cit, vol I, p501
    W. S. Moorsom, *Historical Records of the Fifty-Second Regiment* (London, Richard Bentley, 1860), pp88-92

38 D'Urban, op cit, p154.

Supply and Transport

General

The organisation for the supply of the Army in the Peninsula was probably more efficient eventually than British troops had ever previously enjoyed. The very difficulty of the country, with its many mountainous regions, poor road communications, and limited agricultural resources, made an efficient system necessary, if the Army was to remain concentrated for any length of time. The French, who depended almost entirely on local resources, could not keep a large number of troops together for more than a short period (depending on the time of the year and the agricultural wealth of the region), and Wellington always knew, when he was opposed by a superior force, that his enemy would have to disperse before long to obtain food and forage. Most of the British supplies came by sea, and these were amplified by such fresh food and forage as could be obtained locally. In the earlier days of the campaign an attempt was made to supply the British Army mainly from Portuguese and Spanish sources, but by the end of the Talavera operations the troops were nearly starving as a result; for the Spanish and Portuguese authorities were too lazy, corrupt, and incompetent to organise proper provision. Wellington decided, therefore, to rely principally on ship-borne supplies.

The main base was at Lisbon, and here were located a large proportion of the Commissariat staff; but Oporto was used as well, though as a subsidiary base. In the last year of the war the base ports were moved to Santander and Passages. At the base ports ships unloaded arms, ammunition, stores, and clothing from the United Kingdom, as well as provisions from there and also from Continental Europe, Morocco, Turkey, and the American continent.[1] The successful transport of all these commodities by sea depended, of course, on British naval predominance in the western coastal seas, the Atlantic, and the Mediterranean. The movement of British merchant ships was never threatened until the war with the United States in 1812-14 brought American privateers on to the trade routes.

The unloading, sorting, and storage of these supplies was the task of the Commissariat; who also had to see to their subsequent loading and despatch by regular convoys of pack mules and ox waggons to the forces in the field. The provisions, of course, were such as could be entrusted to a medium or long sea passage without fear of deterioration, such as salt meat, flour, and biscuit. Fresh meat, vegetables, and wine were purchased in the Peninsula by the Commissariat, who also baked bread and biscuit from sea-borne or locally purchased flour.

River transport was preferable by far to that by pack or draught over the Peninsular roads, but there was very little navigable inland waterway. The River Tagus was normally navigable as far as Abrantes, about 100 miles upstream from Lisbon, and this was a very useful route for troops in the Estramadura region. However, Wellington's main force was usually about the Beira frontier, over 200 miles from Lisbon and it was generally only Hill's two divisions that could be supplied by the Tagus. The River Douro was navigable for about 50 miles above Oporto, and in 1811 it was used to transport heavy guns and ammunition for the siege train. In 1812 the Engineers dredged and blasted obstructions to lengthen navigation by another 40 miles to a point north of Almeida.[2]

The roads beyond Coimbra (about 120 miles north of Lisbon) and Abrantes were very rough and badly maintained, whilst side roads were often mere cart tracks. Over the latter the waggons sent from the United Kingdom as the equipment of the Royal Waggon Train and fitted with springs were quite useless, and were soon converted to ambulances to carry the sick and wounded over the better roads. The Portuguese slow and springless ox cart was thereafter used exclusively for the carriage of heavy or bulky loads, but as much as possible was carried on the big pack mules, which moved much faster than the carts.[3]

Commissariat Organisation

Every few days a road convoy left Lisbon commanded by an assistant commissary or a commissariat clerk, consisting of either a long column of creaking ox carts or, more often, a train of pack mules. The mules were led or driven by their owners, who organised themselves into large gangs under the leadership of one of their number elected as *capataz*, or head driver, and there would probably be five of six of these gangs in a convoy. Each of these convoys would have an escort, generally of recovered sick and wounded returning to their units, or of drafts newly arrived at the ports.[4] When the Army was static, commissariat depots were established, often on a scale of one for a division, and at these the convoys unloaded. Regimental quartermasters collected their rations every morning from these depots. Other depots were scattered throughout Portugal, each in charge of a depot commissary, who was responsible for requistioning livestock and provisions over a wide area. These were stored in the depots, pending onward transmission to the field force.[5]

The distribution and duties of commissaries accompanying the army in the field in 1809 were dealt with in the following General Order:

'An Assistant Commissary, with the necessary number of clerks, will be attached to each brigade of infantry, to each regiment of cavalry, to the artillery, and to head-quarters, to whom application must be made for provisions and supplies of all kinds required for the brigade, corps, or department to which he will be attached. No requistions must be made upon the country, excepting by the Commissary General, or his Deputy or Assistants, except in cases of necessity, in which small bodies of troops may be upon the march, unattended by a Commissary; which case of necessity must always be clearly made out to the satisfaction of the Commander of the Forces.

'All requisitions made contrary to this order will be paid for by the Commissary, and the amount charged to the account of the officer who will have signed it.

'The officers of the army must have observed the scarcity of all the supplies, which our army requires in Portugal; at the same time the discipline and efficency of the troops depend upon their regular delivery. The Commander of the Forces trusts, therefore, the General Officers of the army, and the Commanding Officers of regiments, particularly those who may be detached, will communicate constantly with the officer of the Commissariat department attached to their brigades and regiments, and will advise and assist them as far as may be in their power in their endeavouring to procure supplies for the troops.'[6]

The various duties that commissariat officers found themselves performing, particularly if

96

Above: Battle of Barossa, 7 March 1811. In the right foreground is General Sir Thomas Graham directing the battle; in the left foreground the 2nd Hussars KGL are attacking; and in the middle distance on the left the 87th Foot are capturing the French Eagle. / *National Army Museum*

Below: Two features of the Battle of Barossa were the murderous and accurate fire of ten guns of the Royal Artillery, under Major Duncan and the charge of the 87th Regiment (later the 1st Bn The Royal Irish Fusiliers) in which they captured a French Eagle. Duncan's guns are by the trees in the left background, and the fight for the Eagle is shown in the centre foreground. / *National Army Museum*

Above: Battle of Fuentes de Onoro, 5 May 1811. The illustration shows the heavy attack launched by Massena which drove back the British right. Ramsay's Troop RHA, which had been cut off by this withdrawal, has just charged through the French to rejoin the British lines, and the 14th Light Dragoons are charging to cover their retreat. The picture also gives a good idea of the country over which the Light Division operated during the Coa operations of the previous year. The line of trees from right to left marks the River Duas Casas, and beyond that the rolling plain stretches away to the Azava and Agueda Rivers. / *Parker Gallery*

Below: Battle of Fuentes de Onoro. Ramsay galloping his troop through the French. Note the uniform of the Royal Horse Artillery. The horseman on the right is a French hussar.
/ *National Army Museum*

Above: The 57th Foot (later the 1st Bn The Middlesex Regiment) at the Battle of Albuera, 16 May 1811. Out of 570 all ranks, 22 officers and more than 400 other ranks were killed or wounded. They included Lieutenant-Colonel Inglis, the commanding officer, whose exhortation to his regiment to 'die hard' earned them their appellation of the 'Die Hards'. / *National Army Museum*

Below: The 3rd Buffs also suffered severely at Albuera. After the battle the remnants of the 3rd, the 57th, and three other battalions were formed into a single 'Provisional Battalion'. / *National Army Museum*

Above: Troops bivouacked at Villa Velha. This site, on the Tagus between Abrantes and Castel Branco, was frequently used as a staging camp for troops on the march. It lies at the foot of a winding road leading down from the pass of that name. The Light Brigade bivouacked here on its march to Talavera.
/ *National Army Museum*

Below: The storming party of the Light Division mounting the small breach in the assault on Ciudad Rodrigo, January 1812. It was on this occasion that General Craufurd, their commander, was mortally wounded. The men in the foreground belong to the Portuguese 3rd Caçadores. They are carrying hay bags, and they were supposed to precede the stormers to throw the bags into the ditch (from which soldiers on the left are climbing up ladders) but the latter were too impetuous to wait.
/ *National Army Museum*

Above: The storming of the main breach at Ciudad Rodrigo by the 5th, 77th, and 94th Regiments of the 3rd Division. Note the flight of the shells with their fuses lit. / *National Army Museum*

Below: General Sir Thomas Picton at the assault of the Castle at Badajoz by the 3rd Division, April 1812. / *National Army Museum*

Left: The 88th Connaught Rangers of the 3rd Division at the storm of Badajoz Castle, and fighting, by a peculiar coincidence, against the French 88th Regiment. / *National Army Museum*

Below left: The 30th Foot (later 1st Bn The East Lancashire Regiment) assaulting the bastion of San Vincente in the storm of Badajoz. / *National Army Museum*

Right: A private of the 10th Hussars on patrol. He is wearing the new model fur cap, or busby, of reduced height, and the regiment's distinction of white fur on the pelisse. / *National Army Museum*

Below: The 88th Connaught Rangers at the battle of Salamanca, 22 July 1812, capturing the 'Jingling Johnnie' from the French 101st Regiment. The French had captured it from the Moors, who carried it in battle partly as a standard and partly as a musical instrument. The French surmounted it with an Imperial Eagle. In the Connaught Rangers it was carried in the 1st Battalion by the tallest man on parade in front of the band and drums. It is now in the National Army Museum. / *National Army Museum*

Above: The Battle of Salamanca. Wellington is pointing towards the charge of the British heavy cavalry brigade, which broke the French left. The infantry of the 3rd Division are opening their ranks to let the cavalry through. / *National Army Museum*

Below: French prisoners being marched into the town of Salamanca by a British escort after the battle of that name. / *National Army Museum*

Right: Wellington's triumphal entry into Madrid in August 1812. / *National Army Museum*

Below right: General Sir Edward Paget, who had been convalescing in England after losing his arm at Oporto, returned to the Peninsular Army in 1812 to resume his post as second-in-command to Wellington; but he was captured by a French cavalry patrol shortly after his arrival. / *National Army Museum*

Left: A Highlander captured by a French cavalry patrol. The cavalry are hussars, and the similarity of their uniform to that of the British hussars will be noted. It was a similarity of which Wellington complained. / *National Army Museum*

Below: The Battle of Vittoria, 21 June 1813. The illustration shows the end of the battle with British troops amongst the French carriages and baggage waggons. In the distance British cavalry and infantry are pursuing the beaten enemy. In the left background is the town of Vittoria. / *National Army Museum*

Right: The First Battle of Sorauren on 28 July 1813 in the Pyrenees. This shows Soult's attempt to turn the British left. The French infantry are advancing to the attack on the left, and on the right is Wellington pointing with his Field Marshal's baton which he received after his victory at Vittoria. / *National Army Museum*

Below right: An incident at the first battle of Sorauren. Wellington is on the right of the mounted group. An officer wrote that he was wearing his 'grey frock coat, buttoned close up to the chin, with his little cocked hat covered with oilskin, without a feather.' / *National Army Museum*

Above: The storming of San Sebastian on 31 August 1813. The attack on the main breach by Robinson's Brigade of the 4th King's Own, the 47th (later the 1st Bn The North Lancashire Regiment) and the 59th (later the 2nd Bn The East Lancashire Regiment). (As the 4th became in due course The King's Own Royal Regiment (Lancaster), it is an interesting coincidence that all these were eventually Lancashire regiments.) / *National Army Museum*

Below: On 7 October 1813 the 5th Division crossed the River Bidassoa, the frontier between Spain and France, near the sea by three fords, practicable at low tide, and in fishing boats. The illustration shows the right column crossing, with the towering ridge of Andaya in the background.
/ *National Army Museum*

Above: Battle of Nivelle, 10 November 1813.
Wellington, surrounded by commanders and staff
officers, at his command post on La Petite Rhune
mountain. / *National Army Museum*

Below: The 92nd Gordon Highlanders of Hill's
2nd Division crossing the River Nive on
9 December 1813. In the left background a field gun
is in action, with its team of horses and limber
standing behind. / *National Army Museum*

THE BATTLE of ORTHEZ

Above left: The Battle of Orthez, 27 February 1814.
The counter-attack by the 52nd Light Infantry and
the 13th and 14th Light Dragoons against the left
of the French attacking line.
/ *National Army Museum*

Left: The 52nd Light Infantry at the Battle of
Orthez, showing Major the Earl of March (later
Duke of Richmond) wounded at the head of the
leading company and being carried from the field.
/ *National Army Museum*

Above: The Battle of Toulouse, 10 April 1814.
Looking towards the city from the position of
Beresford's 4th and 6th Divisions. In the left
foreground is the right of the British batteries. The
soldier standing in the right foreground is Spanish, a
contingent of which troops were on Beresford's
right. / *National Army Museum*

Below: The Battle of Toulouse. The 3rd Bn The
27th Inniskilling Regiment on the bank of the
Languedoc Canal. / *National Army Museum*

Above: On 14 April the French garrison made a sortie from Bayonne, achieving some surprise and capturing General Sir John Hope, commanding the investing force. The sortie was repulsed, but casualties were heavy — an appalling waste on both sides as hostilities had already officially ceased. / *National Army Museum*

Below: The Battle of Waterloo. French cavalry charging the British infantry squares. The regiment in the foreground are Highlanders. Note the mounted officer in the centre of the square, close to the Colours. / *Parker Gallery*

they had plenty of initiative, covered a very wide range indeed. Schaumann provides plenty of examples. At Zamora, in December 1808, with Moore's army in Spain, he was put in charge of baking biscuits. A great number of the local women were employed and many of the bakers' ovens in the town were requisitioned. Schaumann remarks on the quality of the biscuits, which were as large as pancakes and made of the excellent local flour. They were issued to troops passing through the town.[7] At Zamora he writes: 'Fat General Hamilton of the wagon train has also turned up here with his useless waggon corps.' (This was in reference to the 'spring waggons', as they were called.)[8]

After the capture of Oporto, Schaumann, though still only a commissariat clerk, was appointed commissary to two cavalry regiments, the 14th and 20th Light Dragoons, who were pursuing Soult's retreating army. Schaumann had to collect carts, draw and load salt fish, ship's biscuit, oats, and rum, and then try and catch up with the regiments, followed by a train of slow-moving Portuguese ox carts.[9]

At Talavera the army was desperately short of food and before the battle Schaumann and another cavalry commissary decided to loot from the Spaniards. Immediately opposite the house where they were billeted in the town of Talavera there was a store from which a few Spanish regiments were regularly rationed. The sight was too much for the two commissaries, trying desperately to find provisions for their own hungry regiments, and, taking their dragoon escorts, they ambushed several Spanish convoys approaching Talavera, drove off their convoy escorts, and took possession of the provisions.[10]

General Sir William Payne, Bt, at that time commanding the cavalry, was noted for his eccentricity. During the retreat from Talavera he addressed the cavalry commissaries as follows: 'Owing to the exertions it would entail, a commissary who did his duty in this country could not possibly remain alive. He would be forced to die. Of all my commissaries, not one has yet sacrificed his life; consequently they are not doing their duty.' Schaumann (a German) commented: 'Most Englishmen of high position, particularly when they are serving in a hot climate, are a little mad.'[11]

There is no doubt that in the early part of the Peninsular War some of the officers in the Commissariat Department were incompetent, with the result that the Department as a whole was unpopular. In July 1809 Wellington wrote as follows to Lieutenant-General J. C. Sherbrooke, commanding the 1st Division:

'I am not astonished that you and the General Officers should feel indignant at the neglect and incapacity of some of the Officers of the Commissariat, by which we have suffered and are still suffering so much; but what I have to observe, and wish to impress upon you, is, that they are gentlemen appointed to their office by the King's authority, although not holding his commission; and that it would infinitely better, and more proper, if all neglects and faults of theirs were reported to me, by whom they can be dismissed, rather than that they should be abused by the General Officers of the Army.'[12]

Wellington's inimitable literary art is indeed no better illustrated than by the following letter of dismissal to a Deputy Commissary-General in May 1811:

'It is proper I should inform you that the report of you, which I made to Colonel Gordon, was not founded on any complaint received of you from Mr Kennedy. I made that report because the service had suffered, and is now suffering, the greatest inconvenience, owing to delays in that part of the department of which you are the head; and from which post I ordered that you might be removed, from a thorough conviction, which has since proved to be well founded, that the service would be still further embarrassed if you continued to conduct it.'[13]

On the other hand, Wellington did not fail to give praise where it was due, and in his report to Earl Bathurst on the battle of Salamanca he included the following:

'It is but justice . . . to draw your Lordship's attention upon this occasion to the merits of the officers of the civil departments of the army. Notwithstanding the increased distance of our operations from our magazines, and that the country is completely exhausted, we have hitherto wanted nothing, owing to the dilgence and attention of the Commissary-General, Mr. Bissett, and the officers of the department under his direction.'[14]

Wellington was exasperated at the slowness of the local ox waggons. In January 1812 he wrote to the Earl of Liverpool: 'What do you think of empty cars taking 2 days to go 10 miles on a good road? After all I am obliged to appear satisfied or they would all desert.'[15] Of these carts Schaumann wrote:

'They consisted of rough planks nailed on to a massive pole or shaft. At right angles to the shaft, and under the planks, two blocks of semi-rounded wood were fixed, having a hole in the centre, and through these holes and axles were fitted. It was a live axle fixed firmly to the wheels. As these axles were never greased they make such a terrible squeaking and creaking that the scratching of a knife on a pewter plate is like the sweet sound of a flute beside them.'

The wheels were solid without spokes. The drivers told Schaumann that the oxen would stand still and refuse to move if the axles were greased and the noise stopped. These draught oxen were very large, fine looking, and docile animals. They were harnessed by a wooden yoke, fastened behind their horns, and attached by leather straps to pegs in front of the axle on either side. They were shod with iron shoes.[16]

Both in Spain and Portugal the mule breeding industry was excellent. Schaumann had never seen such fine and powerful beasts. In each gang of mules, either the whole dozen or so were bedecked with little tinkling bells, or else the leader along had a large bell hung round its neck and the others would follow its incessant clanging. Both mules and muleteers had an extraordinary endurance over the rough mountain roads and tracks, and Schaumann often travelled 45 miles in a day with a mule column. The muleteers were big tough men, wearing large black hats with tassels, short jackets, mantles, blue plush breeches, sandals, and blankets with a hole in the middle for the head. They were greedy but cheerful folk, always singing and devoted to a leader who treated them well. Schaumann claimed that many would have faced death for him.[17]

In addition to those in the supply columns, the Commissariat was responsible for providing animals for the transport of the Army. The baggage train of a single division took up over a mile of road, and the order of its march was laid down in General Orders. When more than one infantry division or cavalry brigade marched from the same camp and on the same road, the baggage of each marched at the rear of its own formation, and each baggage train was marshalled in the following order:

1   Oxen for the day's rations.
2   Wheel carriages drawn by horses or mules.

98

3   Wheel carriages with iron axle-trees drawn by oxen.
4   Mules with ammunition.
5   Baggage of the divisional or brigade staff.
6   Mules carrying tents or camp kettles; the baggage of regimental officers (both of these categories being in the order of march of the regiments to which they belonged).
7   Commissariat mules carrying supplies.

Behind all the columns marching on the same road came the slow-moving ox waggons, and the droves of oxen (except those needed for the day's supply).[18]

As regards officers' baggage, the number of mules allowed depended on rank. One mule (or donkey) was allowed for every two subalterns, and for these the Commissariat provided forage. (Junior infantry officers were allowed to ride, but they had to provide their own horses and forage.) Before battle all baggage was sent to the rear, and each infantry brigade detailed an officer to take charge of its own baggage.[19] In most regiments the heavy camp kettles (or 'Flanders cooking pots') which had to be carried on mules, had been replaced by small and light kettles which were carried by the men, thus freeing the mules for the carriage of tents.[20]

Getting sufficient animals for transport, however, always presented a problem. In May 1813 Frazer wrote: 'I hardly know what prevents us taking the field; though the rains may have some effect, I believe our deficiency of transport has more. Nine hundred mules are wanting in the Artillery Department alone, and I believe 3000 or 4000 in that of the Commissariat.'[21]

Rations and Messing

In the Peninsula the scale of rations varied considerably during the war. Lieutenant John Carss, writing from Badajoz on 21 September 1809, said that wine was dear, but to put flesh on his bones he drank two quarts every day at a cost of 10 shillings. The officers drew the same daily rations as the men, for which they were charged sixpence, and which consisted of a pound and a half of bread and a pound and a half of meat. There was no regimental mess for officers of the 2nd Battalion 53rd Foot, but officers messed in little groups. However, when the Battalion moved to Olavenza in Portugal the following month, and into billets instead of huts made from the branches of trees, an officers' mess was established. In August 1810 the ration was reduced to a pound each of meat and bread, and the men no longer got a free issue of wine, as the rough stuff supplied to them had increased in price from threepence a quart to two shillings. (It would appear that this wine was of too inferior a quality to put flesh on Carss's bones!) A year later matters had improved, for the men were now getting meat and biscuit of good quality and there was a pint of wine daily between every three men, even though the price had increased again to two shillings and sixpence a quart.[22] In 1812 each man was getting a pint of wine daily, and the meat and bread rations were a pound and a pound and a half respectively. Troops in Lisbon did not fare so well, because there was no wine on the ration and only salt meat. Fresh beef was difficult to obtain because it was the principal meat of the city's inhabitants, and mutton could only be procured by sending someone far into the country to purchase whole sheep. Frazer, on the march with a party, drew two days rations from a commissariat depot at Villa Franca. The daily ration per head consisted of one pound of salt meat, a pound and a half of bread, and one pint of wine. In addition, there were seven pounds of wood fuel for each of them, and 12 pounds of corn and 12 pounds of straw for each horse.[23]

On the march the rations issued depended very much on the situation, local resources, and the extent to which the commissariat arrangements could keep up with the column. On 20 June 1813 Lieutenant Robert Garrett wrote that because of a rapid advance the 1st Battalion The Royal Fusiliers had been badly supplied for the previous 10 days. (This was the march which culminated in the battle of Vittoria on 21 June.) Sometimes the men got 20 ounces of flour, sometimes a quarter of a pound of bread, at other times raw meat, and sometimes nothing at all. However, the regiment always had plenty of meat of their own, because they were driving a herd of oxen along with them.[24]

In a letter to Dr. James McGrigor, the Inspector-General of Hospitals, on 9 June 1812, Wellington wrote:

'You will likewise see in the General Orders that the attention of commanding officers of regiments has been frequently called to the expediency of supplying soldiers with breakfast; and I believe that in every well regulated regiment they are so supplied when the means can be procurred.

'Their rations are *invariably* delivered to the soldiers daily, except on marches; and the army would be incapable of all movement if I were to order that the soldiers should carry no provisions. The British soldiers, on such occasions, carry 3 days' bread; the Portuguese soldiers, 6 days'; the French soldiers, 15 days' bread.'[25]

There was no supply column when the troops were following Masséna, and each man carried his own kit, which included a blanket, a great-coat, and three days' provisions. The shortage of transport prevented the 4th Foot, The King's Own, from forming a regimental mess, and officers messed in groups of three or four.[26]

Brigadier-General F. P. Robinson gives a most interesting account of rations and messing in his own 2nd Brigade of the 5th Division, during the campaign of 1813.[27] Having taken over command of his brigade in the early part of 1813, his first interest was to examine the state of the men's messing and the hospital. As a result of the former he 'obliged the reluctant Commissary to issue good wine instead of bad rum, bread instead of biscuit, and two ounces of rice per man each day to put in their soup.' He says that as a result of this change in diet 150 of the sick men of the Brigade were restored to the ranks, and adds: 'Wine is so plentiful that you can get the very best for 50 dollars a pipe, and bread is so plentiful and excellent that the whole country for twenty miles round is supplied from hence; and yet our men have been eating hard ship biscuit with jaws scarcely able to crack the livestock in them.' The brigade commissary made many objections to General Robinson's instructions, but all of them, he says, were easily overruled. One hopes that the incompetence of this particular commissary, or perhaps 'red-tape' obstruction by his superiors, eventually reached the ears of the Commander of the Forces!

As regards his own headquarters establishment, which was very low in comparison with other, Robinson wrote that he had:

'12 men employed in various ways, four horses, ten mules, five sheep, two goats, and a large dog — This is besides my Aide de Camp and Major of Brigade who live with me ... Our line of march always remainds me of Abram & Lot; for there is much people and much cattle. The baggage is carried entirely on mules; and that of any one Division occasions a line of at least a mile.'

Schaumann says that the Spaniards were astonished that the English ate so much meat, drank so much wine and so little water, and never slept after the midday meal, but yet remained fresh and healthy. They themselves lived very frugally, believing in plenty of vegetables and water. Their normal morning meal consisted of hot chocolate, toast, and water; whilst a favourite midday meal was a kind of soup or stew, often of two kinds of meat, to which they added a small meat sausage flavoured with pepper and garlic, and vegetables, together with bread and red pepper. They rarely ate beef and drank very little wine.[28] Different eating habits probably contributed to difficulties in rationing from local resources.

Notes

1 C. W. C. Oman, *Wellington's Army* (London, Edward Arnold, 1912), pp307f
2 ibid
3 ibid
4 ibid
5 A. J. F. Schaumann, *On the Road with Wellington*, ed and tr Anthony M. Ludovici (London, William Heinemann, 1924), pp35-9, 221
6 *Selections from the Dispatches and General Orders of Field Marshal the Duke of Wellington*, ed Lieutenant-Colonel Gurwood (London, John Murray, 1861), p254
7 Schaumann, op cit, p84
8 ibid, p87
9 ibid, pp153 54
10 ibid, p172
11 ibid, p198
12 *Selections from the Dispatches*, op cit, p271-72
13 ibid, pp491-92
14 ibid, p614
15 ibid, p563
16 Schaumann, op cit pp8-9
17 ibid, pp223-24
18 *Selections from the Dispatches*, op cit, p699
19 C. T. Atkinson, 'A Subaltern of the 9th in the Peninsula and at Walcheren', *Journal of the Society for Army Historical Research*, vol XXVIII (1950)
20 Colonel L. I. Cowper, *The King's Own* (Oxford, University Press, 1939), p408
21 *Letters of Colonel Sir Augustus Simon Frazer*, ed Major-General Edward Sabine (London, Longman, Brown, etc, 1859), p77
22 S. H. F. Johnson, 'The 2nd/53rd in the Peninsular War', *Journal of the Society for Army Historical Research*, vol XXVI (1948)
23 Frazer, op cit, pp17, 24
24 A. S. White, 'A Subaltern in the Peninsular War', *Journal of the Society for Army Historical Research*, vol XIII (1934)
25 *Selections from the Dispatches*, op cit, pp599-600
26 Cowper, op cit, p375
27 C. T. Atkinson, 'A Peninsular Brigadier', *Journal of the Society for Army Historical Research*, vol (1956)
28 Schaumann, op cit, p206

Medical

Medical Organisation and Ranks

In 1794, for the better administration of the Army's medical affairs, an Army Medical Board was consituted, consisting of a Physician-General, a Surgeon-General, and an Inspector-General of Hospitals. The institution of this board and the selection of its three heads appears to have been due primarily to the Duke of York. Two of them had been surgeons to regiments of Foot Guards; one was Mr Thomas Keate, who was appointed Surgeon-General to the Army, and the other was Mr Francis Knight, who became Inspector-General of Hospitals. Knight had particularly attracted the attention of the Duke of York by the excellent hospital system that he had introduced in the regiment to which he was surgeon. The Duke of York wished a similar system to be used throughout the Army, and in fact Knight's first title after his promotion was Inspector-General of Regimental Hospitals. Sir Lucas Pepys, Bart, was the Physician-General to the Army.

In order to carry out the Duke's wish as regards the Army's hospitals, a class of inspectorial officers was established under Knight's control, and divided into inspectors of hospitals and deputy inspectors of hospitals. The former were intended to take charge of large districts, such as Scotland and the West Indies, and to be appointed to the headquarters of an army in the field; whilst the latter were to look after smaller establishments and areas, such as the various military districts in England. However, for a large command in a theatre of war it became the practice for the senior medical officer to be an inspector-general of hospitals, with under him perhaps inspectors of hospitals, appointed to detached but subordinate commands.

Between the three medical branches there was much overlapping of responsibilities, and consequent jealousies and tensions. The appointment to office of hospital staffs was the responsibility of the Physician-General and Surgeon-General, each within their respective spheres; whilst regimental medical appointments and ranks came under the Inspector-General of Hospitals. Sir Lucas Pepys appointed all the physicians in the Army, and he selected them from all ranks of civil life, without regard to previous military service. Keate followed approximately the same procedure in the selection of staff-surgeons, staff assistant surgeons, and apothecaries to the forces. Pepys made it a rule that all his physicians should be Fellows or Licentiates of the College of Physicians of London, and Keate selected his men from surgeons or pupils in the London hospitals. Knight, on the other hand, appointed his inspectors and deputy inspectors from men who were serving, or who had served, as medical officers in the Army. In fact he said that he would appoint no physician or staff-surgeon to the rank of inspector or deputy inspector unless he had served as surgeon or assistant surgeon of a regiment.

At the beginning of the war with France there were very few medical officers serving in the Army who were qualified by education or talent for appointment to the large hospitals as physicians. During the course of the war, general hospitals were established at home and overseas, to each of which a physician had to be appointed, together with a number of staff surgeons, staff assistant surgeons, and other medical officers of more junior rank styled hospital or surgeon's mates. The physician was the senior in rank and had charge of the hospital.

The regimental surgeons, though in due course a generally competent body of men, were appointed by the colonels of regiments, and frequently purchased their commissions. Most of them did not have high professional knowledge, nor the benefits of university education and scientific qualifications; but it was only from the best of them that promotions into the inspectorate were made. It followed that gentlemen entering the medical service, and wishing to qualify for higher promotion, studied for and obtained the degree of MD at the Universities of Dublin, Edinburgh, or Glasgow, before seeking regimental appointments as assistant surgeon or surgeon's mate.[1] In 1810, for instance, William Dent, newly qualified surgeon and MRCS, began his chosen career in the Army by passing the medical examinations at the Medical Board Office in May of that year. In the same month he was appointed Hospital Mate for General Service, and in July he was ordered to Gibraltar with the 82nd Foot. In November, still at Gibraltar, he was promoted Assistant Surgeon and posted to the 9th Foot. He was not promoted Surgeon until 9 January 1824, after 14 years service. He says that assistant surgeon was equivalent in rank to subaltern, and surgeon to captain.[2]

However, not all regimental medical officers had ambitions, and soon after the beginning of the war the greatest difficulty was experienced in getting qualified doctors. Advertising was resorted to and placards were posted on the college gates at Dublin, Edinburgh, and Glasgow, offering commissions to those students who could pass the Army medical qualifying examination. Those who did pass it were accepted, and were entitled immediately to pay and quarters. This system was continued until the end of the war, but it was very unsatisfactory because the examination standard was low and many persons of poor education and inadequate medical knowledge were admitted into the Service, including apothecaries and druggists' apprentices. The position was made worse, in that some of them, in places where promotion was rapid and medical supervision lax, became regimental surgeons, and even staff surgeons.[3]

A peculiar appointment connected with the medical service was that of Apothecary-General. The office was created in 1747 when George II granted to a private individual the right to be the 'perpetual furnisher, with remainder to his heirs, of all the medicines necessary for the general service of the land forces of Great Britain.' This monopoly was against the best interests of the Army, and during subsequent years it gradually became somewhat eroded. Indeed, regimental surgeons were allowed money, the amount depending on regimental strength, to purchase medicines. If the regiment was healthy its surgeon was able to make a considerable profit, and this was an inducement to him to keep it free from illness. At the end of 1796, however, there must have been a complaint from the hereditary Apothecary-General, for it was again ruled that all medicines should be provided by him. However, a surgeon's pay was increased to compensate for the loss of his profits, but there was no longer a cash incentive to stimulate lazy surgeons, and the Army suffered in consequence — as well as having to pay more for its medicines.

The Physician-General was responsible for the inspection of all medicines supplied by the Apothecary-General, and, in conjunction with the Surgeon-General, he controlled his accounts. The Surgeon-General was concerned with the Apothecary-General's charges for surgical items, and he was entitled to ask the Inspector-General of Hospitals to provide apothecaries and hospital mates to examine these charges.

The Inspector-General of Hospitals appointed to the hospitals, and was responsible for their subsequent promotion, apothecaries, hospital mates, nurses, purveyors, deputy purveyors and hospital servants. He also chose for the hospitals the staff surgeons and staff assistant surgeons from those nominated by the Surgeon-General.[4]

There were two types of medical stores, the apothecary's and the purveyor's. Apothecary's stores included medicines, surgical materials, and surgical instruments. Purveyor's stores consisted of hospital clothing, bedding, articles of comfort for the sick, wines, materials for repair, hospital tents, marquees, and many other 'household' articles.[5] The purveyor's stores came under the Purveyor-General, who was responsible for the administrative running of hospitals, including indenting for supplies on the Commissariat.

The Medical System in Practice

John Moore suffered from a poor regimental surgeon when he took over command of the 51st Regiment in Ireland at the end of 1790. By an extraordinary arrangement, presumably made by Moore's incompetent predecessor in command, the regimental surgeon also acted as regimental paymaster. Moore described him as, 'completely ignorant, dev id of humanity, and a rogue.' He added: 'I have shut up the channels he had for cheating, and have put the Hospital upon a tolerable footing, as far as diet and cleanliness; but against his ignorance I have no remedy, tho' I have daily the grossest instances of it.' Moore wrote to his brother James, who was a doctor, and who had served as a surgeon's mate in the First Guards during the American War, asking him to come temporarily to the 51st, and he also contacted a surgeon's mate of the 22nd Regiment.[6]

The surgeon of the 51st was an example of the very worst type of medical officer. An example of the very best is provided by James McGrigor, who studied at the Universities of Aberdeen, Edinburgh, and Glasgow, and was at Edinburgh elected a Member of the Medical and Chirurgical Society. He chose the Army for his medical career and, going to London, purchased a surgeoncy through the army-agency of Cox and Greenwood in General de Burgh's new Regiment, the 88th or Connaught Rangers, which had been raised in this same year of 1793.[7]

A year later McGrigor was serving with his regiment in the unfortunate campaign in the Netherlands, and his experiences there caused him to comment: 'The want of system in our hospitals, and the inexperience of medical officers in their duties, in which in after years they became so expert, were at this time very striking.'[8]

In 1795 the 88th Foot was posted to Norwich, where there was at this time a strong garrison. Here there was a bad outbreak of typhus, the scourge of all armies at this period. McGrigor, as senior surgeon in the garrison, was ordered to superintend the medical arrangements for all troops in Norwich and to take his orders from the General Officer commanding. Some time later Sir Joseph Gilpin, a Physician to the Forces, arrived wth two hospital mates to take charge. However, obviously pleased with McGrigor's arrangements, he retained him as superintendent of the Norwich hospitals until the 88th Regiment was ordered to march to Chelmsford, and McGrigor perforce, and reluctantly, relinquished his temporary eminence.[9]

The senior medical offical officer in the West Indies, Mr Young, held the rank of Inspector-General of Hospitals, and was stationed in Barbados. McGrigor arrived there in 1796, and, the ship in which he was travelling having become separated from the transports carrying the 88th, he was temporarily out of a job. Young appointed him to hospital duty, but later, apparently impressed with his ability, sent him off with an expedition to Grenada as Principal Medical Officer.[10]

The expedition to Egypt of 1801 is interesting as showing an organisation of the Inspectorate in the field. In 1799 McGrigor had arrived in India with the 88th Foot, and this regiment was included in the force being despatched from India under the command of Sir David Baird. McGrigor was appointed head of the medical staff of Baird's force by the Medical Board of Bombay, with the East India Company's commission as such. However, after the contingent from India had landed at the head of the Red Sea they were joined by British regiments from the Cape, and with these came Dr Shapter an Inspector of Hospitals, who immediately took over from McGrigor. The latter went down the Nile to meet the expedition from Great Britain, now under Hutchinson, and outside Cairo he found Dr Frank, an Inspector of Hospitals under Mr Young who was Inspector-General of Hospitals for the Army in Egypt.[11]

In 1804 McGrigor was transferred from the 88th to the Royal Horse Guards, in succession to Dr Hussey, who had, unusually, been promoted to Deputy Inspector of Hospitals without passing through the intermediate ranks of Staff Surgeon and Physician to the Forces. Before long, McGrigor himself was also promoted to Deputy Inspector of Hospitals, and he too missed the intermediate ranks, thereby passing over the heads of many medical officers senior to him. He was first appointed to the Northern District, which included Yorkshire, Lincolnshire, and part of Northumberland, with headquarters at Beverley. He was not long in that post before he was transferred to the South-Western District, the headquarters of which were at Winchester.[12]

McGrigor's next move was to Walcheren, when he was promoted to Inspector of Hospitals as head of the medical department of the British expediton; the previous holder of the post having succumbed to the Walcheren fever.[13]

Medical Services in the Peninsular Campaign

It was during the operations in the Peninsula under Wellington that the Army medical services first became efficient, and this was entirely due to Dr (later Sir) James McGrigor. Having regard to his ability and integrity, there is little need to refer to sources other than his own personal and very complete account.

The number of soldiers sick and the shortage of medical officers caused Wellington considerable anxiety before he had been very long in command. On 14 November 1809 he wrote to the Earl of Liverpool, saying that the sick amounted to at least ten per cent of his army, and therefore, if he was to have an operational strengh of 30,000 men, he would need an additional 3,000 men, who should be sent out immediately. The medical staff also needed to be increased, not by senior medical officers, but by hospital mates. He wrote:

'The duty of the general hospitals in every active army ought to be done by the general Medical Staff, and the regiments ought to have their surgeons and assistant entirely disengaged for any extraordinary event or sickness that may occur. We have not now one surgeon or assistant with each regiment, instead of three, the others being employed in the hospital instead of hospital mates and we have always been equally deficient. Indeed, one of the reasons which induced me to cross the Tagus on the 4th August, instead of attacking Soult, was the want of surgeons in the army, all being employed with the hospitals, and there being scarcely one for each brigade; and if we had an action, we should not have been able to dress our wounded.'[14]

At the end of 1811 Dr James McGrigor was appointed chief of the medical staff in the Peninsula, with the rank of Inspector-General of Hospitals, in replacement of Dr Frank (whom he had last met in Egypt, and who, it soon transpired, had managed matters very inefficiently). McGrigor arrived in Lisbon on 10 January 1812, and proceeded to make a thorough investigation into medical conditions at the base (of which he had heard bad reports) before reporting to Wellington at his headquarters. A minute inspection of the stores and accounts of the purveyor and the apothecary revealed great irregularities in both. He next turned his attention to the sick and wounded and the medical officers in Lisbon. He found that there were immense numbers of both, and also that there were a great many officers about the town who were reported as sick or wounded. McGrigor therefore compiled a lengthy report for Wellington, stating the great accumulation of sick, and the still greater accumulation of officers, their ladies, and the wives of soldiers; all of which detained in Lisbon a disproportionate number of the Army's medical officers. He proposed, firstly, that only special cases should be sent to the rear and that every regiment should have a temporary hospital where all slight cases should be treated by regimental medical officers under the superintendence of the principal medical officer of their division; and secondly, that, as in future no sick or wounded, except those ultimately destined for England, would be sent to Lisbon, all medical officers there should be ordered up to the Army, except for the small establishment needed for the Lisbon garrison. Finally McGrigor included a statement of the sick he had found in Lisbon and proposed that part of them should be returned to England as not fit for active service, and that the remainder should rejoin their regiments, either as fit for duty or to convalesce under the care of their regimental medical officers.

Wellington sent McGrigor a cordial letter of thanks and requested him to join the Army to talk over the report with him, and also to inspect on his way the large hospital stations at Coimbra and Celorice, and other hospitals that lay on his route. Coimbra, net to Lisbon, was the largest of the hospital establishments, and many of the town's convents, monasteries, and churches had been taken over as hospitals. Celorice, on the other hand, was too miserable and dilapidated to provide comfortable accommodation for the sick and wounded.[15]

Wellington's headquarters was in a small village and some staff branches, which it was too small to accommodate, were installed in other small villages a short distance away. The medical staff were a mile away in a village surrounding a fort, and they consisted, in addition to the Inspector-General of Hospitals, of the Surgeon-in-Chief of the Army, the Purveyor-General of the Army, and the office staff of one chief clerk and four others.[16] McGrigor had a very high opinion of Mr James, the Purveyor-General. He says, 'Never had the public a more honourable and faithful servant. Although I believe nearly half a million had passed through his hands, not a shilling stuck to them.' In consequence he had difficulty in London with a large family, whereas if he had taken the customary advantage of his situation he might have retired in affluence. 'Under similar circumstances,' he adds, 'another public officer suffered the same fate, Sir Robert Kennedy, the worthy and upright commissary-general in the Peninsular service.'[17] (McGrigor thus emphatically contradicts Schaumann's opinion of Kennedy.)

Wellington was very pleased with McGrigor's report and asked him to attend Head-quarters every morning at the same hour as the other heads of departments: the Adjutant-General, the Quartermaster-General, and the Commissary-General. Sir Charles Stewart (jealous as always of the rights of his department) told him that it was unnecessary for him to see Lord Wellington; instead he should come to the Adjutant-General's office before-hand and brief him, Stewart, who would transact McGrigor's business with his Lordship. McGrigor replied that he preferred doing business directly with Lord Wellington, and that it was by his Lordship's request that he was there. At that moment the door of the little inner department was opened by Wellington, who, seeing McGrigor, asked him to come in.

Wellington, says McGrigor, saw immediately after breakfast the Adjutant-General, the Quartermaster-General, the Commissary-General, the Inspector-General of Hospitals, occasionally the Deputy Paymaster-General, and, when at Headquarters, the head of the Intelligence Department, Colonel Colquhoun Grant.

In his daily report, McGrigor gave the total numbers of sick and wounded, the total of these in each hospital station in Spain and Portugal, the numbers killed, the numbers of those fit to march with their regiments, the number of convalescents, the cases of diseases and their causes, and anything else affecting the health of the Army. The mere recitation of these shows the vital importance of the part played by the medical department in the fighting strength and efficiency of the Army.

As regards the proposals in McGrigor's Lisbon report, Wellington agreed that no sick or wounded were to be sent to the rear, unless recommended by a board of medical officers and approved by McGrigor. This restriction did not apply in the conditions following a battle or during a retreat. Wellington would not, however, agree to the establishment of regimental or brigade hospitals for the slightly sick or wounded, on the grounds that they would clog the movements of the Army; nor would he sanction the allocation to regiments of special ambulance wagons, as he wanted no additional transport other than for guns and ammunition.

Having been informed by Wellington that the Army was marching to besiege Badajoz, McGrigor ordered the Purveyor and the Apothecary to establish depots of their respective stores in the vicinity, and he directed superintending medical officers of divisions to see that each regiment sent in requisitions for such medicines and surgical material and instruments as they needed. On the way McGrigor passed various divisions on the march, noting the types of sickness amongst the men who were left at hospital stations en route. He discussed these with the regimental surgeons and all agreed that if they had some kind of conveyance only a few of these men would have to be evacuated to hospitals. Regimental commanding officers were of the same opinion. They were unwilling to part with men when they needed their maximum strength, but they feared censure if they carried the slightly sick with them. However, such practice gradually and unofficially crept in, and before long few regiments were to be seen without a cart to carry soldiers with some minor and short-lived complaint.[18]

During the siege of Badajoz in March and April 1812, McGrigor established his office at Elvas, from whence he rode over daily to report to Wellington. The Commander of the Forces gave orders that a tent should be pitched near his own to accommodate his chief medical officer in case he should be detained too late in the day to ride back to Elvas. Near Badajoz McGrigor established a small field hospital, and secured some of the Waggon Train's spring waggons to carry wounded and sick from the field hospital to the general hospital at Elvas.[19] After the victorious termination of the siege, McGrigor persuaded Wellington to include in his despatch mention of the meritorious service performed in the field by the medical officers. This was the first time in the history of the British Army that their services had been publicly acknowledged, and all medical officers, at home as well as in the Peninsula, were delighted.[20]

In May 1812 Wellington published the following General Order in connection with hospitals and the sick:

'The Commander of the Forces requests that when any of the General Officers of the army pass through or near a town in which an hospital may be stationed, they will be so kind as to visit it, and see that it is conducted as it ought to be, and according to the regulations of the service and orders of the army. He likewise requests that they will see on the parade, the convalescents in charge of the Military Commandant, and will receive from him a return of their numbers, and a report of their state: they are requested to report their observations to the Commander of the Forces.'[21]

It was probably as a result of this order that the following incident is recounted by Private James Dunn of the Black Watch. After the end of the retreat from Burgos, Dunn, like many in his regiment, fell ill with fever. He was sent to a hospital in a village, which he says was very indifferent. To it, early one morning, came, he says, 'our good and kind General Lord Pakenham'. A sergeant appeared and Pakenham asked for a doctor, to be told by the sergeant that none of them had yet arrived. Pakenham expressed surprise and anger that there was not a doctor on duty all night and ordered the sergeant to summon the head doctor immediately. This must have been a regimental hospital (the establishment of which Wellington had just, and at last, approved) for all the doctors arrived and also the commanding officer of the regiment. Dunn continues: 'The General, addressing the Colonel, said, "I am surprised you do not command your doctors attend to their duty and have one here all night." The head doctor said he left instructions with the hospital sergeant what medicine to give, but if a change of medicine was required he was to send for us.' Pakenham was not impressed and said that if he found a similar state of affairs on his next visit he would send the doctor home. He then asked if the patients he could see were all he had. The doctor replied that the worst cases were upstairs, pointing to an outside staircase with a tiled roof. Dunn says: 'His Lordship made a move to go up. The doctor said, "please, my Lord, up there is the worst cases we have." "Aye", said His Lordship, "I see you do not go up there, but walk up before me." So on entering two poor fellows were laying there on a pallet of straw unconscious, and some snow on the floor.'[22] One imagines that an enraged McGrigor would have been on the spot soon after Pakenham had submitted his report to the Commander of the Forces, and that both the medical officer in charge of the hospital and the commanding officer of the regiment would have been on their way to other appointments.

To Dr McGrigor, Wellington wrote on 9 June 1812:

'The only mode I know of removing sick to the rear is in spring waggons, which are all applied to this service and in aid of them, bullock carts. I am aware that the drivers of the spring waggons are very irregular, and take but little care of their horses; but this, like many other evils in the service, which although equally the cause of mortality, you have not noticed and, among other things, the irregularities of the soldiers themselves, it is impossible for me to remedy, till the Military Law and the whole system of the service are altered.'[23]

McGrigor was obviously getting no change out of a request for more suitable vehicles for ambulance waggons.

McGrigor got into hot water with the Commander of the Forces after the battle of Salamanca. On his way to join Wellington, at the latter's request, he found considerable numbers of sick at several places along his route, many of them left there by divisions on the march from Salamanca to Madrid, and others fallen ill from drafts on the way from Lisbon to join the Army. Most of them were suffering from diseases caused by dissipation and drunkenness, and many of these parties were without medical attendance or provisions. McGrigor sent orders to the Principal Medical Officer at Salamanca to send medical and purveying officers to each of these places, and he also wrote to the Deputy Commissary-General at Salamanca informing him of the situation and recommending him to send a store of provisions to each place with proper commissariat officers. However, when McGrigor reported all this to Wellington, he incurred a severe reprimand. Wellington, in fact, lost his temper. He said, 'I should be glad to know who is to command the army? I or you? I establish one route, one line of communication for the army; you establish another, and order the commissariat and the supplies by that line. As long as you live, sir, never do so again; never do anything without my orders.' McGrigor pleaded that there had been no time to consult him if lives were to be saved. Wellington merely instructed him never again to act without his orders. A chastened McGrigor was about to leave when Wellington, in a much milder tone, invited him to dine with him.[24]

The sequel came some months later during and after the retreat from Burgos. Wellington told McGrigor in strict confidence that he would have to retreat and asked what was to become of the sick and wounded. He feared they were numerous, and that many of the wounded could not be removed. McGrigor replied that seeing that Wellington's mind had been occupied with the siege, he had got from the Commissary-General all the carts and mules that had come up with provisions and sent back with them every day all who could be moved to the hospitals he had established at Valladolid. Wellington said: 'Very well indeed; but how many have you now at Burgos hospital?' McGrigor replied that with the conveyances he expected that day he hoped only to leave about 60 officers and other ranks, and these could be severe wounds, recent amputations, and fractures which would not bear movement. Wellington's comment was, 'Admirable'. In reply to another question, McGrigor said that he proposed to leave two medical officers and a deputy purveyor, provided with a sum of money with the sick and wounded, and would write a letter to the French principal medical officer, recommending the wounded and the medical staff to his care.

When the Army reached Valladolid, where McGrigor had more than 2,000 sick and wounded, he hastened the departure of all who could march, and all who could bear conveyance, to Salamanca; and sent pressing orders to the principal medical officers at Salamanca, Ciudad Rodrigo, and Oporto to hurry up the evacuation of those hospitals.

At Valladolid Wellington sent for McGrigor and asked what was to be done with all the wounded there. He repeated: 'What is to be done, for, you see, we must be off from this place and conveyance there is none?' McGrigor said that the number remaining in Valadolid was small, not more than 100, for he had been laying his hands daily on all the carts as well as the mules that he could find to send them on to Salamanca. To this Wellington commented: 'And you have made Salamanca choke full. I cannot stop there.' 'No,' replied McGrigor, 'they are in movement from Salamanca to Ciudad Rodrigo, and from that to the Pise hospital buildings which we erected near the Douro, and move from thence on to Oporto, with instructions to the principal medical officer there to have them in readiness for embarkation should that be necessary.' Wellington said that this was excellent, and now he did not care how soon they were off. McGrigor took the opportunity to remind how much he had blamed him for the steps he had taken, and asked what the consequences would have been if he had not taken them. Wellington said: 'It is all right as it turned out; but I recommend you still to have my orders for what you do.' McGrigor comments: 'This was a singular feature in the character of Lord Wellington.'[25]

From the first returns made by divisions after the retreat from Burgos, the number of men missing was prodigious, but in the course of a fortnight a great number of stragglers turned up. Many of them who, from intoxication, irregularities, or fatigue, had dropped behind, were found in a state of disease. Typhus infected a large part of the Army and the loss was great.

In reference to the disorderly scenes during the retreat from Burgos, Wellington said to McGrigor: 'I never knew till now, nor believed, how unjustly poor Moore had been dealt with in the outcry raised against him in England about his retreat. I consider him the worst used man that ever lived. Nothing is so unmanageable as a British army in retreat or when foiled.'

There was a great shortage of doctors to deal with the very large numbers of sick, and Wellington forwarded to England McGrigor's demand for medical officers of every class. As a temporary measure, McGrigor offered to any Spanish doctors, or any French prisoner of war medical officers, British rates of pay if they would work in British military hospitals. All the French medical officers accepted, and they were sent to hospitals in the rear where they would not be tempted to desert. Only a few Spaniards were obtained, but they proved very useful.

To meet the acute need for hospitals, McGrigor at last got approval for regimental hospitals, and he sent orders to every regiment to construct its own hospital, under the superintendence of the staff surgeon of the brigade or division to which the regiment belonged, and directed the purveyor to supply them with such stores as each regimental surgeon required. In a short time the movement of sick from regiments to the general hospitals in rear stopped; and not before time, because many had died on the way.[26]

Hospitals

McGrigor told Wellington that the regimental hospitals were working well, but added that if the operations of the next campaign were extended, there would be a need for buildings to provide general hospitals for the reception of such cases as would not bear conveyance to the rear. The following day Wellington said that he had discussed the matter with the Chief Engineer who thought that temporary buildings might be constructed, at no great distance from the existing Headquarters, which might be moved when the Army advanced. McGrigor mentioned that in the West Indies the Government had sent out wooden buildings for hospitals, the frameworks of which only needed to be put together by carpenters, and that one day sufficed to erect a strong wooden building. Wellington did not appear to take much notice, but not long afterwards, when McGrigor paid his usual morning visit, Wellington told him that his hospitals were on the way, loaded in three vessels, with two master carpenters and 12 carpenters, who would teach the Army's artificers to put them up and take them down. He added: 'You must let me know at what places you would wish to have them; they will be landed at Oporto, but you must have them at no great distance from the Douro, for I have no conveyance to a distance.' McGrigor selected a spot near Castello Rodrigo within a short distance of the Douro, where stores could be brought up from Oporto. The hospital when erected consisted of several streets of small houses.

Through the exertions of medical officers, particularly at the larger hospitals, a very number large number of men were returned to their units fit for duty before the start of the 1813 campaign. Even during the advance of the Army considerable bodies of soldiers were joining the regiments daily from the hospitals; and it was said by one eminent soldier that he thought the extraordinary exertions of the medical officers of the Army might be said to have decided the day at the battle of Vittoria, for they had added the strength of a full division to Wellington's command.[27]

After the cessation of hostilities, McGrigor sought, and obtained, Marshal Soult's permission to visit the French military hospitals; but he found it impossible to do so, for so many obstructions were placed in the way. From much conversation with the French medical officers who had worked in the British military hospitals, and from the condition of the sick and wounded French soldiers who fell into British hands, and also from the hospitals in which they had been left behind by the retreating French Army, he believed that the hospitals that he had proposed to visit were in poor condition and that the French did not want him to inspect them. But he did envy their ambulances for the transport of sick and wounded, and wished that Wellington had approved his request for such vehicles.[28]

Postscript

A letter from the Treasury, of September 1859, stated that in the college that had recently been founded in honour of the memory of the Duke of Wellington (ie Wellington College, in Berkshire), niches and places had been provided for the reception of the statues and busts of the principal officers, contemporary statesmen, and personal friends of the late Duke of Wellington, and that the name of Sir James McGrigor had been selected for this distinction.

Notes

1 Sir James McGrigor, Bart, *Autobiography and Services* (London, Longman, Green, Longman, & Roberts, 1861), pp170-77
2 Leonard W. Woodford, 'War & Peace — The Experiences of an Army Surgeon 1810-24', *Journal of the Society for Army Historical Research*, vol XLIX (1971)
3 McGrigor, op cit, pp93-4
4 ibid, ppxix-xx
5 ibid, p266
6 Carola Oman, *Sir John Moore* (London, Hodder & Stoughton, 1953), p73
7 McGrigor, op cit, pp5-11
8 ibid, p32
9 ibid, pp41-2
10 ibid, pp53-4
11 ibid, pp107-16
12 ibid, pp170-71, 179-80, 191
13 ibid, p228
14 *Selections from the Dispatches and General Orders of Field Marshal the Duke of Wellington*, ed Lieutenant-Colonel Gurwood (London, John Murray, 1861), pp317-19
15 McGrigor, op cit, pp254-60
16 ibid, pp260, 319
17 ibid, pp261-65
18 ibid, pp266-68
19 ibid, pp268-69
20 ibid, p278
21 *Selections from the Dispatches*, op cit, p592

22 Dr R. H. Roy, 'The Memoirs of Private James Gunn', *Journal of the Society for Army Historical Research*, vol XLIX (1971)
23 *Selections from the Despatches*, p600
24 McGrigor, op cit, pp300-03
25 ibid, pp306-11
26 ibid, pp319-23
27 ibid, pp325-31
28 ibid, pp352-53

The Light Division

This chapter deals firstly with the earlier history of the formation which became the famous Light Division of Wellington's Peninsular Army, and secondly with the period during which this highly skilled division, acting alone, held Wellington's outpost line between the Rivers Coa and Agueda, and then fought a successful rearguard battle to cover its withdrawal across the Coa. The chapter ends with some comments on the Light Division's remarkable commander, Robert Craufurd.

Earlier History

'Oh, you will do; I see you are a good cut of a Light Infantry man, — come and dine with me.' The speaker was General Sir John Moore and he was addressing a subaltern, George Napier, who had just been posted to Moore's Regiment, the 52nd Light Infantry.[1] The subaltern was later to be General Sir George Napier, one of three eminent soldier brothers. The eldest of the three was in the 95th Rifles, and he became famous in later life as General Sir Charles Napier, the conqueror of Scinde. William, the youngest of the three is best known as General Sir William Napier, the historian of the Peninsular War. He joined George in the 52nd, but Moore later got him a company in the 43rd; so that each regiment of the original Light Brigade had a Napier brother. George tells an amusing story of competition between William and himself in recruiting for their respective regiments. Soon after he himself had been promoted captain, the two went to Limerick to get volunteers from an Irish militia regiment. They were approached by 'ten very handsome militia soldiers, six feet high' who said that they would volunteer for the regiment whose recruiting officer (there were others besides George and William) could beat them in running and jumping. George failed, but William, says George, 'with his cursed long legs beat the men both in running and jumping, and they, being honourable fellows, as most Irishmen are, kept their word, and he took them all ten into the 43rd.'[2]

On Moore's appointment to command in Spain, he selected George as his ADC. The 1st Battalion 43rd Light Infantry, the 2nd Battalion 52nd Light Infantry, and the 2nd Battalion 95th Rifles were formed into a Light Brigade under the command of Robert Craufurd, and were part of the force which sailed from Falmouth, under the command of Sir David Baird, in October 1808, to Corunna, to reinforce Moore's army.

Craufurd was a comparatively junior officer, and he was worried as to whether he would be able to keep his command. As soon as he landed at Corunna he wrote to Moore to ask if his position was secure. Moore replied from Salamanca on 13 November:

'My dear Colonel,
'I had the pleasure of your letter of the 3rd. I hope you do not doubt my wish to oblige you. I feel how unpleasant it would be to descend from a rank once held, and I should have much satisfaction in relieving you from that, as any other thing that was disagreeable

to you; but you are notified to me, not as Brigadier, but as Colonel upon the Staff. Not only so, but it has been added that, as this may be disagreeable to you, to descend from a rank you once held, it has been signified to you that, if you choose it, you have the Duke's permission to return to England. I should be most sorry, were you to accept this alternative, and I hope to give you a command you will like . . . '

However, Moore apparently succeeded in getting Craufurd confirmed both in his rank of Brigadier-General and in his command.[3]

After the junction of Baird's troops with the remainder of the army, Moore reorganised the whole as described in Chapter 7. Craufurd's command formed one of the two 'flank' brigades; the other, commanded by Alten, consisted of the two Light battalions of the King's German Legion. (The Reserve included the 1st Battalion 52nd and the 1st Battalion 95th; whilst the 2nd Battalion 43rd was in the 3rd Division.)[4]

During the first stage of the retreat, Craufurd's Brigade was the rearguard on one of the two roads by which the army moved, and Alten's on the other. On 31 December, however, the two flank brigades were separated from the main body at Bonillas, near Astorga, and were directed to march via Orense to Vigo, in order to lessen the pressure on the commissariat and to cover the southern flank. The Reserve took over as rearguard to the main body. According to William Napier, 'The separation of his [Moore's] light brigades, reluctantly adopted on the bad counsel of his quarter-master-general Murray, had weakened the army by three thousand men.'[5] (William Napier was, at the time, in the 1st Battalion 43rd under Craufurd.)

On the return of the troops to England, the Light Brigade was reconstituted, again under Craufurd's command, and it now consisted of the 1st Bn 43rd, 1st Bn 52nd, and 1st Bn 95th.[6] The regiments were ordered to prepare for service with the least possible delay. Equipped for active service, each man had to carry from 60 to 80 rounds of ammunition, musket or rifle, greatcoat, blanket, knapsack (packed with shoes, shirts, etc), canteen, haversack with rations, bayonet and belts.

On 25 May 1809 the Light Brigade embarked at Dover, but bad weather prevented the transports from reaching Lisbon until 28 June. After landing, time had to be spent in purchasing horses, mules, pack saddles, and other items required for campaigning in the Peninsula.[7]

When the Light Brigade (now accompanied by Captain Ross's Troop of Horse Artillery) was ready to march, the infantry were embarked in flat-bottomed boats and launches to be towed up the Tagus to Vallada, 40 miles from Lisbon; whilst the artillery and regimental animals were sent by road to Santarem. The boats started late at night on 2 July, when the tide was flowing up the river, and 24 hours later they arrived at Vallada, by which time the men's legs were terribly cramped from being squeezed so tight in the boats.[8] From Vallada the infantry marched to Santarem, where they were joined on 7 July by the road party. On 9 July the reunited brigade marched to Abrantes. Lieutenant-Colonel J. Leach, then a Captain in the 95th, writes:

'General Craufurd at this period issued a long string of standing orders and regulations to his brigade: many of them were undoubtedly excellent, and well calculated to insure regularity, on the march, in camp, and in quarters; but they were so exceedingly numerous, and some so very minute and tedious, that a man must have been blessed with a better memory than falls to the general lot of mortals to have recollected one half of them.'[9]

The brigade marched chiefly during the night or in the very early morning, owing to the great heat; usually starting soon after midnight, so that the day's work could be finished by eight or nine in the morning.[10]

On 28 July the Light Brigade was on the move before dawn, and before long distant gunfire could be heard. At mid-day they reached Oropesa, and here orders were awaiting Craufurd to make a forced march to join the Army. Anxious as he was to push on, he considered a short stop for a meal necessary, and he ordered regimental commanding officers to leave at Oropesa any men they thought incapable of making a forced march, for he had decided to march without halting until he reached Wellington's army, which, from the continuous cannonade, was obviously hotly engaged. After the troops had eaten the march was resumed, and soon Spanish, and a few British stragglers, were encountered, both wounded and unwounded, and these, presumably to justify their flight, reported disaster. There was a short halt at 10pm beside a muddy pool, where all ranks quenched their raging thirst, and then the march was continued without further halt until the Light Brigade arrived at Talavera to find the battle over and Wellington victorious. They were promptly ordered by the Commander of the Forces to occupy some woods in front and take charge of the outposts.

Leach writes that in 24 hours the brigade had 'passed over upwards of fifty miles of country; as extraordinary a march, perhaps, as is to be found on record.'[11] William Napier was taken ill a few days earlier and his brother George got him into a bullock cart and took him to a hospital which had been established in Placentia. He then started off to overtake his regiment. He reached Oropesa to find that they had marched, and went off in pursuit. He says:

'At about twelve or one o'clock, I began to be very tired, when I saw a light glimmering at some distance, and making towards it I was glad to find an officer of the Rifle Corps in a hut, with some sick men and some baggage. I got some wine from him and a bit of something to eat, and lay down for half an hour, when I awoke and jumped up, and seizing my sword and cap I started off, having dreamt that my company was in action with the enemy; and I never halted till about eleven the next morning when I overtook the brigade and marched on to Talavera's bloody field . . . Our brigade arrived on the field of battle, after having marched *fifty miles in twenty-two hours*, every man having at least forty pounds weight upon his back!'[12]

There have been various estimates as to the length of this march, and some disagreement as to its starting point. William Napier in his history[13] says that the Light Brigade:

'had been after a march of twenty miles, hutted near Malpartida de Plasencia, when the alarm caused by the Spanish fugitives spread to that part; Craufurd, fearing for the army, allowed only a few hours rest, and then withdrawing about fifty of the weakest from the ranks, re-commenced the march . . . The troops . . . leaving only seventeen stragglers behind, in twenty-six hours crossed the field of battle in a close and compact body; having in that time passed over sixty-two English miles in the hottest season of the year.'

Moorsom says that the brigade:

'arrived at Oropesa in the forenoon of the 28th, having that morning performed a tiresome march of twenty-four miles . . . As soon as the men had cooked and eaten their dinners the march was resumed, and these regiments arrived in the vicinity of Talavera before daylight, on the morning of the 29th, having performed a forced march of forty-eight miles in excessively hot weather, in addition to the twenty-four miles of the preceding day; in all, sixty-two miles in twenty-six hours.'

Of the narrators of the march, only Leach kept a daily journal, and he was the only one who actually took part in it, and his story is therefore probably the most dependable. Any differences from it may, perhaps, be fairly ascribed to faulty memories some years after the event. In any case the march was a very notable achievement.

Leach of the 95th Rifles had a great regard for his commanding officer, Lieutenant-Colonel Sidney Beckwith. During the period after the retreat from Talavera, Craufurd ordered that all regiments of his division should be marched frequently to the River Caya, about four miles away, to bathe. Leach says that every regiment except his own marched fully armed and accoutred. Beckwith, however, directed that the men should take no arms or accoutrements, but should wear light fatigue dress and foraging caps and carry sticks. Officers were ordered to take fowling pieces and greyhounds. As soon as the battalion was out in the country, the men were extended in a long line in skirmishing order, and made straight across the plain towards the river. Hares, rabbits, and partridges were soon started up, and these were shot, caught by the greyhounds, or knocked on the head with the sticks. After bathing the process was repeated on the way back. The troops had an enjoyable day's sport and a welcome addition to their rations.[14]

The Light Division and the Coa

At the end of the year 1809 Wellington was preparing for the French attempt to invade Portugal, which he knew must be made. It would be made, furthermore, in considerable strength; and the only suitable road for a large army, which did not entail forcing the line of the Tagus, lay through the Spanish frontier fortress of Cuidad Rodrigo, and the opposite Portuguese one of Almeida. Wellington was certain, therefore, that it was an advance by this route that he would be forced to face. The plan that he adopted was to station the bulk of his army around the upper Mondego valley, one division in the south to watch the approaches from Badajoz and the upper Tagus, and one division holding an outpost line beyond the River Coa.

At this time Craufurd was commanding the 3rd Division, in place of Major-General Mackenzie, who had been killed at Talavera, and it consisted of his own Light Brigade, and the brigade of Brigadier-General Mackinnon (1st Bn 54th, 5th Bn 60th, and 1st Bn 88th). Wellington selected Craufurd to command the troops allocated to the lengthy outpost line. The tasks required of him were to obtain information of enemy movements; to prevent the French from penetrating the outpost line to obtain information about British locations and movements; to keep contact with, and encourage the Spanish garrison of Ciudad Rodrigo; and to keep communications open with Almeida.

Ciudad Rodrigo lies on the River Agueda and Almeida is about two miles east of the River Coa. These two rivers flow northwards to join the River Douro, and are, on an average, about 20 miles apart. The country between them is mostly plain, and is crossed by three minor tributaries of the Agueda, also flowing mainly north, which, from east to west, are the Azava, the Duas Casa, and the Turon. From the junction of the Agueda with the Douro, the former river was crossed by only four bridges in a length of 25 miles. These, from the Duoro, were at Barba del Puerco, Ciudad Rodrigo, Villar, and Navas Frias. The Agueda was not fordable when in flood (and this could happen quickly after

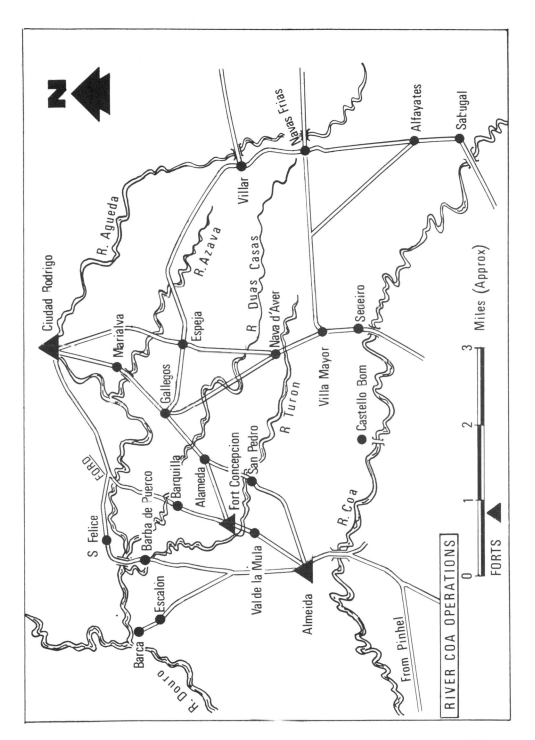

RIVER COA OPERATIONS

FORTS ◄

0 1 2 3

Miles (Approx)

N

Ciudad Rodrigo

R. Agueda

R. Azava

R Duas Casas

Villar

Navas Frias

Alfayates

Sabugal

Marialva

Espeja

Nava d'Aver

Sedeiro

Gallegos

Villa Mayor

R Turon

Castello Bom

San Pedro

Fort Concepcion

Barquilla

Alameda

Barba de Puerco

FORD

S Felice

Escalon

Barca

R. Douro

Val de la Mula

Almeida

R. Coa

From Pinhel

heavy rain), but there were fords in several places when the water was low. However, it was dangerous to rely on the flooded river making the fords impassable for long, because the water level could fall several feet in a night without apparent cause, and fords that were unusable in the evening could be traversed again by early morning.

At the beginning of January 1810 Craufurd's division was at Pinhel, about 10 miles north-west of Almeida and west of the Coa. On 3 January 1810 Wellington wrote to him:

'We have a store of provisions in Almeida, from which you will draw what you require, if it should be necessary, but don't use it until it is so . . . I wish that you would desire Captain Campbell, and any other officers in your Division that are capable of it, to examine the course of the Coa which runs by Almeida, and to report upon it, and if possible let me have a plan of it; likewise, if the position of the enemy will allow of it, the course of the Agueda . . . Hereafter I shall fix my head-quarters at Vizeu, and will go forward to pay you a visit.'[15]

To assist Craufurd in his task, Wellington placed the 1st Hussars, King's German Legion, under his command, the best trained cavalry regiment in the Army in reconnaissance and outpost duties. For his artillery, he still had Ross's Troop RHA. Initially Craufurd kept most of his force at Pinhel, sending the 1st Hussars KGL and the 95th Rifles forward to carry out a reconnaissance of the area.

On 31 January Wellington wrote to Craufurd, giving him a broad directive on the action he expected of him; he said:

' . . . I don't think the enemy is likely to molest us at present; but I am desiring of maintaining the Coa, unless he should collect a very large force, and obviously intends to set seriously to work on the invasion of Portugal. If that should be the case, I don't propose to maintain the Coa, or that you should risk anything for that purpose; and I beg you to retire gradually to Celerico, where you will be joined by General Cole's Division. From Celerice I propose that you should retire gradually along the valley of the Mondego upon General Sherbrooke's Division and other troops which will be there. If you should quit the Coa, bring the Hussars with you.'

Wellington may have felt that the above instruction might lead Craufurd to withdraw from the Coa to readily, for on 4 February he wrote:

'As my views in the positions which the army now occupy, are to take the offensive in case of the occurrence of certain events, I wish not to lose possession of the Coa; and I am anxious, therefore, that you and General Cole should maintain your positions upon that river, unless you find that the enemy collect a force in Castille which is so formidable as to manifest a serious intention of invading Portugal.'[16]

In the light of these two letters a considerable responsibility was laid on Craufurd in arriving at a correct decision. He was to maintain his positions on the right bank of the Coa, unless it was obvious that the French were preparing to invade Portugal with a large force. It seems strange that Wellington should have placed that responsibility on Craufurd, instead of taking the decision himself in the light of the information that Craufurd supplied him.

Early in February Craufurd reported to Wellington that Ney was moving towards Ciudad Rodrigo. Wellington replied on 18 February, and his letter is of particular interest because it contains the reorganisation he had been compelled to make because of the arrival in the theatre of war of Picton, an officer considerably senior to Craufurd, and at the same time shows his confidence in Craufurd as a commander of light troops and his determination to keep him in command of the outposts. Wellington wrote:

'I don't understand Ney's movement, coupled as it was with a movement on Badajoz from the south of Spain. The French are certainly not sufficiently strong for two sieges at the same time; and I much doubt whether they are in a state even to undertake one ... In answer to your letter of the 1st, I have only to assure you that in any event I should have taken care to keep your command distinct, as I am convinced that you will be able to render most service in such a situation. You will have heard that General Stewart is gone to Cadiz; but General Picton is coming to the army, which will render necessary a new arrangement, and will oblige me to deprive you of Mackinnon's Brigade. But I will make up for you the best corps I can, including your own Brigade of which you shall continue in separate command.'[17]

Wellington's 'new arrangement' was to give Picton command of the 3rd Division, from which the Light Brigade was removed and replaced by another British brigade and a Portuguese brigade; and on 22 February a General Order announced that: 'The 1st and 2nd battalions of Portuguese Chasseurs are attached to the Brigade of Brigadier-General Craufurd, which is to be called the *Light Division*.'[18] The distribution and command of the British divisions became as follows: 1st Division (Spencer, in place of Sherbrooke invalided home) at Viseu; 2nd Division (Hill) at Abrantes and Portalegre (watching the southern flank and approaches from Badajoz); 3rd Division (Picton) at Celerico; 4th Division (Cole) at Guarda; Light Division (Craufurd) at Pinhel; Cavalry (Cotton) in the valley of the Mondego.[19]

The choice of the Portuguese Chasseur (ie Caçador) battalions for Craufurd was not a happy one. D'Urban writes:

'Dec. 18-19. Abrantes ... The Marshal [Beresford] inspected the 1st, 2nd, and 3rd Regiments of Chasseurs ... The progress of Lt Col Elder in forming and training the 3rd is perfectly wonderful. Dec 30. Lord Wellington ... inspected the Chasseurs at Turcos, — the Villa Real Regiment by the exertions of Lt Col Elder are in a state of discipline altogether excellent. March 21. The 1st and 2nd Chasseurs marched to join the British Army. April 10. The Brigade of Chasseurs (1st and 2nd), which were sent to General Craufurd, are returned unfit for service; this does not astonish me. Why they were sent I wonder — certainly the worst in the Army.'[20]

In view of Wellington's promise to Craufurd, and after his inspection of these units, it seems strange that they should have been selected for the Light Division; particularly as after their rejection Craufurd had only his original three infantry battalions. Both the Portuguese battalions now underwent a further period of training. Craufurd asked for the 3rd Chasseurs under Elder, but this application, for some reason, was at first unsuccessful.[21]

Craufurd, in the meantime and as the campaigning season approached, had been moving his troops forward across the Coa. His ADC, who was later General Sir James Shaw Kennedy, kept a diary of this period. In a letter to Lord Frederick Fitzclarence on outpost duties, Shaw Kennedy explained the object of the Light Division's operations. He says that in order to encourage the Governor of Ciudad Rodrigo and to keep the communications with Almeida open as long as possible, Craufurd decided to hold all the country beyond the Coa up to the left bank of the Agueda. To hold such an extensive area with the original force of about 2,500 infantry, 400 cavalry, and six light guns, was, he adds, a bold and hazardous operation. Later the Portuguese battalion increased the infantry strength to 3,500, and the cavalry was augmented, first by some squadrons of the 16th Light Dragoons, and then during the last days before withdrawal by the whole of the 14th and 16th Light Dragoons. The 1st Hussars KGL were, says Shaw Kennedy, exceptionally good at outpost duties, but Craufurd himself planned in detail their most difficult tasks, and, speaking German fluently, he dealt directly with the troop commanders.[22]

On 27 February the first company of the 95th Rifles, commanded by Captain Creagh, was ordered to march from Escarigo and to reconnoitre the village of Barba del Puerco, near to the junction of the Agueda with the Douro and having a bridge over the former. Creagh encountered a strong detachment of French cavalry and infantry in the village and, after a skirmish, fell back in accordance with his orders to Escarigo. There Leach joined him with his company. A third company of the 95th was sent forward in support. The next day Leach was ordered to reconnoitre Barba del Puerco again. He found that the French had vacated the village, so he established a piquet there and sent a party down the steep road which ran through a pass in the hills to the bridge. On the far side of the bridge there was a French post of infantry and cavalry detached from a force located at St Felices on the far side of the Agueda. Leach says that the local priest told him that at Felices there were 3,000 infantry, cavalry and artillery belonging to General Loison's Division.

The whole of the 95th Rifles were now ordered to the lower Agueda and posted in villages from whence they could command the fords between Ciudad Rodrigo and the Douro. Barba del Puerco, with its bridge, was the only post held right down on the river bank, and here Beckwith stationed himself with four companies. A post on the right of the sector was also manned with four companies, whilst two other posts, including one at Escalhao by the junction of the Agueda and Douro, were each held by one company. Patrols of the 1st Hussars were active along the river bank, and the 1st Hussars alone watched the river above Ciuded Rodrigo, where the enemy was less likely to appear in force, as far as the bridge at Navas Frias. To keep the 95th on the alert and enable every officer in the battalion to make himself acquainted with the line of the river and the roads leading from it to the Coa, as well as the general features of the area, the companies frequently exchanged posts.[23]

The remainder of Craufurd's infantry, the 43rd Light Infantry and the 52nd Light Infantry, were held further back in general support, occupying villages between the Coa and the Agueda. Ross's Troop was in Fort Concepcion, and the Caçadores, when they were in the area, were kept in reserve. Shaw Kennedy says that the posts of the bulk of the infantry were based upon the time that Craufurd calculated he would need to withdraw them to the Coa after receiving information of an enemy advance in force. By the distribution of his troops he was able to watch enemy movements, keep the country clear of French foraging parties, and encourage the defence of Ciudad Rodrigo. Shaw Kennedy writes:

'If we are to properly understand the operations of General Craufurd, the *calculation* as above stated, must never be lost sight of; for it was upon the *calculation* that he acted all along. The cause of hazarding the four comapines at Barba del Puerco forms a separate consideration. It was formed upon the belief that the pass there was so difficult that four companies could defend it against any numbers, and that, if turned higher up the river, the Hussars would give Colonel Beckwith warning in ample time to make a safe retreat.'[24]

The bridge at this place was a special case and was to be defended, whilst the other posts were to be evacuated if he enemy appeared in force.

William Napier adds that when the Agueda was fordable, 'Craufurd concentrated his division, yet to do so safely required from the troops a promptitude and intelligence the like of which had seldom been known. Seven minutes sufficed to get under arms in the night, a quarter of an hour, night or day, to gather them in order of battle at the alarm posts, with baggage loaded and assembled at a convenient distance in the rear; and this not upon a concerted signal and as a trial, but all times certain and for many months consecutively.'[25] William Napier writes with first hand experience, for he was serving there in his own regiment, the 43rd.

Craufurd was acting within the very broad instruction contained in the following letter of 8 March from Wellington:

'The line of cantonments which we took up, principally with a view to the accommodation of the troops during the winter, and their subsistence on a point on which it was likely that it might be desirable to assemble the army, will not answer our purpose of assembling on the Coa, if eventually that should be deemed an object. Neither does our position, as at present occupied, suit the existing organisation of the army. For these reasons, I have long intended to alter our dispositions, as soon as the season would permit the troops occupying the smaller villages on the Coa, and as I should be able to bring up the Portuguese light troops of your Division to the front. Since we took the position which we now occupy, our outposts have come in contact with those of the French; and although there is some distance between the two, still the arrangement of our outposts must be made on a better principle, and the whole of them must be in the hands of one person, who must be yourself. I propose, therefore, as soon as the weather will allow of an alteration of the disposition of the advanced corps, that your Division, with the Hussars which will be put under your orders, should occupy the whole line of the outposts, and, with this, the Portuguese corps shall be brought up to the front as soon as the state of the weather will allow them to march. I am desirous of being able to assemble the army upon the Coa, if it should be necessary; at the same time I am perfectly aware that if the enemy should collect in any large numbers in Estremadura, we should be too forward for our communications with General Hill even here and much more so upon the Coa. But till they will collect in Estremadura, and till we shall see more clearly than I can at present what reinforcements they have received, and what military object they have in view, and particularly in the existing disposition of the army, I am averse to withdrawing from a position so favourable as the Coa affords, to enable us to collect our army and prevent the execution of any design upon Ciudad Rodrigo. I wish you, then, to consider of the parts to be occupied in front of and upon the Coa, to enable me to effect that object. The left should probably be at Castello Roderigo; and I believe you must have a post of observation as far as Alfayates on the right. However, you must be a better judge of the details of this question than I can be; and I wish you to consider it, in order to be able to carry the plan into execution when I shall send it to you. I intend the Divisions of General Cole and General Picton should support you on the Coa without waiting for orders from me, if it should be necessary; and they shall be directed accordingly.'[26]

It would appear that Shaw Kennedy was not aware of the contents of this letter, and that the real reason for Craufurd holding such a large extent of territory was to cover the deployment of Wellington's main army on the plain between the two rivers in the event of the French making an attempt on Ciudad Rodrigo with a comparatively small force. The plan to which Wellington refers is presumably that for the movement and deployment of the army if that event should occur.

At midnight on 19 March the French General Ferrez, commanding at St Felices, launched a sudden attack on the 95th Rifles' post at Barba del Puerco, at the head of 600 picked grenadiers and light infantry. He first concealed this force as close to the bridge as he could get it. The two British sentries on the other side of the river did not see the French, and the noise made by the river tumbling over the rocks drowned the sounds of their approach. Once ready, the attackers dashed across the bridge, driving the sergeant's picquet before them, and pushed on up through the pass. They were half way to the village before the alarm was given, and the companies of the 95th had only time to seize their arms and accoutrements, and the men ran out in their shirts with belts and cartridge boxes slung over them. Beckwith led them, clad in his dressing gown and slippers and wearing a red nightcap. There followed an extraordinary conflict in the mountain pass. The French were driven headlong down it and across the bridge, where they took cover behind General Ferrez's reserve of infantry. Leach says, 'Colonel Beckwith received a shot through his cap, whilst in the act of rolling a huge piece of rock down on the fugitives, by way of accelerating their retreat.'[27]

A few days later the post was reinforced by one company of the 43rd and two of the 52nd; but the day after their arrival all the infantry at Barba del Puerco were withdrawn to a village further from the river and replaced by a party of the 1st Hussars. Beckwith received a letter from Wellington expressing his appreciation of the conduct of his regiment and Craufurd, never lavish in his praise, issued a complimentary order.[28]

On 26 March Wellington wrote to Craufurd: 'By this time you will have been joined by the two battalions of Caçadores, and will be the best judge what to do with them.'[29] As already narrated, Craufurd sent them straight back again!

On 17 April 1810 an Imperial Decree was issued from Compiègne, stating that three army corps in Spain, the II, VI, and VIII, together with certain other troops, were to form, an Army of Portugal under the command of Marshal Masséna, Duke of Rivoli and Prince of Essling. The II and VI Corps were already observing Portugal, the former under Reynier with headquarters at Talavera, and the latter under Ney, whose headquarters were at Salamanca. The II Corps had two divisions and was 18,000 men strong, whilst the VI Corps had three divisions and a total strength of 33,000. The VIII Corps numbered about 20,000 men and was composed mostly of newly raised battalions.[30] Napoleon was indeed building up a very strong force with the aim of conquering Portugal and driving Wellington's army into the sea. French cavalry had already been active in trying to pierce Craufurd's outpost line. There had been 3,000 of them along the Agueda in March and April, and by May this number had increased to 5,000. They were backed by bodies of infantry, some only three or four miles east of the Agueda. The Light Division's Cavalry were vastly outnumbered by those of the enemy, yet Craufurd's outpost line was never pierced.

During most of April there was heavy rain and the Agueda was only passable at the bridges. On 26 April French troops moved up close to Ciudad Rodrigo, drove in the Spanish outposts, and blockaded it on three sides. The bridge over the Agueda, however, was kept open by the garrison and communications were maintained with the Light

Division. On 30 May the main body of Ney's VI Corps arrived before the fortress, and a little later Junot's VIII Corps took over the line of the lower Agueda from VI Corps troops. Craufurd was now faced by 57,000 French soldiers.[31]

At about this time the Portuguese Caçador battalions rejoined the Light Division. D'Urban writes: 'June 1 . . . B. Genl. Craufurd's Portuguese Brigade to Mello. June 21 . . . The 2nd Chasseurs are thought unfit for service.' On 23 June he noted that the 2nd Chasseurs would arrive at Reteiro on the Mondego the following day and would halt there until Beresford inspected them, which he proposed to do on 25 June. The regiment had been returned because Craufurd had considered them as unfit to take the field. He had also reported the 1st Chasseurs as unfit because of the 'bad and weak physical qualities of the men.' Beresford, however, had always considered them satisfactory in this respect, having regard to the low physical standards of the country. Furthermore, he believed that the discipline of the 1st Chasseurs must have improved because Craufurd had used them on outpost duty, and he accordingly sent D'Urban to inspect them. The upshot was that Craufurd retained the 1st Chasseurs, and on 25 June Beresford at last sent him the 3rd Chasseurs in place of the 2nd. On 5 July D'Urban wrote that Lieutenant-Colonel Elder 'brought his Portuguese Chasseurs into fire for the first time with excellent effect.' When Craufurd was attacked on 24 July and driven over the Coa, D'Urban says that, 'Elder's Chasseurs behaved perfectly well.' His remarks about the 1st Chasseurs are obliterated; a practice of his when he did not wish to leave a record in his journal of anything unpleasant.[32]

Meanwhile, on 1 June Ney had constructed a bridge across the Agueda a mile and a half above Ciudad Rodrigo. On 3 June Massena arrived, took over command and ordered Reynier with the II Corps to advance on Coria, threatening Castel Branco. (Wellington, foreseeing this, had ordered Hill to leave Portalegre and concentrate the 2nd Division at Villa Velha; and shortly after this he used newly arrived British battalions and some Portuguese ones to form a 5th Division under Leith, which was available to support Hill.) On 5 June Ney built a second bridge across the Agueda, below Ciudad Rodrigo. He then pushed strong forces across the river, driving back the piquets of the 1st Hussars and cutting Craufurd's communications with Ciudad Rodrigo. The French now busied themselves with the siege of the fortress and action against the Light Division was limited to harassment.[33] Leach says, 'The French cavalry were eternally in motion in large bodies towards our chain of posts, and we as often under arms waiting for them.'[34]

As the French were now across the Agueda, Craufurd concentrated the bulk of his division at Gallegos and Espeja, commanding the two roads leading eastwards from Ciudad Rodrigo towards Almeida and the Coa; he was thus well placed to stop any minor thrust or to fight a delaying action against an advance in force. On 10 June the level of the Agueda dropped and its fords became passable, but Craufurd maintained a position which was now in danger of being outflanked in order to encourage the garrison or the beleagured fortress.

George Napier was commanding a piquet at a ford over the Azava, in front of Gallegos, when he saw a French general and his staff coming down the road on the opposite bank towards the ford. The river was narrow and George Napier called across it to the general to go back or he would fire. The latter took no notice, so Napier ordered a solider to shoot one of the horses. This had the desired effect and the party wheeled about and went off at a trot. The General, it later transpired, was Marshal Ney. On another day, at the same place, some French soldiers, mounting a piquet on the opposite bank, asked Napier's leave to come across and get some tobacco from his men as they had none. He allowed two of them to come, provided they swam across, as he would not let them try the ford. He says they 'got the tobacco, told us all the news from France, and returned quite happy.'[35] These were fairly typical instances of the civilities exchanged between the two sides during the Peninsular War.

On 25 June the French siege batteries opened fire on Ciudad Rodrigo, and French cavalry closed up in strength on the Azava River. Craufurd accordingly drew back his piquets, and on 1 July Wellington increased the Light Division's cavalry strength by placing the whole of the 14th and 16th Light Dragoons under Craufurd's command. Leach says that at this stage they were still occupying Gallegos by day, but that every evening Craufurd 'marched his infantry to a wood on some heights behind the village, towards the river Duas Casas, where we bivouacked, and returned soon after daybreak to the village. This I presume was a precautionary measure, fearing the enemy might attempt a night attack on the village, which their extreme proximity rendered probable.'

Leach gives the following interesting account of the Light Division's withdrawal from this advanced position, which was becoming increasingly untenable. Wellington, accompanied by General Spencer, commanding the 1st Division, had come up recently to see things for himself. Leach writes:

'From some commanding ground in the French lines, the return of our division from the heights of the village could plainly be perceived; and possibiy being decieved on that point, mistaking us for reinforcements sent across the Coa to join General Craufurd, Massena ordered General Junot to cross the Azarva at Marialva Bridge on the 4th July, with, it was supposed, about fifteen thousand men; and, by a close reconoissance, to ascertain how matters really stood.

'4th July. — Being under arms, as usual, an hour before day-break, on the heights, some shots were heard from our cavalry pickets at Marialva, who shortly afterwards retired slowly and in excellent order, keeping up a continued skirmish. Captain Kraukenberg, of the 1st German Hussars, an officer of the highest merit, distinguished himself on this occasion. Forming his squadron on some eligible ground near a small narrow bridge over a rivulet which runs through Gallegos, he waited until as many of the French dragoons had crossed as he thought proper to permit, when he instantly charged and put them into confusion, killing and wounding many of them, and bringing some prisoners with him to the heights, where General Craufurd had drawn out the Light Division in line. The horse artillery opened with effect on the head of Junot's troops, who advanced with caution; but General Craufurd having ascertained their great superiority of numbers, decided on retiring across the Duas Casas. This movement was covered by some cavalry and our battalion, who skirmished with the advance of the French until we had passed the river, which was effected with a very trifling loss on our part. Two hundred riflemen and some cavalry were left on the heights of Fort Conception as a picket, the remainder being placed in a position near the Portuguese village of Val de la Mula, behind the rivulet called the Turon, which is here the boundary of the two countries.'[36]

On 8 July Wellington wrote to Craufurd: 'I agree with you in thinking that the enemy will not attack Almeida; and it is not improbable that, after Ciudad Rodrigo will have fallen, they will direct their march upon Castello Branco, and endeavour to cut in between General Hill and me; but I have in some degree provided for the movement.'[37] The last phrase of the letter refers to the move of Hill's 2nd Division to Villa Velha.

Ciudad Rodrigo fell on 10 July, and on the same day there occurred an incident that resulted in widespread criticism of Craufurd. French foraging parties had been busy in the villages between the Azava and Duas Casas Rivers, and Craufurd decided to try and surprise some of these troops. He marched from Val de la Mula after dark with seven companies of the 95th, two of the 52nd, six squadrons of cavalry (three of the 14th Light Dragoons, two of the 16th Light Dragoons, and one of the 1st Hussars), and two of Ross's guns. Before daybreak this force was drawn up on rising ground about half a mile from the village of Barquilla, where there was a French detachment of two troops of dragoons and 200 men of the 22nd Regiment, covering the activities of the foragers. At daylight, when the enemy saw British troops deployed and ready to attack, they began a rapid retreat. Craufurd promptly ordered his two leading squadrons, one of the 16th Light Dragoons and the one of the 1st Hussars, to charge. The French infantry halted in a corn field and formed square to received them. The two squadrons, after galloping a mile, and disordered by enclosures through which they had had to pass, made no impression on the square, and, swinging to right and left of it, went after the French cavalry, cutting down some and making most of the rest prisoners. Craufurd, had despatched his next squadron, one of the 14th Light Dragoons, in support of the first two. Led by Lieutenant-Colonel Talbot, commanding the regiment, it went straight for the square, but failed to break it, and Talbot was amongst those killed. Before another attack could be mounted the French had slipped away.

The firing was heard by another squadron of the 1st Hussars and the remaining squadron of the 14th Hussars, both of which were on outpost duty, and they rode towards it. Unfortunately they were mistaken for French cavalry coming to rescue the infantry, so that no effort was made to pursue the latter. Leach, who was with the companies of his regiment, was puzzled as to why the British infantry were not ordered to advance, or why the two horse artillery guns had not been sent forward with the cavalry, because, as he says: 'A few discharges of grape-shot would either have annihilated the square in ten minutes or caused it to surrender.'[38] However, Wellington did not think criticism justified. In a letter to Craufurd on 23 July he said that the charge would have succeeded, 'notwithstanding the gallantry and steadiness of the French infantry, if various accidents had not prevented the execution of he plan as first formed; and I have stated this, as my opinion, in the report which I have made upon the business.'[39]

Charles Napier went to the French army with a flag of truce about some business a few hours after the action, and met the French General Loison, to whose division the infantry concerned belonged. Charles Napier says he commented on 'how gallantly and skilfully the captain and his little band had behaved, which pleased them very much.'[40]

On 11 July Wellington wrote to Craufurd, acknowledging his report of the fall of Ciudad Rodrigo, and giving him instructions and advice as to his future activities, as follows:

'The fall of Ciudad Rodrigo was to be expected and the defence has been greater than we had a right to expect ... I have looked over my instructions to you, and see nothing to add excepting the word threaten in the fourth paragraph; that is to say, it will run, in case the enemy should threaten to attack General Craufurd instead of in case the enemy should attack General Craufurd. In short, I don't wish you to risk anything beyond the Coa; and indeed ... I don't see why you should remain any longer at such a distance in front of Almeida. It is desirable that the communication with Almeida should be kept open as long as possible, in order that we may throw into that place as much provisions as possible; and therefore I would not wish you to fall back beyond that place, unless it should be necessary. But it does not appear that you should be so far, and it will be safer that you should be nearer, at least with your infantry.'[41]

Wellington's intention that Craufurd should withdraw across the Coa as soon as an attack on him was threatened, is clear; but the Commander of the Light Division may have reflected that by the time the threat was apparent there might not be time to withdraw without fighting.

Presumably appreciating Craufurd's difficulties, Wellington wrote to him on 13 July: 'I shall be obliged if you will direct your posts on the left to report all extraordinaries to Major-General Picton's posts on the Coa; and they might fall back on them if necessary.' (Picton's headquarters were now at Pinhel, and he had piquets thrown forward on the left bank of the Coa below Almeida.) This advice certainly envisaged a possibly hurried departure.

On 16 July Wellington wrote again to Craufurd, slightly modifying his previous instructions; he said: 'It is desirable that we should hold the other side of the Coa a little longer; and I think that our doing so is facilitated by our keeping La Concepcion. At the same time I don't want you to risk anything to remain at the other side of the river, or to retain the fort; and I am anxious that, when you leave it, it should be destroyed.'[42] On receipt of this, and on the same day, Craufurd, leaving his cavalry about Fort Concepcion and Val de la Mula, pulled his infantry back close to the Coa and Almeida. Three days later French cavalry patrols clashed with the British cavalry outposts, and a few enemy prisoners were taken.[43]

At dawn on 21 July the 95th and Ross's Troop RHA were ordered forward to the Turon River to support the cavalry, who were falling back before a superior force of infantry, cavalry and artillery. The remainder of the Light Division took up a position flanking Almeida. The mines which the Engineers had installed in Fort Concepcion were now fired, and the works completely destroyed. On the following day the covering force fell back on to the remainder of the Light Division, with the exception of cavalry piquets which were left to observe the various roads across the great plain in front.[44]

Craufurd has not as yet been threatened with attack. If the enemy advance was merely a reconnaissance in force, a withdrawal across the Coa at this juncture would be premature, and, in any case, against his instructions. His position was one which few commanders would envy, particularly in the light of those instructions. There was only one bridge by which he could cross the Coa, and this was approached by a steep and winding road. One rather feels that, although Wellington said that he did not wish to risk anything, he was by his instructions doing just that. Perhaps the Commander of the Forces felt the same thing, because at 8pm on 22 July he wrote to Craufurd: 'I order two battalions to support your flanks; but I am not desirous of engaging in an affair beyond the Coa. Under the circumstances, if you are not covered where you are, would it not be better that you should come to this side, with your infantry at least.'[45] It is not known at what time Craufurd received this letter, but it took the responsiblity out of his hands as to when he should cross the Coa. It may have been too late to do anything that night, but it seems likely that orders were issued on 23 July for a retreat the next day, because William Napier, who was with his regiment, the 43rd writes that on the morning of 24 July: 'The troops, drenched with rain, were under arms before daylight, expecting to retire, when some pistol shots in front, followed by an order for the cavalry reserves and the guns to advance, gave notice of the enemy's approach.'[46]

On 21 July Ney had advanced with a sizeable portion of his Corps, consisting of

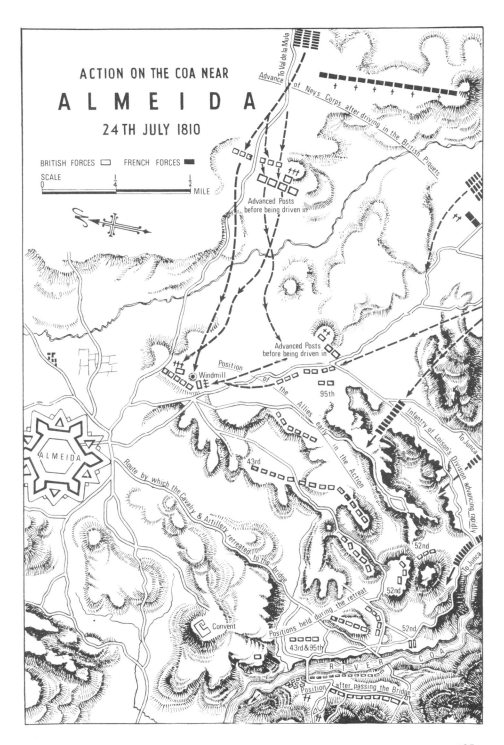

ACTION ON THE COA NEAR

ALMEIDA

24TH JULY 1810

BRITISH FORCES ☐ FRENCH FORCES ▬

SCALE

0   ¼   ½

MILE

Advance of Ney's Corps after driving in the British Piquets

To Val de la Mula

Advanced Posts
before being driven in

Advanced Posts
before being driven in

Position

of

the

Allies

early

in

the

Action

Windmill

95th

Infantry of Loison's Division advancing rapidly

To Junca

ALMEIDA

Route by which the Cavalry & Artillery retreated to the Bridge

43rd

52nd

52nd

To Junca

52nd

Convent

Positions held during the retreat

43rd & 95th

R I V E R   C O A

Position after passing the Bridge

127

Loison's Division and Treillard's Cavalry Brigade; but he moved with some caution and halted on 22 July, some three miles from Craufurd's position.[47] So far the force he had deployed was not very much stronger than Craufurd's.

On the night of 23 July there was a thunderstorm and torrential rain. Leach was on piquet with his company amongst some granite rocks as a support to the 1st Hussars who were on the plain in front. He says: 'A more tremendous night of thunder, lightning, and rain, I never remember before or since, from which our only shelter was the lee side of the rocks.'[48]

By the morning of 24 July Ney had concentrated the whole of VI Corps. 24,000 infantry were formed in one wide deep column, and in front of them were Lamotte's and Gardanne's Cavalry Brigades. Loison's Division of 13 battalions led the infantry; behind them came Mermet's Division of 11 battalions; and Marchand's Division (less four battalions garrisoning Ciudad Rodrigo) formed the reserve.[49]

The French infantry had been reorganised by Napoleon in 1808. Each regiment now consisted of five battalions, of which one was a depot battalion. A battalion consisted of six companies — one grenadier company, one light infantry company, and four fusilier companies (the last being the equivalent of the 'battalion' companies in the British Army). Each company comprised 140 all ranks. A favourite attack formation for a regiment was a column of double fusilier companies, which were called 'divisions' (not to be confused with the large formation of that name). A four-battalion regiment would provide a column of eight such divisions (each division in line and one behind the other). The four light infantry companies of the regiment would be deployed as skirmishers across the front of the column, and the four grenadier companies would probably be grouped as a regimental reserve.[50] The column relied on the weight of its attack and its moral effect, but against steady troops it had the disadvantage that only the leading division could use its fire power.

In response to a bragging and mendacious report by Masséna about the action on the Coa, Craufurd wrote a letter to *The Times* on 21 November 1810 giving his own account of the action. He gives the following description of his position:

'Almeida is a small fortress situated at the edge of the declivity forming a right bank of the valley of the Coa, which river runs from the south to the north, and the bridge over it is nearly an English mile west of the town. From July 21 to 24 the chain of our cavalry outposts formed a semi-circle in front of Almeida, the right flank being appuyé to the Coa, near As-Naves, which is about three miles above the place, and the left flank also appuyé to the river near Cinco-Villa, which is about three miles below the fortress. The centre of the line was covered by a small stream; and on the principal roads by which it was expected the enemy would advance, namely, on the right and centre of the position, the cavalry posts were supported by piquets of infantry. The only road which our artillery and the body of our cavalry could make use of, to retreat across the Coa, was that which leads from Almeida to the bridge. The nature of the ground made it difficult for the enemy to approach this road on our left, that is to say, on the north side of the town; and the infantry of the Division was, therefore, placed in a position to cover it on the right or south side, having its right flank appuyé to the Coa above the bridge, its front covered by a deep and rocky ravine, and its left in some enclosures near a windmill, which is on the plain, about eight hundred yards south of the town. The governor had intended to mount a gun upon the windmill; and one was actually in it, but quite useless, as it was not mounted. Another gun, also dismounted, was lying near the mill.'[51]

Neither the bridge nor the river are visible from Almeida, and the guns of the fortress could not therefore give covering fire on the approaches to the bridge. The ground that the Light Division was holding, however, presented difficulties to an attacking force. A high rocky spur runs south from Almeida, roughly parallel to the Coa, and from it a series of ragged spurs run down to the banks of the river, which flows in a deep ravine. The spurs were crossed by many stone walls, providing excellent cover, and along one of these spurs was Craufurd's infantry line. The right of the line rested on the river and the left was covered by Almeida's guns. The total length of the front was about a mile and a half. The 52nd were posted in craggy country on the right, except for a half company which was detached and placed in the old stone windmill tower on which the left flank rested, and at which were also posted two of Ross's guns. Craufurd was mistaken, however, in thinking that the gun in the windmill had not been mounted. It was a Spanish garrison gun and had in fact been mounted, but so badly that it broke through the floor of the mill on the first discharge.[52] Next to the tower, on its right, were the 43rd, and on their right were the 95th Rifles. The 1st and 3rd Caçadores held the rest of the front, connecting with the 52nd on the right.[53]

The action started with French cavalry attacking the infantry piquets on the road leading from Almeida to Val de la Mula. The piquets were supported by the 14th Light Dragoons and two of Ross's guns. The initial French attack was driven off, but soon the head of a large column with guns was seen and the piquets were withdrawn. The French, continuing their advance, passed the rivulet running across the British front and formed a line of 15 squadrons of cavalry, distant about a mile from the windmill. Artillery took post in front of this line of cavalry, and a division of about 7,000 infantry were coming up on their right. Against the British right, other troops could be seen advancing in the distance. As it was evident to Craufurd that he was about to be attacked by the French in very superior strength he decided to withdraw across the Coa immediately. He accordingly ordered the artillery and cavalry to move off by the road leading from Almeida to the bridge, and the infantry to follow, retiring in echelon from the left; it being necessary to hold the right to the last to prevent the enemy approaching the bridge by the road which led to it from the south, following the bottom of the valley and close to the river.[54]

Before this movement was well under way, the French infantry came on to the attack in an impetuous rush; the skirmishers being followed by drums beating the *pas de charge*, and led by officers calling to their men: '*Allons, enfants de la Patrie, le premier qui s'avancera, Napoleon le recompensera*'[55] As usual, the steady fire of the British infantry sent this onslaught reeling back. This was quickly followed, however, by a charge by the French 3rd Hussars against Craufurd's left flank, at a point where some companies of the 95th were in a vineyard, enclosed by a high stone wall which should have made them quite secure against cavalry. Unfortunately, during the night the men had pulled the wall down in many places in order to build shelters against the rain; so that, after the cavalry and artillery had moved off as ordered, there was no defence against a mounted attack, and one company was almost wiped out.[56]

It was perhaps at this juncture that the 1st Caçadores failed in their duty, and the 3rd Caçadores may have been ordered to follow them in order to rally them on the far side of the bridge. Anyhow, Leach writes:

'The baggage, artillery, cavalry, and the two Portuguese light battalions, were directed to retire instantly to the bridge over the Coa, and to gain the opposite bank without delay. Those who have seen and know this narrow and difficult defile, need not be informed, that to keep at bay as many thousand infantry as Marshal Ney might think proper to send forward, whilst the road was choked with troops, baggage, and artillery, which it was absolutely necessary should be covered and protected, during a retreat of a mile or more, and until they had crossed the bridge in safety, was no easy matter.

'Troops destined to cover the retreat consisted of our own battalion, and a considerable part, or the whole, of the 43rd and 52nd regiments. No further description of this rocky defile is necessary, than that the road is very narrow, and as bad as the generality of mountain roads in the Peninsula are; and, moreover, that it is overhung by huge rocks in many places, from which, had our pursuers been permitted to possess themselves of them, they might have annihilated the troops underneath, without their being able to retaliate.'[57]

The enemy cavalry attack was checked by riflemen firing from behind a stone wall, but the left flank was no longer secure. William Napier, fighting with his regiment, the 43rd, says that they were within an enclosure of solid masonry 10 feet high on the left of the road that ran towards the bridge from a point near the windmill, and which had only one narrow outlet. The firing in front soon became heavy, the cavalry, artillery, and the Caçadores, passed in retreat, 'and the sharp clang of rifles was heard along the edge of the plain above'. Those of the 43rd who were in this enclosure were nearly trapped, for the narrow exit would not have allowed them to withdraw quickly enough; but some large stones were loosened and by a simultaneous effort the men pushed the wall down and joined the 95th in the withdrawal. Eventually the 43rd, 95th, and 52nd were fighting as a mass of skirmishers in small parties, 'under no regular command, yet each confident in the courage and discipline of those on his right and left.'[58]

The cavalry and artillery had now been ordered to gallop to the bridge, with the Caçadores following close behind them, in order that the rearguard action being fought by the three British battalions should be as short as possible. The approach to the bridge was difficult, because, although there were shorter tracks down the hillside, the only one practicable for wheeled vehicles ran almost parallel to the river in its descent, with a hairpin turn near the bottom to make its final 300 yards approach to the bridge. In the hurry a horse artillery ammunition wagon overturned in the road, and on Craufurd's orders some of the 43rd, the 95th, and the 3rd Caçadores were thrown rapidly across a knoll which commanded the road near the bridge.[59] Leach writes of this incident: 'As the rearguard approached the Coa, we perceived that a part only of our cavalry, infantry, and artillery, had yet crossed the bridge; it became, therefore, indispensably requisite for us to keep possession of a small hill looking down on, and perfectly commanding the bridge, until everything had passed over cost what it might.'[60] A charge by a company of the 52nd recovered the ammunition waggon, which Lieutenant McDonald of Ross's Troop brought off.[61] The knoll was held until everything was over the bridge. Leach writes:

'I trust I shall be pardoned for saying that the soldiers of the old and gallant 43rd, and that part also of our own battalion whose lot it was to defend this important hill, against a vast superiority of numbers, proved themselves worthy of the trust.

'In ascending the hill, a musket-shot grazed the left side of my head, and buried itself in the earth close by. Both my subalterns, who were brothers, were severely wounded in the defence of this hill; and we had but barely time to send them, with other wounded officers and men, across the river, ere we were obliged to retire, and to make a push in double quick time to reach the bridge.'

Leach pays tribute to the gallantry of Major M'Leod of the 43rd, who was the senior officer on the spot. He says that he charged on horseback at the head of 'a hundred or two skirmishers' of the 43rd and 95th, all mixed up together against a wall lined with French infantry and drove them off.[62] William Napier also mentions M'Leod's action, saying that he rallied four companies on the hill whilst Craufurd's Brigade Major, Rowan, posted two companies on another hill to the left, flanking the road. He adds:

'The French, gathering in great numbers, made a serious rush and forced the companies back before the bridge could be cleared, and while a part of the fifty-second was still a considerable distance from it. The crisis was imminent, but M'Leod, a young man endowed with a natural genius for war, immediately turned his horse round, called on the troops to follow, and waving his cap, rode with a shout towards the enemy... A mob of soldiers rushed after him, cheering and charging as if a whole army had been at their backs; the enemy's skirmishers... stopped short, and before they could recover from their surprise, the fifty-second had passed the river: M'Leod followed at a run and gained the other side without a disaster. It was a fine exploit.'[63]

Craufurd says that the 43rd, being on the left of the line, were the first to reach the bridge, and he ordered the battalion (less those companies flung on to the knoll) to cross it and take up a position on the heights on the other side of the river.[64] William Napier says that as the infantry passed the bridge, they formed up in 'loose order' on the side of the mountain, whilst Ross's Troop RHA came into action on the summit. The cavalry were directed to cover all the roads on the right of the position and to watch some fords two miles upstream and the bridge at Castello Bom, in case Junot should cross the river in an attempt to get between the Light Division and Celorico.[65] However, after the rainstorm during the night all the fords were at the moment impassable. The only way in which the French could continue their attack was across the narrow bridge over which the Light Division had now successfully withdrawn, and on which Craufurd's infantry and artillery could now concentrate a devastating fire.

George Napier was very ill with fever the night before the battle, and he says that both the doctor and his brother thought he would die. By morning, however, he was a little better. Suddenly he heard firing and was told that the enemy were advancing with their cavalry. This, apparently, accelerated his convalescence, for by the time that the infantry had completed their withdrawal across the bridge, he was back in the field and commanding his company. He says that his regiment, the 52nd, was sent more to the right to bring flanking fire to bear on the enemy, and also to act as a reserve to support the other regiments or cover their retreat. He continues:

'I was detached with my company to the right, close upon the edge of the river, to defend a part that was fordable. In a short time the enemy moved down a heavy column of infantry to force the passage over the bridge, but were received so steadily and gallantly by the 43rd and Rifle Regiments, that after three desperate attempts, and pushing better than half way across, they gave up the point with great loss both in killed and wounded. We also suffered severely. My brother William was wounded in the hip in the last attack and effort to gain the bridge; his colonel and several other officers were killed.'[66]

Leach, describing the attacks on the bridge, writes: 'An incessant fire was kept up across the river by both parties, and after it had continued for some time, the French sent a party of grenadiers to storm the bridge . . . They advanced most resolutely across the bridge, but few, if any, went back alive . . . This experiment was repeated, and it is almost needless to add, that it met the same fate each time.' It appears that by this time the 1st Caçadores, if they had indeed given way in the initial French attack, must have been rallied, for Leach continues:

'The French officer who directed those attacks on the bridge, might have known, before he caused the experiment to be made, that a few hundred French grenadiers, advancing to the tune of "Vive l'Empereur!", "En avant, mes enfants!", and so forth, were not likely to succeed in scaring away three British and two Portuguese regiments, supported by artillery.'[67]

The attacks on the bridge appear to have been due entirely to Ney; Ever an optimist, he presumably thought that the British troops were in too much disorder to stand firm on the far side of the bridge and that it could be carried with a rush. The initial attack had been carried out by the 66th Regiment, led by its grenadiers. When this failed, Ney apparently lost his temper and ordered his ADC, Sprünglin, to take command of a battalion of light infantry and seize the bridge at all costs. The result was that out of a battalion a little over 300 strong, 90 men were killed and 147 wounded in less than 10 minutes.[68]

The half company of the 52nd, under Lieutenant Dawson, which had been cut off at the windmill, remained there till nightfall without being observed by the enemy. Dawson then withdrew his men, past the Almeida glacis, and downstream along the right bank of the Coa. He then crossed the river at a ford and eventually rejoined his regiment near Pinhel.[69]

There was a curious incident during the battle. It will be remembered that Wellington, in his letter of 8 March, had said: 'I intend the Divisions of General Cole and General Picton should support you on the Coa without waiting for orders from me, if it should be necessary; and they shall be directed accordingly.' Picton, from his headquarters at Pinhel, heard the firing on the morning of 24 July and rode to the Coa bridge, arriving as Craufurd was organising the defence on the left bank. Craufurd asked him to bring his 3rd Division up to support the Light Division. Picton, it is said, refused abruptly, and told Craufurd he could get out of his own scrape. There was a bitter altercation, and Picton rode away to order the 3rd Division to prepare to retreat.[70]

Craufurd's letter to *The Times* includes a fitting summary of the battle; he writes:

'To retire in tactical order over such ground, so broken, rocky, and intersected with walls, as that which separated the first position from the second, would have been impossible, even if not under fire from the enemy; and the ground on the other side of the river was equally unfavourable for reforming the regiments. Whoever knows anything of war, knows that in such an operation, and upon such ground, some derangement of regular order is inevitable; but the retreat was made in a military, soldier-like manner, and without the slightest precipitation. In the course of it the enemy, when he was pressed, was attacked in different places by the 43rd, 52nd, and 95th Regiments and driven before them.'[71]

The Light Division's losses in this very successful rearguard action were extraordinarily small. They amounted to four officers and 32 men killed, 23 officers and 191 men wounded, and one officer and 82 men missing. The heaviest casualties were in the 43rd and 95th, each regiment losing 129 all ranks. Totals for the remainder were 52nd 25, 1st

Caçadores 16, 3rd Caçadores 29, and the Cavalry seven.[72] William Napier puts the French losses in round figures as 1,000 men.[73] Craufurd, more cautiously, says that it was difficult to say what the French loss was because no French official report ever contained true figures.[74]

Craufurd has been criticised, not only by most of his contemporaries, for fighting this action instead of withdrawing across the Coa in time to avoid it, but also by the majority of military historians. William Napier says that Craufurd had,

'kept a weak division for three months within two hours march of sixty thousand men, appropriating the resources of the plains entirely to himself; but this exploit, only to be appreciated by military men, did not satisfy his feverish thirst of distinction; he had safely affronted a superior power, and forgetting that his stay behind the Coa was a matter of sufference not real strength, he with headstrong ambition resolved, in defiance of reason and of the reiterated orders of his general, to fight on the right bank.'[75]

George Napier says that Wellington had left Craufurd merely to watch the enemy and give him information, whilst he had forbidden him to commit himself by any engagement, but to retreat across the Coa without firing a shot.[76] Leach writes that he had never heard it doubted or denied that Wellington had given Craufurd positive orders to withdrawn across the Coa on the fall of Ciudad Rodrigo, or on the first sympton of Massena's advance on Almeida.[77] The Committee who directed the publication of the *Historical Record of the Fifty-Second Light Infantry* restricted themselves to the milder comment that Craufurd seemed to have felt himself bound to prevent the investment of Almeida if possible, and therefore to have 'clung to a false position longer than sound military judgment would have dictated if unfettered by such a view.'[78] Sir Charles Oman writes that 'Wellington was justly displeased with Craufurd for accepting the wholly unnecessary combat: if the Light Division had been withdrawn behind the Coa on the 22nd, as he had advised, no danger would have been incurred.'[79]

As regards the comments of Leach and the Napier brothers, they were all company commanders at the time, and it is unlikely that they ever saw Wellington's letters to Craufurd. Oman's comment is more surprising. We have seen that Wellington's letter, to which he refers, was only written at 8pm on 22 July, and therefore Craufurd could not possibly have acted on it quickly enough to withdraw that day. Wellington was certainly annoyed by the affair, and in a private letter of 31 July he wrote:

'I had positively forbidden the foolish affairs in which Craufurd involved his outposts, . . . and repeated my injunction that he should not engage in an affair on the right of the river . . . You will say in this case, "Why not accuse Craufurd?" I answer, "Because if I am to be hanged for it, I cannot accuse a man who I believe has meant well, and whose error was one of judgement, not of intention".'[80]

Wellington, in fact, knew that Craufurd had not disobeyed an order, and it is possible, even likely, that in his heart he knew that if there was any error it was his own; for within the general guide lines of his instruction, which Craufurd had observed, he had given his subordinate the responsibility of deciding the correct moment to withdraw, and should therefore have supported whatever decision he made. Indeed, in the light of Wellington's instruction, one might well ask, 'When should Craufurd have withdrawn across the Coa, and for what reasons?'

Craufurd's handling of the battle at the Coa was, indeed, brilliant. In the face of an enemy in overwhelming strength, he had retreated over a single mountainous road and bridge at the cost of remarkably few casualties. His confidence that his division could undertake such a hazardous operation resulted from his own training methods and the high standard that he set. Building on the three infantry regiments which Moore had trained, and the elite cavalry and artillery placed under his command, Craufurd had welded the whole into the superb Light Division, the finest fighting formation on either side in the Peninsular campaign, and one of the finest in British military history. When Craufurd was killed at the storming of Ciudad Rodrigo the Light Division was never quite the same again.

Robert Craufurd

George Napier, who had an arm amputated after being wounded at Ciuded Rodrigo, was lying in great pain in a hospital in which, in the room over his, Robert Craufurd was dying. Napier says that Craufurd was suffering terribly, and that his moans were the more distressing to him in that Craufurd was almost hourly sending messages to know how he was and to express his approval of his conduct and his regret that he would never see him again.[81]

This was one side of Craufurd's nature: yet many officers detested him. He was a very strict disciplinarian who would not tolerate the slightest deviation from the very strict standards that he set. His temper was quick, and a rebuke could be delivered with a bitter sarcasm which the recipient found hard to forget. Other officers were devoted to him, and he possessed the confidence of probably the majority of the rank and file, and the affection, even, of many of them. George Napier called him a very unpopular man, but added that every officer under his command acknowledged that it was to his efforts that the Light Division owed its high standard of discipline and a knowledge of the duties of light troops that was never equalled by any division in the British Army or surpassed by any division in the French Army. Napier mentions, as a proof of the high standard of all ranks, the extraordinary number of privates in the Light Division who were commissioned as officers, and who, the moment they joined their new regiments, were made adjutants.[82]

George Napier gave the following character sketch of Craufurd:

'Brilliant as some of the traits of his character were, and notwithstanding the good and generous feelings which often burst forth like a bright gleam of sunshine from behind a dark and heavy cloud, still there was a sullenness which seemed to brood in his inmost soul and generate passions which new no bounds. As a general commanding a division of light troops of all arms, Craufurd certainly excelled. His knowledge of outpost duty was never exceeded by any British general, and I much doubt if there are many in any other service who know more of that particular branch of the profession than he did. He had, by long experience, unwearied zeal, and constant activity, united to practice, founded a system of discipline and marching which arrived at such perfection that he could calculate to the minute the time his whole division, baggage, commissariat, etc., etc., would take to arrive at any given point, no matter how many days' march. Every officer and soldier knew his duty in every particular, and also knew how he must perform it. No excuse would save him from the general's rage if he failed in a single iota. As a commissary he was perfect, and if provisions were to be got within his possible reach his division was never without them. His mental activity was only surpassed by his physical powers. The moment his division was at its ground for the night he never moved from his horse till he had made himself master of every part of his post, formed his plans for defence if necessary, and explained all his arrangements to the staff officers and the field officers of each regiment, so that if his orders were strictly obeyed a surprise was impossible.'[83]

One of Craufurd's instructions was that troops on the march must never make a detour to avoid fordable steams or deep mud, nor break ranks to pick the shallowest water or the easiest walking. The reason for this order was that any diversion caused an unacceptable delay to rapid movement. He had even had men flogged for straggling, whilst fording a stream, to fill water bottles or to take a drink. On the march back from Craufurd's funeral, the leading company of the Light Division came to an excavation, at the rear of the Ciudad Rodrigo siege works, which was half filled with mud and water. The men hesitated for a moment, and then marched straight through it, with the step and bearing of a parade ground review. The whole of the Light Division followed in the same way. It was the soldier's tribute to their old commander.[84]

Notes

1 *Passages in the early Military Life of General Sir George T. Napier*, ed General W. C. E. Napier (London, John Murray, 1884), p11

2 ibid, pp21-2

3 Alexander H. Craufurd, *General Craufurd and his Light Division* (London, Griffith, Farran, Okeden, & Welsh, 1891), pp36-37

4 Major-General Sir W. F. P. Napier, *History of the War in the Peninsula and in the South of France* (London, Frederick Warne & Co.) vol I, p501

5 ibid, pp311, 313

6 W. S. Moorsom, *Historical Record of the Fifty-Second Regiment (Oxfordshire Light Infantry)* (London, Richard Bentley, 1860), p115

7 Craufurd, op cit, p65

8 Lieutenant-Colonel J. Leach, *Rough Sketches of the Life of an Old Soldier* (London, Longman, Rees, Orme, Brown, & Green, 1831), p71

9 ibid, pp74-5

10 ibid, p75

11 ibid, pp80-4

12 George Napier, op cit, pp107-09

13 W. F. P. Napier, op cit, vol II, pp168-69

14 Leach, op cit, pp108-10

15 Craufurd, op cit, pp82-3

16 ibid, pp83-4

17 ibid, pp84-5

18 Moorsom, op cit, p117

19 W. F. P. Napier, op cit, vol II, p394

20 *The Peninsula Journal of Major-General Sir Benjamin D'Urban*, ed I. J. Rousseau (London, Longmans, Green, & Co, 1930), pp77-8, 93, 97

21 Charles Oman, *A History of the Peninsular War*, vol III (Oxford, Clarendon Press, 1908), p232

22 Craufurd, op cit, pp88-92

23 Leach, op cit, pp124-25

24 Craufurd, op cit, pp96-7

25 W. F. P. Napier, vol II, op cit, pp404-05
26 Craufurd, op cit, pp86-8
27 Leach, op cit, pp127-29
28 ibid, p129
29 Craufurd, op cit, p101
30 Oman, op cit, pp199, 202-03
31 ibid, pp238-43
32 D'Urban, op cit, p109f
33 Oman, op cit, pp246-8
34 Leach op cit, p134
35 W. F. P. Napier, op cit, pp114-15
36 Leach, op cit, pp137-39
37 Craufurd, op cit, p111
38 ibid, pp111-12
39 *Selections from the Dispatches and General Orders of Field Marshal the Duke of Wellington*, ed Lieutenant-Colonel Gurwood (London, John Murray, 1861), pp370-71
40 George Napier, op cit, p123
41 Craufurd, op cit, p122
42 ibid, pp122-24
43 Leach, op cit, pp144-45
44 ibid, p145
45 Craufurd, op cit, pp122-24
46 W. F. P. Napier, op cit, pp411-12
47 Oman, op cit, p258
48 Leach, op cit, p145
49 Oman, op cit, p259
    Craufurd, op cit, p140
50 Colonel H. C. B. Rogers, *Napoleon's Army* (London, Ian Allan, 1974), pp61-2, 69-72
51 Craufurd, op cit, pp141-42
52 Moorsom, op cit, pp119-20
53 ibid, p120
54 Craufurd, op cit, pp142-43
55 Oman, op cit, p77
56 ibid, p260
    Craufurd, op cit, p143
57 Leach, op cit, pp147-48
58 W. F. P. Napier, op cit, p412
59 Oman, op cit, pp260-61
    Craufurd, op cit, p143
    Moorsom, op cit, p120
60 Leach, op cit, pp148-49
61 Moorsom, op cit, pp120-21
62 Leach, op cit, pp149-50
63 W. F. P. Napier, op cit, pp413-14
64 Craufurd, op cit, p143
65 W. F. P. Napier, op cit, p414
66 George Napier, op cit, pp130-31

67 Leach, op cit, p121
68 Oman, op cit, p263
69 Moorsom, op cit, p121
70 Oman, op cit, p266
   W. F. P. Napier, op cit, pp415-16
71 Craufurd, op cit, p144
72 Oman, op cit, p544
73 W. F. P. Napier, op cit, p415
74 Craufurd, op cit, p144
75 W. F. P. Napier, op cit, p411
76 George Napier, op cit, p129
77 Leach, op cit, p147
78 Moorsom, op cit, p119
79 Oman, op cit, p266
80 ibid, p266
81 George Napier, op cit, p223
82 ibid, p224
83 ibid, p225-26
84 C. W. C. Oman, *Wellington's Army* (London, Edward Arnold, 1912), p149

Index